Manchester United

The Red Army

Manchester

United
The Red Army

Ivan Ponting

hamlyn

ACKNOWLEDGMENTS

The author would like to thank the following:
Pat, Rosie and Joe Ponting for embracing foot-
ball as part of their lives with such heartening
enthusiasm; Steve Small for the original idea
and design of Manchester United Player By
Player, the title of this book in its first four
editions; Bob Bickerton, the Sage of Gresty
Road, for consultancy without fees; Cliff
Butler for never tugging his forelock; John
Doherty for sharing his wisdom yet again;
David Sadler, David Herd, Paddy Crerand, Bill
Foulkes, Arthur Albiston, Stuart Pearson,
Paddy Roche, Albert Scanlon, Graham Hart
and Chris and Jo Forster for earlier contributions; Tarda Davison-Aitkins for unremitting
composure under fire; Julian Brown and
Trevor Davies for their patience; Les Gold for
his friendship and generosity; Barry Hugman
for his statistical wizardry; Rod Towers for his
encouragement; and, crucially, all at
Colorsport, especially Andy Cowie, undoubtedly 'The Guv'nor' when it comes to tracking
down elusive pictures.

Illustrations: The vast majority are from
Colorsport, with other contributions from Cliff
Butler of Manchester United, Associated
Sports Photography and Cumbrian
Newspapers. Every effort has been made to
trace the copyright holders of all photographs
used in this book. We apologise for any omissions, which are unintentional, and would be
pleased to include appropriate acknowledge-
ment in any subsequent edition.

First published by The Crowood Press in 1989
Second edition published by Tony Williams
publications 1994
Third and fourth editions published by Hamlyn
1997 and 1998

Redesigned and updated in 1999 by Hamlyn.
Revised and updated in 2000 by Hamlyn, an
imprint of Octopus Publishing Group, 2–4
Heron Quays, London E14 4JP

Text copyright © 2000 by Ivan Ponting
Design (Darren Kirk) copyright © 2000
Hamlyn

Printed and bound in Spain by Grafos SA

ISBN: 0 600 60178 1

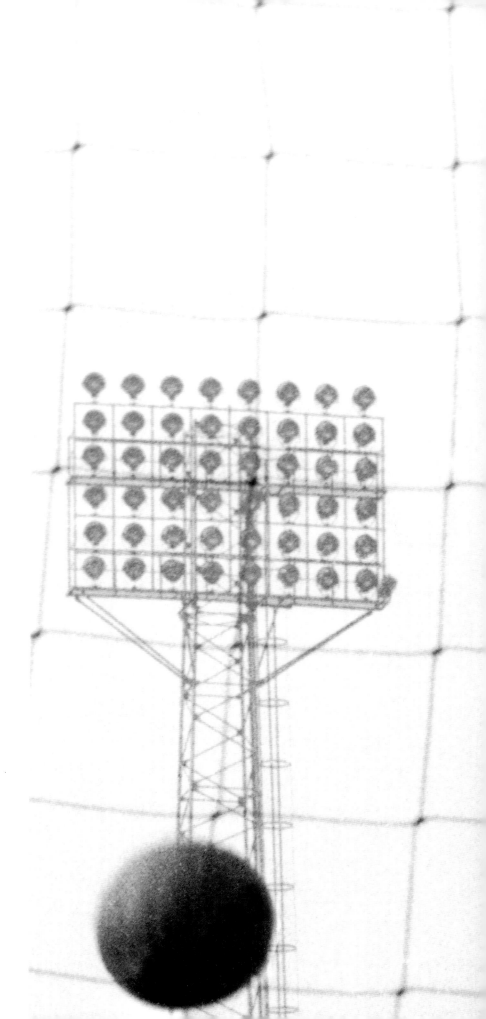

Seasons come and seasons go but it seems inconceivable that there will ever be another to match Manchester United's momentous 1998/99 campaign. However, any rivals who hoped that the epoch-making treble might breed complacency at Old Trafford had their illusions shattered comprehensively by the events of 1999/2000. Though the European Cup slipped away and the FA Cup, regrettably, was not contested, the Premiership crown was retained in overwhelmingly dominant fashion, an 18-point victory margin and nearly a century of goals ramming home the crushing domestic superiority of Sir Alex Ferguson's enchanting side.

Introduction

Happily, the romance and the thrills seem never-ending for followers of the Old Trafford club. Since the first edition of this book in 1989, we have experienced 11 seasons of compelling excitement encompassing two European trophies, six Championships, four FA Cup victories and a success in the League Cup. These glories have been attained through the efforts of a glittering cavalcade of performers, from the likes of Bryan Robson and Mark Hughes during the early years of Alex Ferguson's reign through to the host of fresh faces in the late 1990s. Indeed, 'fresh' is the operative word with the gratifying involvement of so many youngsters. An uplifting parallel can be drawn with the era of the Busby Babes and writing about these latest achievements has been pure pleasure.

But the march of the new must never obscure what has gone before. Thus a major function of Manchester United: The Red Army is to record and pay tribute to men who are Red Devils no more, whether heroes like Law and Best, or lads who didn't quite make the Old Trafford grade and left to try their luck elsewhere. During this process, many of the previous entries have been developed and revised for this sixth edition to offer a volume which is both comprehensive and as up-to-date as publishing deadlines would permit.

As I wrote in my initial introduction a decade ago, my first hero was Davy Crockett, king of the wild frontier ... but Bobby Charlton was not far behind. I began supporting United as a wide-eyed youngster in the mid-1950s, my starting point for the main section of this book. No matter that, in those days before motorways criss-crossed the country, trips to Old Trafford from deepest Somerset were rare treats and that I spent more time watching the Bristol clubs than the Busby Babes. There was never any doubt where my heart resided. As I grew up I became a regular visitor to Manchester and formed the impressions that I have set down here.

Accordingly, everyone who has kicked a ball for the Reds since 1955/56 – in the League, FA Cup, League Cup (in its various guises), European competition and now the Club World Championship – is included. There is a photograph of each man and, in most cases, an assessment of his merits and his place in the club's history, Where an individual has taken part in so few matches as to render such treatment inappropriate, a brief statistical resume of his United career appears with his picture. All records are complete to 20 May, 2000. I have attempted to depict in words the essence of each player and kept the emphasis on footballing rather than personal matters. Also I have tried to keep figures to a minimum, though I have included all the basic facts, such as games played (consolidated to include substitute appearances), goals scored etc, alongside each assessment. The United figures refer to all matches (a breakdown for each competition begins on page 248) but under the heading of 'Other Clubs', the games and goals are in the League only. The dates in large type refer to the seasons in which the player appeared in the first team, not when he joined or left the club. Under 'Honours' I have included only those won at United, except in the case of international caps, the figures for which cover each man's complete career to date. Transfer fees are those favoured in the press.

Though I deal in detail with 1955/56 onwards, I have not ignored the years that went before. The club has been in existence since 1878, so to set the scene I have recalled the Victorian era as well as the post-war pomp of Matt Busby's first great side, in which the likes of Johnny Carey, Stan Pearson and Jack Rowley held sway. I'd like to think there is something here for everyone whose imagination has been captured down the decades by the indefinable aura of the Red Devils.

Of course, the story goes ever on and I hope this will not be the final edition of the book. The feats of recent seasons will be well-nigh impossible to emulate, let alone surpass, while the intensity and scale of the task in the years ahead will be magnified by increased emphasis on the European and world scene. But the essential challenge, to be the best, will remain. The Red Army can hardly wait.

Ivan Ponting
Chewton Mendip
August 2000.

CONTENTS

The early years

Manchester United have not always been the most glamorous club in English football. Indeed, after their foundation as Newton Heath in 1878, early financial struggles drove them to the edge of extinction and no major honours were won until the first decade of the 20th century.

The breakthrough came with the League title in 1907/08, the FA Cup the following season and another Championship in 1910/11. Between the wars there followed a yo-yo period during which United suffered three relegations to the Second Division, and although they made a rapid return to the top flight after each demotion, there was no real hint of the glory to follow.

And then came Matt Busby ...

FA CUP WINNERS 1909

STANDING (LEFT TO RIGHT)

ERNEST MANGNALL (secretary-manager 03–12).

F BACON (trainer).

JACK PICKEN (05/06–10/11, inside-forward, 121 games, 46 goals).

HUGH EDMONDS (10/11–11/12, goalkeeper, 50 games, 0 goals).

Mr MURRAY (director).

HARRY MOGER (03/04–11/12, goalkeeper, 264 games, 0 goals).

JOHN HENRY DAVIES (chairman).

TOM HOMER (09/10–11/12, centre-forward, 25 games, 14 goals).

Mr LAWTON (director).

ALEX BELL (02/03–12/13, left-half, 306 games, 10 goals).

Mr DEAKIN (director).

SITTING

BILLY MEREDITH (06/07–20/21, outside-right, 332 games, 35 goals).

DICK DUCKWORTH (03/04–13/14, right-half, 251 games, 11 goals).

CHARLIE ROBERTS (03/04–12/13, centre-half and captain, 299 games, 23 goals).

SANDY TURNBULL (06/07–14/15, inside-forward, 245 games, 100 goals).

ENOCH 'KNOCKER' WEST (10/11–14/15, centre-forward, 181 games, 80 goals).

GEORGE STACEY (07/08–14/15, full-back, 267 games, 9 goals).

ON GROUND

ARTHUR WHALLEY (09/10–19/20, half-back, 106 games, 6 goals).

LESLIE HOFTON (10/11–11/12 and 20/21, full-back, 18 games, 0 goals).

HAROLD HALSE (07/08–11/12, forward, 124 games, 50 goals).

GEORGE WALL (05/06–14/15, outside-left, 316 games, 98 goals).

MISSING FROM PICTURE

VINCE HAYES (1900/01–04/05 and 08/09–10/11, full-back, 128 games, 2 goals).

JIMMY TURNBULL (07/08–09/10, centre-forward, 76 games, 42 goals).

SECOND DIVISION CHAMPIONS 1935/36

STANDING (LEFT TO RIGHT)

JAMES GIBSON (chairman).

RON FERRIER
(35/36–37/38, inside-forward, 19 games, 4 goals).

JACK GRIFFITHS
(33/34–39/40, full-back, 176 games, 1 goal).

JACK BREEDON
(35/36–39/40, goalkeeper, 38 games, 0 goals).

TOM CURRY (trainer).

JACK HALL (33/34–35/36, goalkeeper, 67 games, 0 goals).

BILLY PORTER
(34/35–37/38, full-back, 65 games, 0 goals).

TOM MANLEY
(31/32–38/39, outside-left, 195 games, 41 goals).

SCOTT DUNCAN (manager 32–37).

SITTING

JACK CAPE (33/34–36/37, outside-right, 60 games, 18 goals).

GEORGE MUTCH
(34/35–37/38, inside-forward, 120 games, 49 goals).

TOMMY BAMFORD
(34/35–37/38, centre-forward, 109 games, 57 goals).

JAMES BROWN
(35/36–38/39, wing-half, 110 games, 1 goal).

HARRY ROWLEY
(28/29–36/37, inside-forward, 180 games, 55 goals).

BILL McKAY (33/34–39/40, left-half, 184 games, 15 goals).

GEORGE VOSE
(33/34–39/40, centre-half, 211 games, 1 goal).
On ground

BILLY BRYANT
(34/35–39/40, outside-right, 160 games, 44 goals).

BILL ROBERTSON
(33/34–35/36, right-half, 50 games, 1 goal).

BILL OWEN (34/35–35/36, outside-left, 17 games, 1 goal).

HUBERT REDWOOD
(35/36–39/40, full-back, 96 games, 4 goals).

Prelude to the Babes

When Matt Busby became manager of Manchester United after the war he created a crack side which lifted the FA Cup in 1948. The reborn Reds were First Division runners-up four times in five seasons before finally taking the title in 1951/52.

Here are the men who took part in those triumphs and who played during the subsequent seasons leading to the Busby Babes' first great achievement, the 1955/56 League Championship, where our story really begins.

FA CUP WINNERS 1948

BACK ROW (LEFT TO RIGHT)

JIMMY DELANEY (46/7–50/1, winger, 183 games, 28 goals).
JACK WARNER (38/9–49/50, wing-half, 118 games, 2 goals).
STAN PEARSON (37/8–53/4, inside-forward, 345 games, 149 goals).
JACK CROMPTON (45/6–55/6, goalkeeper, 211 games, 0 goals).
JOHN HANLON (38/9–48/9, centre-forward, 70 games, 22 goals).
JACK ROWLEY (37/8–54/5, centre-forward, 422 games, 208 goals).
SAMMY LYNN (47/8–49/50, centre-half, 13 games, 0 goals).
ALLENBY CHILTON (39/40–54/5, centre-half, 390 games, 3 goals).
JIMMY MURPHY (coach).

FRONT ROW:

JOHNNY MORRIS (46/7–48/9, inside-forward, 92 games, 35 goals).
JOHN ANDERSON (47/8–48/9, wing-half, 39 games, 2 goals).
JOHNNY CAREY (37/8–52/3, full-back and captain, 344 games, 18 goals).
JOHN ASTON (46/7–53/4, full-back, 282 games, 30 goals).
HENRY COCKBURN (45/6–54/5, wing-half, 275 games, 4 goals).
CHARLIE MITTEN (46/7–49/50, winger, 161 games, 61 goals).

TOP TO BOTTOM: JACK ROWLEY, JOHNNY CAREY, CHARLIE MITTEN, STAN PEARSON

PICTURED LEFT TO RIGHT, ABOVE:

JOHN DOWNIE (48/9–52/3, inside-forward, 115 games, 36 goals).

REG ALLEN (50/1–52/3, goalkeeper, 80 games, 0 goals).

BILLY McGLEN (46/7–51/2, wing-half, 122 games, 2 goals).

TOM McNULTY (49/50–53/4, full-back, 59 games, 0 goals).

HARRY McSHANE (50/1–53/4, winger, 57 games, 8 goals).

DON GIBSON (50/1–54/5, wing-half, 114 games, 0 goals).

Babes in waiting

The Manchester United youngsters who lifted the European Youth Cup in 1954, not all of whom graduated to the first team. Three of those who did – Liam Whelan, Eddie Colman and David Pegg – were to lose their lives at Munich. Left to right are Ivan Beswick, Tony Hawksworth, Peter Pearce, Bryce Fulton, Liam Whelan, trainer Arthur Powell (with trophy), Mr Hartley (supporter), Bobby Harrop, Ada (supporter), Eddie Colman, Eddie Lewis, Wilf McGuinness, Gordon Clayton, Tommy Littler, Bobby Charlton, Alan Rhodes (behind Charlton), Albert Scanlon and David Pegg.

Football managers provoke a variety of emotions among players and supporters. Few, though, inspire reverence. But that's really the only word to describe the feeling for Sir Matt Busby among the people who were close to him – and many more who never met him – during his 48 years at Old Trafford.

Matt Busby

TEAM MANAGER: 1945–1969
GENERAL MANAGER: 1969–1971
DIRECTOR: 1971–1982
PRESIDENT: 1980–1994

Matt made Manchester United. It's as simple as that. True, when the former Manchester City, Liverpool and Scotland wing-half took over, the Red Devils could already look back on 60 years of history. But the United the world knows today, the club with an indefinable aura of magic which transcends its periodic traumas, is essentially a creation of the miner's son from Lanarkshire. After the war he inherited a bankrupt outfit with a bombed-out ground, and almost immediately he breathed life into the place. Donning a tracksuit to work alongside his new charges, he built a dashing side and soon he was lifting English football's major honours: the FA Cup in 1948, the League title four years later, to say nothing of finishing as runners-up in four seasons out of five.

Matt's creed was to entertain. He had a clear vision of how the game should be played and the ability to communicate it to his players. But there was more to the man than his flair and charisma. By demolishing his first Championship side to bring together the Busby Babes – a label of which he was never enamoured – he demonstrated a rare combination of steel and judgement.

His young side shook the soccer world. After winning two League titles with a squad which could weather the most ruinous injury crisis, a decade of dominance beck-oned. The Munich air disaster in 1958 put paid to that, but Matt was not done. He fought back from the brink of death to build a third wonderful team, taking two more Championships and the FA Cup in the 1960s.

Ultimately there was that most glittering prize, the European Cup, something of a holy grail to the United boss who had blazed the British trail in Europe after refusing to bow his knee before the Football League's stern opposition to participation. How he wanted that trophy for the lads who had died. The triumph, when it came in 1968 and following which he was knighted, was glorious and deserved, and with that last great battle won, soon he handed over to Wilf McGuinness.

The new man was not a success and many have criticised Matt for letting the side grow old together. He was even called soft. But, as anyone who played under Busby will testify, he was a hard man. He proved this in breaking up one fine side to build a better one in the 1950s, by dealing summarily with a wage revolt by Denis Law in the 1960s and by quietly dispensing iron discipline throughout his reign.

Perhaps he felt it fair to let his successor do his own weeding and plant his own seeds for the future. Unfortunately it didn't work, and Matt resumed control briefly until the appointment of Frank O'Farrell.

It was a pity that such a monumental tenure should end in anti-climax, but Matt's reputation was unassailable. The man who set the trend for modern management, then went on to become first a director and then president of his great club, would never cease to be held in respect, even awe, throughout the football world. Importantly, he was a gentleman first and a soccer boss second, reflecting the absolute truth of Law's declaration that he was the greatest ambassador the game had ever known.

Almost until the end of his life, he graced Old Trafford with his presence, revelling in the exhilarating fare served up by the new Red Devils. When he died, aged 84 in January 1994, millions of people around the world mourned his passing. Sir Matt Busby was one of a kind, and Manchester United owe him everything.

The truth is that Roger Byrne was one of the most accomplished defenders in British soccer history.

1951/52–1957/58

277 19

GAMES GOALS

BORN ● Manchester, 8.2.29.
HONOURS ● League Championship 51/2, 55/6, 56/7. 33
England caps (54–57).

If a manager from another planet, attracted by Roger Byrne's exalted reputation, had sent a scout to watch him train there would have been one very confused alien when he perused the report. It might have read something like this: heading – poor; tackling – ordinary; right foot – good; left foot – average (very); general impression – disillusioned. But if that same scout, wary of making too hasty a decision, had decided to stay for a match he would have torn up his notes and advised his boss to beam Roger up without delay.

Roger Byrne

The truth is that Roger Byrne was a superlative performer, one of the most accomplished defenders in British soccer history, but that his game defied detailed and logical analysis. Break his attributes down and he could be made to sound a bad player; but watch him in action and he was a master.

He started as a wing-half and was converted to a left-winger, the berth he filled when breaking through in United's junior sides. However, he was switched to left-back as an experiment during a training session and it was in the number-three shirt that he made his senior debut, against Liverpool at Anfield. That was in the Championship-winning season of 1951/52 and Roger was so impressive that he retained his defensive job until six matches from the end of the campaign.

Then, after a couple of defeats, Matt Busby opted to experiment and the newly-created full-back found himself back at outside-left. He responded by scoring seven goals in six games as United romped to the title without losing again. The following season Roger reverted to left-back, made the position his own and went on to play the same role for England on 33 consecutive occasions, from his debut against Scotland at Hampden Park in April 1954, through that summer's World Cup Finals in Switzerland, and thereafter until his death at Munich.

Roger, who succeeded Johnny Carey as United skipper, was a man who made a nonsense of soccer convention. To begin with he played on the left despite being right-footed. Even more significant was his propensity for attack in an era when most British full-backs thought their place was in their own half and there they must remain. Truly, here was a player ahead of his time.

His great asset was speed, both mental and physical. There were few opponents he could not outwit with his inspired anticipation and cool reading of the game, and it was a rare winger – Peter Harris of Portsmouth is the only one who comes to mind – who could make him struggle for pace.

Beyond the example he set on the field, Roger was a born leader in every other way. Though only 28 when he died, he was a father figure to the youngsters in the first-team squad. A man of integrity, he had their respect and if at times his tongue could seem sharp they accepted his discipline. Roger Byrne exuded class and charisma. He would have stood out in any company, in any era.

JOHNNY BERRY

1951/52–1957/58

273 **44**
GAMES GOALS

BORN — Aldershot, Hampshire, 1.6.26.
HONOURS — League Championship 51/2, 55/6, 56/7. 4 England caps (53–56).
OTHER CLUBS — Birmingham City 47/8–51/2 (103, 5).

When Johnny Berry was a Birmingham City player, Matt Busby was sick of the sight of him. Every time the tiny, but tough, right-winger faced United he tortured the Reds' defence. In the end the Old Trafford boss decided the only way to put an end to the torment was to sign the tormentor.

Even that wasn't as simple as it sounded. Birmingham were understandably reluctant to part with a performer who was gifted with both feet and who, had he not played in the era of Stan Matthews and Tom Finney, would have added considerably to his handful of England caps.

United had to wait 18 months before getting their man for £25,000, and what an inspired acquisition he proved to be. Johnny came into the team as the first wave of Busby Babes were making their debuts, and his experience and willingness to help the youngsters played an important part in their development.

Of course, his contribution went way beyond that. He was a tremendous performer in his own right, a classical flankman whose game was to make for the byline and get the ball into the middle with as little fuss as possible, although sometimes he appeared moody and had his off days.

Johnny was as brave a wingman as any who ever pulled on a red shirt. When full-backs handed out punishment – and there were certainly some ferocious customers among First Division defenders of the 1950s – there were many forwards who would jump for their lives. That was not Johnny's way; he would bite back, competing to the death, and the fans loved him for his courage.

He was to win three Championship medals with United before injuries sustained at Munich brought his career to an untimely end. Johnny died in September 1994.

With Tom Finney approaching the end of his illustrious career, David Pegg was seen by many as the man most likely, in the long term, to step into his international boots.

Then came Munich. Although Albert Scanlon was keeping him out of the United side at the time of the disaster, there was plainly a great deal more to come from David, who was only 22 when he died.

A one-time schoolboy prodigy who had been a target for every top club, he made his debut in 1952/53 at the age of 17. He had become one of the most respected left-wingers in the Football League when he suffered a loss of form towards the end of 1957 which let Albert in. He also enjoyed an enviable reputation in Europe, being held in particularly high regard by Real Madrid, who are said to have once signed a new defender specifically to combat his talents.

David, who twice won Championship medals, was more of a ball-playing winger than an out-and-out runner. Full-backs found him elusive to mark as he was in the habit of jinking inside, where he did much of his best work. On these penetrative sorties he was such a smooth mover that he seemed to glide over the ground, yet despite this delicate grace he possessed a left-foot shot of destructive force.

He was also a precise crosser of the ball, a boon to the likes of Dennis Viollet, with whom he formed a lethal partnership on the left flank, and centre-forward Tommy Taylor.

David Pegg had won only one full cap when he lost his life but England, as much as Manchester United, were robbed of a priceless asset on that bleak February day in 1958.

DAVID PEGG

1952/53–1957/58

 148 **28**
GAMES GOALS

BORN · Doncaster, Yorkshire, 20.9.35.
HONOURS · League Championship 55/6, 56/7. 1 England cap (57).

There was nothing that could be done on a football field that this young giant couldn't do better than anyone else.

1952/53–1957/58

175	21
GAMES	GOALS

BORN Dudley, Worcestershire, 1.10.36.

HONOURS League Championship 55/6, 56/7. 18 England caps (55–57).

The legend of Duncan Edwards was a short time in the building but, as long as men gather together to kick a football, it will never die. Duncan was a soccer titan, a once-in-a-lifetime phenomenon who thundered on to the First Division scene in the early 1950s and was snatched away just five years later, leaving the football world aching for what might have been. He had been in the United side at 16, the England team two years later, and there seemed no limit to what he would achieve.

Duncan Edwards

Duncan Edwards was that hitherto mythical being, the complete player. There was nothing that could be done on a football field that this young giant couldn't do better than anyone else. His ball control, with both feet, was masterful; his passing and tackling were exemplary; his shooting was awesome, both in power and accuracy; in the air he was a king; his reading of the game was startling in its maturity. The catalogue of his playing attributes was comprehensive.

And that's barely the half of it. Then there were his bravery, loyalty and dedication, and – perhaps the most crucial of the lot – a temperament that ensured he would never squander the gifts with which he was so bounteously endowed.

From the moment he arrived at Old Trafford, there was no doubt that Duncan was going to be very special. He was aware of this himself but was not one to sit back and let it all happen. His devotion to the game bordered on the fanatical and he would often practise until the ball had to be dragged away from him. Duncan would have played all day for the love of it if he could and was the embodiment of the Corinthian spirit.

Most of his games for United were at wing-half, a position from which he could lend his dominance to the defence but could also storm into the attack at every opportunity. Defenders seemed to bounce off him when he set off on one of those surging runs, an apparently unstoppable force. His last League match, the Reds' epic victory over Arsenal at Highbury by the odd goal in nine, saw one of his typical strikes when he arrived late on the edge of the penalty box to wallop a pass from Dennis Viollet past the Gunners' custodian, Jack Kelsey.

It's a testimony to his stature that respected judges who saw such men as Best, Law and Charlton in their prime nevertheless place Duncan above them. As Bobby Charlton himself once put it: 'If I had to play for my life, and could take one man with me, it would be Duncan Edwards.'

When he died at Munich – after a courageous two-week fight for life during which he joked with Jimmy Murphy about being fit for the next game – he had won two Championship medals and had played 18 times for England. He was only 21, his vast potential barely tapped. Those who saw Duncan Edwards play will treasure the memory. He was a young leviathan, and his like will not be seen again.

Mark was the archetypal pivot, broad of beam, crushing in the tackle and majestic in the air.

1950/51–1957/58

120 GAMES **1** GOALS

BORN ● Long Valley, near Barnsley, Yorkshire, 15.6.33.
HONOURS ● League Championship 55/6, 56/7.

'The Gentle Giant' was a nickname coined for the mighty John Charles, but it was just as apt to describe Mark Jones, that seam of Yorkshire granite standing between marauding centre-forwards of the 1950s and the Manchester United goal.

Mark Jones

Mark was the archetypal pivot, broad of beam, crushing in the tackle and majestic in the air. He was an uncomplicated sort of player and rarely ruined his ball-winning efforts by squandering possession with over-ambitious distribution. A simple pass to Duncan Edwards or Eddie Colman was his preferred option.

The doughty stopper, who won two Championship medals with United, relished the physical challenge presented by such craggy characters as Nat Lofthouse and Trevor Ford, yet off the field he was a mild-mannered family man who had more in common with Clark Kent than Superman. Mark was a fellow without an ounce of malice and his gentleness was a byword. He liked nothing better than a natter about his beloved budgerigars, of which he was an avid collector, and reacted amiably to being dubbed 'Dan Archer' by team-mates in reference to his pipe-smoking habit.

His football life was complicated by a continual battle for the centre-half spot with Jackie Blanchflower, the best man at his wedding. First one looked to have it sewn up, then the initiative would pass to the other. The Irishman edged selection for the 1957 FA Cup Final, but by the time of the Munich disaster, Mark had regained his place and was playing the best football of his career. Even the slightest injury to either man would mean a lengthy spell on the sidelines because of the other's excellence, though respected contemporary pundits reckoned that Mark was perhaps the best long-term bet.

The big, blond ex-bricklayer, a former captain of the England schoolboys team, had joined United from Yorkshire junior football and turned professional in the summer of 1950. That autumn, still only 17, he tasted League action for the first time in a home victory over Sheffield Wednesday, but then faced a four-year wait for a regular place. Duly he emerged from the shadow of his boyhood hero, Allenby Chilton, who played an important and selfless part in the youngster's development, helping to iron out initial crudeness in the Jones technique.

Thereafter Mark made steady progress, but was never to realise his lifelong ambition of playing for England. The nearest he came was a place on the reserves' bench, but had he not perished at Munich, then surely that elusive cap would have been his before long.

JACKIE BLANCHFLOWER

1951/52–1957/58

116 GAMES **27** GOALS

BORN · Belfast, 7.3.33.
HONOURS · League Championship 55/6. 12 Northern Ireland caps (54–58).

A thoroughbred footballer imbued with the spirit of adventure, Jackie Blanchflower did not always get the credit he deserved. While plaudits were rained – rightly enough – on the heads of Duncan Edwards and company, often Jackie's name was absent from dispatches.

A utility man of style and subtle skills and the younger brother of the more famous Danny, he made an impressive United debut as a wing-half at Anfield in 1951/52, but then suffered a knee injury which put him out of immediate contention. By the time he had fully recovered, there had appeared a new wave of exquisitely talented youngsters – with the aforementioned Mr Edwards at its crest – and the consequently ferocious competition for places forced him temporarily to one side.

But Jackie – known as Twiggy by colleagues who took grave liberties with his name, long before the emergence of a certain stick-like lady – was too sure of his own worth merely to fade away. Thus he returned to the reckoning as a creative inside-forward, contributing 24 goals over two campaigns before pocketing a title medal in 1955/56.

However, blessed as he was with a golden crop of outstanding young attackers, Matt Busby decreed that centre-half should be Jackie's premier position and thereafter, until the Munich tragedy, the Ulsterman waged war with Mark Jones for the number-five shirt.

Jackie brought enviable qualities to that duel: he had a fine touch with both feet, was combative in the air and possessed a formidable footballing brain. His most marked defect was a distinct lack of pace which, in his early days at Old Trafford, caused much ribbing.

A natural all-round sportsman, he demonstrated his versatility when he took over in goal for the injured Ray Wood in the 1957 FA Cup Final. He gave a sound display and blame for neither of Aston Villa's goals could be laid at his door.

Jackie, who received the last rites at Munich, survived the accident but was unable to resume his career, a bitter loss to United and Northern Ireland. He died in 1998.

COLIN WEBSTER ▲

1953/54–1958/59

79	31
GAMES	GOALS

BORN	Cardiff, 17.7.32.
HONOURS	League Championship 55/6.
	4 Wales caps (57–58).
OTHER CLUBS	Swansea Town 58/9–62/3 (159, 65);
	Newport County 62/3–63/4 (31, 3).

A bout of flu may have saved Colin Webster's life. The Welsh international utility forward was due to travel with the side that was to meet catastrophe at Munich but he was too ill to make the trip. In fact, Colin would have gone only as a reserve. His first-team opportunities were severely limited due to the strength in depth at Old Trafford. Eight players, for example, were in serious contention for the three places in the middle of the attack.

Though not in the top bracket, Colin was a respected member of the club. He played all across the front line, won a Championship medal in 1955/56 and, despite his lazy, loping action, he was deceptively quick and a rumbustious competitor. His goals-to-games ratio was impressive, too, his most important strike being the winner against West Bromwich Albion in the 1958 FA Cup fifth-round replay. After the crash Colin did get an extended run and faced Bolton in the FA Cup Final before moving to Swansea Town the following season.

JOHN DOHERTY ▼

1952/53–1957/58

26	7
GAMES	GOALS

BORN	Manchester, 12.3.35.
HONOURS	League Championship 55/6.
OTHER CLUBS	Leicester City 57/8 (12, 5).

There was a time, when John Doherty's star was rising, that he looked the equal of any promising young inside-forward in the country. John was blessed with an astute football brain, skill aplenty in both feet and a shot to compare with Bobby Charlton's.

An outstanding youth player, he made his debut in 1952/53. But competition was fierce among the Busby Babes and John had a knee injury which would never quite clear up, so he was denied a settled run in the team until 1955/56. That season he won a Championship medal on merit with 16 appearances. But that gammy knee continued to plague him and Liam Whelan, originally brought to England to fill in for an unfit John in an FA Youth Cup Final, had developed into an irresistible performer.

A future that had once beckoned so invitingly no longer seemed so bright and the unlucky Mancunian moved to Leicester shortly before limping out of the game for good. John, and United, were left to ponder what might have been.

A tiny bundle of creative energy, Eddie was the wing-half with the wiggle and his prospects appeared to be limitless.

1955/56–1957/58

107 **2**
GAMES GOALS

BORN ● Salford, Lancashire, 1.11.36.
HONOURS ● League Championship 55/6, 56/7.

Watching Eddie Colman on a football pitch was like spying on a precocious small boy scrumping apples from his teacher's garden while playing truant from school. There was the same jaunty swagger spiced with a dash of daring which made him an irresistible figure to the denizens of the Old Trafford terraces, especially the Stretford End. But, by the time the Munich disaster took the life of this irrepressible local lad, he had very much come of age as a football talent.

Eddie Colman

A tiny bundle of creative energy, Eddie was the wing-half with the wiggle – the press dubbed him 'Snakehips' for his mesmeric body swerve – and his prospects appeared to be limitless. He had been a fixture in the team since making his debut, aged 19, in November 1955 against Bolton. In that match he had astonished seasoned campaigners such as Nat Lofthouse with his skill and confidence, and he improved rapidly with experience.

Eddie's influence on the United side that won the Championship in consecutive seasons, 1955/56 and 1956/57, was enormous. So many of their most effective moves owed plenty to his wickedly incisive passing and devastating dribbling ability. His eye for an opening was unerring and he was particularly adept at curling perfect passes around stranded defenders to set up his forwards.

Sometimes, like George Best in later years, he would madden team-mates by hanging on to the ball too long. But they knew Eddie was a player who needed a free rein. To have shackled him to a rigid team plan would have stifled the inspiration which made him priceless.

In another set-up Eddie Colman might have struggled to express himself, but with the Busby Babes he was in his element. So much of his success was thanks to the manager's golden gift of creating the right blend. Although tough enough for his size and a plucky tackler, Eddie needed to play alongside a man of dominating physical presence – and who better than Duncan Edwards?

One element missing from the Colman game was goals. He managed only two in his career, though one of those was a crucial effort in the 1957/58 European Cup quarter-final against Red Star Belgrade. Part of the reason for this drought was that he wasn't the strongest striker of the ball, his glorious passes owing more to deftness than power, but that hardly qualifies as a criticism when he did so much to boost his team-mates' tallies.

Eddie Colman will be remembered as a crowd-pleaser supreme whose best days were yet to come. He was only 21 when he died and yet to appear for England. Country, as well as club, was thus deprived of a diamond.

JACK CROMPTON ▼

1945/46–1955/56

211	0
GAMES	GOALS

BORN ○ Manchester, 18.12.21.
HONOURS ○ FA Cup 47/8.
OTHER CLUBS ○ MANAGER: Luton Town (acting, 62); Barrow (71–72).

Jack Crompton, one of Manchester United's most valued servants, is included in this section of the book only on the strength of one game in 1955/56 when he stood in for the injured Ray Wood. His heyday was in the immediate post-war years, during which he made more than 200 senior appearances.

A steady, dependable 'keeper rather than a brilliant one, he won an FA Cup medal in the classic 1948 encounter with Blackpool but played only a handful of games in the title season of 1951/52, having been displaced by Reg Allen.

On retirement he became a coach at Luton before returning as United trainer after Munich, staying at Old Trafford until the early 1970s. After spells as manager at Barrow and assistant to Bobby Charlton at Preston, he made a brief return to United as reserve team trainer. Jack completed his Old Trafford service as caretaker boss during the interregnum between Dave Sexton and Ron Atkinson in the summer of 1981.

JEFF WHITEFOOT ▲

1949/50–1955/56

95	0
GAMES	GOALS

BORN ○ Cheadle, Cheshire, 13.12.33.
HONOURS ○ League Championship 55/6.
OTHER CLUBS ○ Grimsby Town 57/8 (27, 5); Nottingham Forest 58/9–67/8 (255, 5).

More than a handful of well-informed observers of the Old Trafford scene in the 1950s were mystified by Jeff Whitefoot's failure to become a United star. The obvious answer was that this skilful wing-half, one of the original Babes who made his debut at 16, lost out through the emergence of Eddie Colman, but that alone is not a satisfactory solution.

Quite clearly, Eddie was a marvellous player who merited his place but the way the club was developing, particularly on the European front, meant that a large squad of quality performers was needed; and the football fates being what they are, it seemed likely that opportunity would come again for Jeff. But, after winning a Championship medal in 1955/56, he moved to Grimsby and then Nottingham Forest, where he carved himself a successful niche.

After Munich, many thought that United would turn again to Jeff, an accomplished passer with both feet and an effective tackler, but Stan Crowther was signed instead.

A freezing November night in Dortmund is not the time or place most players would choose to have their finest hour, but so it was with **Ray Wood**. It happened in 1956, well before the days when television brought instant worldwide glory for any performer who excelled in a big match.

Ray was keeping goal in the second leg of the European Cup first-round tie against Borussia. United took only a one-goal lead with them, an advantage which looked increasingly slender as the Germans took control. Borussia created chances galore and must have been confident that goals would come, but they were destined to be disappointed thanks to the inspiration of Ray Wood, who gave the performance of a lifetime.

In fact, Ray was always a top notch shot-stopper, but his handling of crosses was not of quite the same calibre and he was eventually replaced by Harry Gregg. He will be remembered always as the man whose injury in a sickening collision with Peter McParland in the 1957 FA Cup Final probably cost United the League and FA Cup double. He deserves a better epitaph than that and can justifiably point to two Championship medals and three England caps.

Ray, who joined United from Darlington, survived Munich and then moved on to Huddersfield when it became clear he would not regain his place. A measure of Matt Busby's professional regard for the likeable Wood was that the Old Trafford boss tried unsuccessfully to re-sign him when Gregg suffered a serious shoulder injury.

RAY WOOD

1949/50–1958/59

 205 **0**
GAMES GOALS

BORN Hebburn, County Durham, 11.6.31.
HONOURS League Championship 55/6, 56/7. 3 England caps (54–56).
OTHER CLUBS Darlington 49/50 (12, 0); Huddersfield Town 58/9–64/5 (207, 0); Bradford City 65/6 (32, 0); Barnsley 66/7–67/8 (30, 0).
MANAGER: Los Angeles Wolves, USA, 68; Cyprus national team 69–72; Apoel, Cyprus, 72–73; Trikkala, Greece, 73; Salymia, Kuwait, 73–74; Kenya club and national teams 74–78; United Arab Emirates clubs 78–82.

He could smack the ball with his forehead more forcefully and accurately than many players could kick it.

1952/53–1957/58

189	128
GAMES	GOALS

BORN ● Barnsley, Yorkshire, 29.1.32.
HONOURS ● League Championship 55/6, 56/7. 19 England caps (53–57).
OTHER CLUBS ● Barnsley 50/1–52/3 (44, 26).

When Tommy Taylor powered home a header from outside the penalty area against Preston North End in his first game for Manchester United, Reds supporters sensed they were in the presence of an extraordinary talent. The following five years, until he lost his life at Munich, were to prove them emphatically correct.

Tommy Taylor

Tommy was arguably the greatest centre-forward England, let alone United, ever had. He was certainly one of the most underrated and his scoring record would have been staggering in any era. For the Red Devils he managed two goals every three matches; put another way, he found the net once every two hours or so that he spent on a football pitch.

On top of that he weighed in with a further 16 in 19 games for England and there was every reason to believe that, at 26, he was still approaching his peak. Yet when the all-time greats are mentioned, his name does not always crop up – outside Old Trafford circles, I hasten to add.

Tommy, a big, raw-boned Yorkshire lad, was snapped up from Barnsley for what was then a record fee of £29,999 – as is generally known, Matt Busby did not want him burdened with a £30,000 tag and gave the extra pound to a tea lady. Soon it was apparent that United had got a bargain. The new boy, an ebullient character who quickly became popular with fans and colleagues alike, scored twice on his debut and by the end of the 1952/53 campaign he had notched seven in just 11 games.

Unquestionably his greatest gift was for aerial combat, in which he had no contemporary peer. He could smack the ball with his forehead more forcefully and accurately than many players could kick it, his timing was uncanny and his bravery knew no bounds. This spectacular talent tended to obscure his other attributes, which were considerable. Perhaps because of his size, he could look clumsy on the ball but this belied excellent control and a sharp line in first-time distribution which made him devastating, particularly in tandem with Dennis Viollet.

A strong, selfless player who had the stamina to spend 90 minutes at full stretch, Tommy was often at his best when drifting wide to the right, pulling defenders with him and interchanging positions with Johnny Berry. Such a ploy produced Johnny's unforgettable winner against Atletico Bilbao in the quarter-final of the 1956/57 European Cup.

Tommy's growing stature in the world game was illustrated immediately after the 1957 FA Cup Final, in which he scored United's goal, when Inter Milan made the then-astronomical offer of £65,000 for his services. The manager rejected the bid; his dashing young centre-forward was not for sale at any price. What a tragic shame that Matt was unable to enjoy the full fruits of his judgement.

If this dream of a dribbler had only possessed pace he would have ranked as one of football's all-time greats.

1954/55–1957/58

96 **52**
GAMES GOALS

BORN — Dublin, 1.4.35.
HONOURS — League Championship 55/6, 56/7. 4 Republic of Ireland caps (56–57).
OTHER CLUBS — Home Farm, Republic of Ireland.

Liam Whelan was a soccer artist whose brain moved faster than his legs. On the ball he could look awkward, even clumsy, yet he had the knack of ghosting past opponent after opponent with the merest of shimmies. And once within shooting distance he was a man to respect, as his record of better than a goal every two games testifies. Indeed, in 1956/57 Liam netted 33 times in 53 senior outings – and he wasn't even playing as an out-and-out front man.

Liam Whelan

A vivid example of his talent came in the quarter-final of the European Cup in Bilbao that same season. He picked the ball up deep, shuffled half the length of the pitch leaving five defenders in his wake and scored with precision.

The quietly-spoken inside-forward, whose engagingly modest personality was never altered by his success with United and the Republic of Ireland, played his football with a deceptively relaxed air. Certainly there was nothing casual about his work in the penalty area and he could be especially lethal with his back to goal. One of soccer's more persuasive dummy salesmen, he found an unwilling customer in the shape of a bemused Wrexham defender in January 1957. The subtle flick which found the net when no danger seemed imminent was the work of a conjuror.

If this dream of a dribbler had only possessed pace he would have ranked as one of football's all-time greats, even though his career – and his life – ended at Munich. As it was Liam didn't always get the credit he deserved and didn't realise just how good he was.

United's coaching staff, however, were under no such misapprehension, right from the moment he was signed as an 18-year-old from Home Farm with the urgent initial task of replacing the injured John Doherty in the 1953 FA Youth Cup Final against Wolves. Liam – or Billy as he quickly became known to Mancunians – starred in a 7–1 first-leg victory and was marked down for an illustrious future. Indeed, so eye-catching were his gifts that, following a fabulous display in a youth tournament in Switzerland, the club received a discreet inquiry from Brazil about his availability. Needless to say, further interest was not encouraged.

The boy's development continued apace; soon he was a major creative and goal-scoring force at senior level and the honours began to mount. Yet such was the wealth of talent available to Matt Busby in that glorious era that, at the time of the Munich disaster, the 22-year-old Dubliner was being kept out of the side by one of his closest friends, Bobby Charlton. Of course, he had so much to give that, sooner or later, he must have reclaimed a place, even if it had not been at Bobby's expense.

Liam was a devout Roman Catholic and, to the last, his faith never wavered. As United's plane made its fateful third attempt at take-off from that slushy German runway, he was heard to murmur: 'If this is the end, then I am ready for it.' The tragedy was that the soccer world was far from ready to lose Liam Whelan.

ALBERT SCANLON

1954/55–1960/61

127 **35**
GAMES GOALS

BORN ● Manchester, 10.10.35.
OTHER CLUBS ● Newcastle United 60/1–61/2 (22, 0); Lincoln City 61/2–62/3 (47, 11); Mansfield Town 62/3–65/6 (108, 21).

Albert Scanlon was something of an enigma. A dashing winger of skill and verve who could wreak havoc with both feet, he didn't build the lengthy career at Old Trafford that his ability appeared to warrant.

After a creditable run in the side as a rather overawed teenager in 1954/55, he found himself largely in the shadow of David Pegg for the next two years. The two made a fascinating contrast: David blessed with more intricate skills and a more consistent player, Albert quicker and perhaps more exciting but with an unpredictable streak.

Halfway through the 1957/58 campaign the young Scanlon forced his way back in and he was still there on merit at the time of Munich. One of his most memorable performances was in the last League game before the disaster, a stirring 5–4 triumph over Arsenal at Highbury. That day he laid on three goals and generally tantalised the Gunners' defence with a display of speed and flair which had the pundits talking about an international future that, alas, never came to pass.

The crash sidelined Albert for the rest of the season but he came back strongly the next year to be an everpresent and score 16 goals as, astonishingly, the new United finished runners-up. By now he was playing the best football of his career, but there was always the feeling that a couple of blinders could be followed by a stinker.

By 1960/61 Matt Busby had temporarily converted Bobby Charlton into an outside-left, and Albert moved on to Newcastle before seeing out his career at Lincoln and Mansfield. Those who recall him in his prime know he had much more to offer.

GEOFF BENT ▲

1954/55–1956/57

12	0
GAMES	GOALS

BORN ◇ Salford, Lancashire, 27.9.32.

Geoff Bent was perhaps the unluckiest player to die at Munich on that ill-fated journey home from Belgrade. As a reserve full-back he had not been going to make the trip for the European Cup encounter with Red Star until Roger Byrne suffered a slight strain in the match at Highbury the previous Saturday. In the event, Roger was fit to face the Yugoslavians so Geoff was not needed, which made the events that followed all the more poignant.

In fact, if he had been with any other club in the First Division, Geoff Bent would have been an automatic first choice. He was an aggressive tackler who could play on the left or right side of defence and who boasted speed, a cool head and good distribution among his assets. Life in the shadow of Roger must have been frustrating but it never affected Geoff's enthusiastic approach or his loyalty.

KENNY MORGANS ▼

1957/58–1960/61

23	0
GAMES	GOALS

BORN ◇ Swansea, Glamorgan, 16.3.39.
OTHER CLUBS ◇ Swansea Town 60/1–63/4 (55, 8),
Newport County 64/5–66/7 (125, 46).

The odd case of Kenny Morgans poses a mystery. Before the Munich disaster Kenny, a nippy winger who could play on either flank, was in the first team on merit. He had displaced Johnny Berry in the December, had a six-week purple patch and, come February, looked set for a lengthy run.

Then came the crash, which the chirpy Welshman survived. He was passed fit and returned to the side by April. Yet he never recaptured his form or the confidence that was his hallmark and was not picked for the FA Cup Final against Bolton Wanderers. And that was just about that. Soon he moved to Swansea and then Newport, where he saw out his playing days.

So what went wrong? With much of the competition for places so tragically removed he had been expected to prosper at Old Trafford. Perhaps he had hinted at more than he could deliver, or maybe he had rushed back into action too soon without giving the mental scars left by the disaster a chance to heal. Either way, a promising career at the top level was cut short before it really got going.

One of the most prolific goal-scorers in Old Trafford history, Viollet luxuriated in the space created by the ever-bustling Taylor.

1952/53–1961/62

291 **178**
GAMES GOALS

BORN ● Manchester, 20.9.33.
HONOURS ● League Championship 55/6, 56/7.
2 England caps (60–61).
OTHER CLUBS ● Stoke City 61/2–66/7 (182, 59);
Baltimore Bays, USA, 67-68;
Linfield, Northern Ireland, 69/70.
MANAGER: Crewe Alexandra (71).

Dennis Viollet was a steel dart of a player. Slim, even frail of appearance, he was possessed of magnetic control and sudden, searing pace which could slice to the heart of the stoutest defence. Yet one of soccer's absurdities is that he played only twice for his country.

Dennis Viollet

In the middle and late 1950s, at a time when the deceptively wiry inside-forward and his partner-in-goals Tommy Taylor were terrorising First Division defences, England deigned to select only half of the free-scoring United double-act. Never mind that Tommy was at his most lethal alongside his clubmate, or that Dennis himself was as gifted and resourceful a front-man as could be found in Britain. It was deemed desirable for the coveted white shirt to be placed on the backs of a series of worthy but uninspired individuals.

But if England fans were denied the chance to revel in the talents of such an exciting entertainer, United supporters faced no such deprivation in those heady, adventurous pre-Munich days. One of the most prolific goalscorers in Old Trafford history, Viollet luxuriated in the space created by the ever-bustling Taylor who, in turn, fed voraciously off opportunities fashioned by his Manchester-born cohort. In terms of a striking duo they were the dream ticket, but anyone who doubted that Dennis was an outstanding performer in his own right was soon furnished with ample proof after Tommy was killed.

Viollet was laid low by the after-effects of the crash until the end of 1957/58 – he recovered just in time to appear in the FA Cup Final against Bolton – but then bounced back with 21 goals the following term. But it was in 1959/60 that he really demonstrated his quality, rattling in 32 goals in 36 League matches, more strikes in one campaign than any United player before or since.

Stop to consider a few of the men Dennis Viollet has outscored – take Jack Rowley, Stan Pearson, Tommy Taylor, Bobby Charlton, Denis Law and George Best for starters – and the scale of his achievement is apparent. Yet there was more to his game than that. He had the distribution and all-round ability to succeed in a deep-lying role, in which he operated at times for United and, more frequently, after his transfer to Stoke in January 1962. His only discernible defect was a lack of aerial ability, not serious when playing alongside the likes of Taylor.

A man who lived life to the full, Dennis surprised many people with his £25,000 move, which was completed not long after his two belated England appearances. Perhaps fittingly for an individual so continuously under-valued in his own country, he finished his football career as a coach in the United States. Dennis died in 1999, following a long illness.

FREDDIE GOODWIN ▼

1954/55–1959/60

106	8
GAMES	GOALS

BORN Heywood, Lancashire, 28.6.33.
OTHER CLUBS Leeds United 59/60–63/4 (107, 2); Scunthorpe United 65/6 (6, 1).
MANAGER: Scunthorpe United (64–67); New York Generals, USA (67–68); Brighton and Hove Albion (68–70); Birmingham City (70–75); Minnesota Kicks, USA (76–79 and 80–81).

Freddie Goodwin was a lanky, cool, almost languid wing-half whose misfortune it was to be at Old Trafford at the same time as Eddie Colman and Duncan Edwards. A good passer, particularly adept at one-twos, he was a kind of lesser, six-foot version of Colman without the flair.

He made his debut in 1954/55 but, until Munich, never surpassed the status of reserve, though he was one of the classiest stand-ins in the First Division. In the wake of the crash he made the right-half position his own, appearing in the 1958 FA Cup Final and earning considerable distinction as an ever-present in the side which finished as runners-up the following season.

After that Freddie's star began to fall as Matt Busby began building a new team, and in March 1960 he joined Leeds, whom he served with consistency for five seasons.

A former county cricketer with Lancashire, Freddie went on to take up soccer management, serving a series of clubs in Britain and the United States, with his spell at Birmingham City being the most notable.

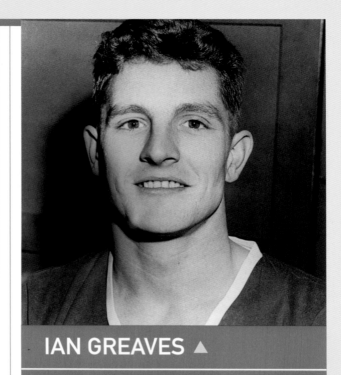

IAN GREAVES ▲

1954/55–1959/60

75	0
GAMES	GOALS

BORN Oldham, Lancashire, 26.5.32.
HONOURS League Championship 55/6.
OTHER CLUBS Lincoln City 60/1(11, 0); Oldham Athletic 61/2–62/3 (22, 0).
MANAGER: Huddersfield Town (68–74); Bolton Wanderers (74–80); Oxford United (80–82); Wolverhampton Wanderers (82); Mansfield Town; (83–89)

One inspired spell was enough for Ian Greaves to win a Championship medal, and he did it on merit in the pre-Munich days of white-hot competition. Admittedly Ian got his chance at right-back when the redoubtable Bill Foulkes was injured, but he performed so well that Bill could not win back his place until the following season. After the crash the versatile Ian took over at left-back, a position in which he picked up an FA Cup finalist's medal, then kept the job during the next term, only for a knee injury to effectively end his Old Trafford sojourn.

Ian was a tall, sturdy, inelegant defender who looked all arms and legs. He linked well with his half-backs and was brave but never, except in that one purple patch, looked likely to make the very highest grade. If he was not in the top bracket as a player, however, there is ample evidence of his excellence as a manager. There was even a time, during his splendid spell at Bolton, when he was tipped to take over from Tommy Docherty at United. And there are those who believe that had he done so, the wait for the title would have been considerably shorter . . .

ERNIE TAYLOR ▼

1957/58–1958/59

30 GAMES **4** GOALS

BORN	Sunderland, 2.9.25.
HONOURS	1 England cap (53).
OTHER CLUBS	Newcastle United 47/8–51/2 (107, 19); Blackpool 51/2–57/8 (217, 53); Sunderland 58/9–60/61(68, 11).

Ernie Taylor arrived at Old Trafford, did the job that was expected of him and departed – all within a matter of ten months. Acting manager Jimmy Murphy bought the vastly experienced little schemer from Blackpool for £8,000 immediately after Munich. His task: to hold together a gang of raw lads at the most emotional time imaginable.

In the first game after the crash, an FA Cup tie against Sheffield Wednesday, he worked like a Trojan as United chalked up a heart-swelling 3–0 victory. This set the tone for his brief but vital stay. Sometimes cajoling, at other times driving, this voluble little general was the youngsters' inspiration on the field, as Jimmy was off it.

And he wasn't all talk; Ernie Taylor had the talent to lead by example. He was an ingenious, instinctive passer and a crowd-pleasing improviser, full of flicks and backheels. He played in the 1958 FA Cup Final but lost his place early in the next campaign. There was talk of a job helping the reserves but instead he moved to Sunderland for £6,000, his task completed. Ernie died in 1985.

STAN CROWTHER ▲

1957/58–1958/59

20 GAMES **0** GOALS

BORN	Bilston, Staffordshire, 3.9.35.
OTHER CLUBS	Aston Villa 56/7–57/8 (50, 4); Chelsea 58/9–59/60 (51, 0); Brighton and Hove Albion 60/1 (4, 0).

Stan Crowther was a trier but he never looked likely to have a long-term future with Manchester United. Bought for £35,000 as an emergency measure after Munich, he was a tough winghalf who lacked the all-round ability to succeed at the top level.

Stan had an effective game for Aston Villa against United in the 1957 FA Cup Final, displaying just the grit and vigour which Jimmy Murphy needed for his team after the crash. Though he was cup-tied with the Midlanders come February 1958, the FA waived the rule and he helped to tide the Reds over the immediate crisis, picking up a Wembley loser's medal in the process. Stan lost his place to Wilf McGuinness at the outset of the 1958/59 campaign and soon moved on, first to Chelsea for £10,000 and then to Brighton, without managing to make much of a mark.

During his spell at Villa, he won England under-23 recognition but that early promise was never fulfilled.

WILF McGUINNESS

1955/56–1959/60

85 GAMES **2** GOALS

BORN	Manchester, 25.10.37.
HONOURS	2 England caps (58–59).
OTHER CLUBS	**MANAGER:** Manchester United (69–70); Aris Salonika, Greece (71–73); Panaraiki Patras, Greece (73–74); York City (75–77); Bury (acting, 89).

If there were a prize for the keenest footballer ever to play for Manchester United then it would have to go to Wilf McGuinness. He was possessed by an all-consuming enthusiasm — passion is perhaps a more apt word — for football in general and the Old Trafford club in particular.

A defensive wing-half whose rather limited skills were outshone by a phenomenal work rate, Wilf was granted few senior opportunities during his early professional years, due to the omnipotent presence of his chum, one Duncan Edwards.

However, when the England star fell foul of flu in October 1955, up stepped the 17-year-old McGuinness to make his debut at home to Wolves, then a major power. Faced with the cunning wiles of schemer Peter Broadbent, the newcomer did an efficient job, signalling to Matt Busby that here was yet another confident young fellow with the nerve to rise to a big occasion.

Just over two years later, having earned a title medal in 1956/57 mainly as Duncan's deputy, Wilf had been due to be part of the ill-fated expedition to Belgrade, only to withdraw because of knee problems.

Yet even the depredations of Munich did not guarantee him a place and the arrival of emergency signing Stan Crowther signalled new competition. But, his eagerness undiminished, Wilf ousted Stan at the start of 1958/59 and missed only three games in the whole campaign. Perhaps surprisingly, considering his inexperience, the former captain of England Schoolboys was rewarded with two full caps that same term.

Then, while seemingly poised on the brink of a glittering future, the lion-hearted 22-year-old was struck down. A shin injury had been limiting his effectiveness and he was seeking to test it in a reserve clash with Stoke City when he went into a routine tackle with Peter Bullock and emerged with a shattered leg.

An optimist by nature, he strove for two years to regain fitness but he never came back, a chronic blow to a manager in the throes of major team reconstruction. On a personal level it was a crushing setback to the self-assured McGuinness, who had been looking forward to another decade's active service in the Old Trafford cause.

Recognising Wilf's burning desire to serve the club, Matt Busby employed him as a youth coach and he built on that, eventually becoming influential in the England set-up under another former United man, Walter Winterbottom.

In 1966/67 there was just the whiff of a comeback, when the fit-again 29-year-old got as far as the first-team substitute's bench but, sadly for a man still desperate to play, he progressed no further.

Still to come, of course, was a traumatic reign as manager of the club he loved so much it hurt, of which more follows later. After that, Wilf went on to boss York before becoming a physiotherapist.

If Alex Dawson had not been allowed to leave United to become 'The Black Prince of Deepdale', might he one day have donned a yet more majestic crown at Old Trafford? It's impossible, of course, to say. But this tank of a centre-forward's striking rate makes the question well worth the asking.

There are fearsome characters in any era but it is difficult to imagine a more blood-curdling sight for a defender than the Red Devils' bull-necked battering ram. He would fix his eye on the ball and go for it; whatever, or whoever, was in his way usually bounced off him. As he has admitted since, there wasn't much he wouldn't do to put the ball in the net, though he maintained that he was fundamentally fair and never maimed anybody!

An England schoolboy international, having crossed the border from Aberdeen to Hull as a child, Alex joined United as a winger in the mid 1950s. Conversion to spearhead followed and, after helping to win the FA Youth Cup in two successive seasons, he netted on his senior debut at home to Burnley on Easter Monday 1957.

He registered in the next two games, too, as United clinched the title and there was talk that, with Tommy Taylor carrying an injury, young Dawson might face Aston Villa in the FA Cup Final.

The call never came that season, but Alex did find himself at Wembley a year later as the post-Munich Reds defied the odds to reach a second successive final, thanks in no small measure to the burly Aberdonian's hat-trick in the rousing 5-3 semi-final replay victory over Fulham at Highbury.

But despite continuing to demonstrate his endearing penchant for hitting the target – in his last two full seasons he managed 31 goals in 50 outings – he found a regular place hard to command.

Possibly his development as a rounded performer was adversely affected through being rushed into regular first-team action in the wake of the disaster, but whatever the reason, Matt Busby was not completely satisfied with Dawson's progress and recruited the formidable David Herd.

While Alex was no overall match for the Scottish international, he was stronger in the air and could point to his own fine record. However, and perhaps inevitably, Matt was proved right as David went on to contribute ever more impressively as the years went by.

Meanwhile, in October 1961 Alex was sold to Preston for £18,000, going on to earn that regal title before performing further gallant deeds for Bury and others.

ALEX DAWSON

1956/57–1961/62

93 GAMES   54 GOALS

BORN   Aberdeen, 21.2.40.
OTHER CLUBS   Preston North End 61/2–66/7 (197, 114); Bury 66/7–68/9 (50, 21); Brighton and Hove Albion 68/9–70/1 (57, 26); Brentford 70/1 (10, 6).

Harry Gregg was a superb entertainer blessed with courage, pride and character in ample measure.

1957/58–1966/67

247 **0**
GAMES GOALS

BORN	Derry, Northern Ireland, 25.10.32.
HONOURS	25 Northern Ireland caps (54–63).
OTHER CLUBS	Linfield, Northern Ireland; Coleraine, Northern Ireland; Doncaster Rovers 52/3–57/8 (93, 0); Stoke City 66/7 (2, 0). MANAGER: Shrewsbury Town (68–72); Swansea City (72–75); Crewe Alexandra (75–78); Carlisle United (86–87).

Harry Gregg was arguably the best goalkeeper Manchester United ever had – yet he has no honours to show for it. The best that the big, flame-haired Irishman can point to after a decade with one of Europe's most successful club sides is an FA Cup finalist's medal.

Harry Gregg

The bane of Harry's footballing life was a series of shoulder injuries which cost him more than 100 appearances and, often, untold agony when he did turn out. There were times towards the end of his career when he could hardly lift his arm above his head, yet he soldiered on, displaying the same raw bravery which saw him through the ordeal of Munich and other personal tragedies.

When Harry arrived at Old Trafford from Doncaster Rovers in December 1957 for £23,500, then a world record fee for a 'keeper, he stunned the United defence. They were used to Ray Wood, as good a shot-stopper as could be found but a man who often left defenders to their own devices on crosses. Not so Harry. He was out to command his whole area, going for every ball with total commitment and then, whenever possible, setting an instant counter-assault in motion. If there could be such a thing as an attacking goalkeeper then, most definitely, this vociferous acrobat was it.

At first there were the inevitable collisions. Harry was no respecter of reputations or feelings. If England men Roger Byrne and Duncan Edwards got in his way then they found out about it quickly – and sometimes painfully. But as the defence grew accustomed to their dashing new custodian, understanding and confidence grew.

Then came Munich and the football world was never the same again. From being a sports hero, in the superficial parlance of the back page, Harry became a real hero, rescuing a woman and her baby from the wreckage of United's devastated plane.

Within 13 days he was back in goal and at the top of his form as the Red Devils somehow continued their unlikely march towards Wembley by beating Sheffield Wednesday in the FA Cup. The campaign was to end in gallant defeat and controversy when Nat Lofthouse thundered into Harry, knocking him unconscious and sending him and the ball into the net. A goal was given and United lost, gloriously. A few months later Harry was voted top 'keeper in the World Cup Finals as he helped Northern Ireland reach the last eight.

Then at the zenith of his powers, he was seen by Matt Busby as a cornerstone of the new United. But although Harry was a magnificent all-round athlete, often his shoulder let him down. As a result he was absent at crucial junctures, missing out on the FA Cup triumph of 1963 – he was fit in time for the final but the manager opted not to change a winning team – and the Championship two years later.

When Alex Stepney arrived, Harry, by then aged 34, joined Stoke but soon went into management, serving various clubs in the lower divisions before putting in a stint as goalkeeping coach at Old Trafford. Despite the Herculean modern achievements of Peter Schmeichel, there remain many veteran observers of the Old Trafford scene who continue to identify Gregg as the yardstick by which all United custodians should be judged, and they contend fiercely that it will be a momentous day when, finally, one matches him in every respect. Harry Gregg was a superb entertainer blessed with courage, pride and character in ample measure. But when it came to the luck of the Irish, his was nearly all bad.

HAROLD BRATT

1960/61

DEFENDER

1 0
GAMES GOALS

BORN:
Salford, Lancashire, 8.10.39.

OTHER CLUBS:
Doncaster Rovers 61/2–62/3
(54, 0).

BOBBY HARROP

1957/58–1958/59

DEFENDER

11 0
GAMES GOALS

BORN:
Manchester, 25.8.36.

OTHER CLUBS:
Tranmere Rovers
59/60–60/1 (41, 2).

RONNIE BRIGGS

1960/61–1961/62

GOALKEEPER

11 0
GAMES GOALS

BORN:
Belfast, 29.3.43.

HONOURS:
2 Northern Ireland caps
(62–65).

OTHER CLUBS:
Swansea Town 64/5 (27, 0);
Bristol Rovers 65/6–67/8
(35, 0).

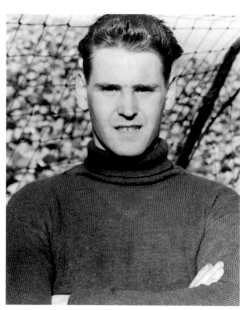

TONY HAWKSWORTH

1956/57

GOALKEEPER

1 0
GAMES GOALS

BORN:
Sheffield, 15.1.38.

OTHER CLUBS:
Tranmere Rovers
59/60–60/1 (4, 0).

GORDON CLAYTON

1956/57

GOALKEEPER

2 0
GAMES GOALS

BORN:
Wednesbury, Staffordshire,
3.11.36.

OTHER CLUBS:
Tranmere Rovers
59/60–60/1 (4, 0).

Died 1991.

TOMMY HERON

1957/58–1960/61

FULL-BACK OR WINGER

3 0
GAMES GOALS

BORN:
Irvine, Ayrshire, 31.3.36.

OTHER CLUBS:
Queen's Park; Portadown,
Northern Ireland; York City
61/2–65/6 (192, 6).

REG HUNTER
1958/59

WINGER

 1 GAMES | 0 GOALS

BORN:
Colwyn Bay, Denbighshire, 25.10.38.

OTHER CLUBS:
Wrexham 59/60–61/2 (34, 3).

MIKE PINNER
1960/61

GOALKEEPER

 4 GAMES | 0 GOALS

BORN:
Boston, Lincolnshire, 16.2.34.

OTHER CLUBS:
Aston Villa 54/5–56/7 (4, 0); Sheffield Wednesday 57/8–58/9 (7, 0); Queen's Park Rangers 59/60 (19, 0); Chelsea 61/2 (1, 0); Swansea Town 61/2 (1, 0); Leyton Orient 62/3–64/5 (77, 0).

PETER JONES
1957/58

FULL-BACK

 1 GAMES | 0 GOALS

BORN:
Manchester, 30.11.37.

OTHER CLUBS:
Wrexham 59/60–66/7 (227, 7); Stockport County 66/7–67/8 (54, 1).

JOHN SCOTT
1952/53–1955/56

WINGER

 3 GAMES | 0 GOALS

BORN:
Belfast, 22.12.33.

HONOURS:
2 Northern Ireland caps (58)

OTHER CLUBS:
Grimsby Town 56/7–62/3 (241, 51); York City 63/4 (21, 3).
Died 1978.

EDDIE LEWIS
1952/53–1955/56

FORWARD

 24 11 GAMES | GOALS

BORN:
Manchester, 3.1.35.

OTHER CLUBS:
Preston North End 55/6–56/7 (12, 2); West Ham United 56/7–57/8 (31, 12); Leyton Orient 58/9–63/4 (142, 4).

WALTER WHITEHURST
1955/56

WING-HALF

 1 0 GAMES | GOALS

BORN:
Manchester, 7.6.34.

OTHER CLUBS:
Chesterfield 56/7–59/60 (92, 2); Crewe Alexandra 60/1 (3, 1).

WARREN BRADLEY ▼

1958/59–1961/62

66	21
GAMES	GOALS

BORN ● Hyde, Cheshire, 20.6.33.
HONOURS ● 3 England caps (59).
OTHER CLUBS ● Bury 61/2–62/3 (13, 1).

From non-League Bishop Auckland to Manchester United to the England side, all in the space of 15 months – that was the barely credible experience of Warren Bradley after he answered the Old Trafford club's SOS following the Munich tragedy. And even though this sturdy, hard-running right-winger was no greenhorn – he was already an established amateur international – his rise was nothing less than meteoric.

Perhaps Warren wasn't the classiest of performers, and his progress to full international status startled some observers, but there was no denying the success of his term at United.

A tough little character who, in the manner of Johnny Berry, was always willing to tackle back, he could also point to an outstanding goal-scoring record for a flank player. In his first season, when United finished as runners-up, he managed 12 goals in 24 games. Indeed, during that campaign he and Albert Scanlon were the highest-scoring pair of wingers in the First Division.

But he was not part of Matt Busby's long-term plans and in 1962, having completed an admirable holding job for United, he joined Bury before going on to concentrate on his teaching career.

MARK PEARSON ▲

1957/58–1962/63

80	14
GAMES	GOALS

BORN ● Sheffield, 28.10.39.
OTHER CLUBS ● Sheffield Wednesday 63/4–64/5 (39, 9); Fulham 65/6–67/8 (58, 7); Halifax Town 68/9 (5, 0).

As a youngster Mark Pearson looked a top footballer in the making. 'Pancho' – the nickname was a consequence of his sideburns and was bestowed on Mark at a time when its subsequent and better-known possessor, Stuart Pearson, was still wearing short trousers – was one of the best natural tacklers ever seen at Old Trafford; he was also a sharp, instinctive passer and was at his most effective as a foraging inside-forward, linking defence with attack.

But his potential was never fulfilled and there is no shortage of theories for that sad circumstance. Some would have it that Mark was a victim of his own aggressive temperament. He certainly got into his share of scrapes, being inanely dubbed a teddy boy by Bob Lord after one acrimonious clash with Burnley. Others pointed to the fact that he was pitched into the limelight before he was ready – his debut was in that emotional FA Cup tie with Sheffield Wednesday straight after Munich – while still more reckon that his unenviable injury record dragged him down.

Whatever the answer, he was not destined to make the grade with United and his later spells with Sheffield Wednesday and Fulham also proved disappointing.

RON COPE ▲

1956/57–1960/61

106	2
GAMES	GOALS

BORN ○ Crewe, Cheshire, 5.10.34.
OTHER CLUBS ○ Luton Town 61/2–62/3 (28, 0).

For most of his time at Old Trafford Ron Cope was an uncomplaining reserve, albeit a classy one. With the likes of Allenby Chilton, Mark Jones, Jackie Blanchflower and, later, Bill Foulkes ahead of him in the centre-halves' pecking order, he needed to be an outstanding player to claim a long-term first-team spot – and he was never that.

Ron's opportunity came after Munich and to his credit he kept his place for two seasons, a run that included a polished and staunch performance in direct opposition to Bolton Wanderers' Nat Lofthouse in the 1958 FA Cup Final.

A loyal clubman, Ron was a footballing central defender who invariably attempted to play his way out of trouble rather than apply the big boot, but he lacked the ruthlessness and cutting edge to succeed at the top level.

Nevertheless he can look back on a worthy United career of more than 100 matches and a subsequent short stint with Luton Town, whom he joined for £10,000 in the summer of 1961.

JOE CAROLAN ▼

1958/59–1960/61

71	0
GAMES	GOALS

BORN ○ Dublin, 8.9.37.
HONOURS ○ 2 Republic of Ireland caps (59–60).
OTHER CLUBS ○ Brighton and Hove Albion 60/1–61/2 (33, 0).

Joe Carolan was the quiet man of Old Trafford. Unassuming both by nature and in the way he played his football, he was United's regular left-back for a season and a half. During that time the club finished as runners-up and seventh in the First Division and the Republic of Ireland international did not let them down, performing competently and unflashily without ever suggesting that he had the necessary class to become a long-term fixture in the side.

Joe, who managed quite adequately on the left despite being right-footed, eventually lost out with the arrival of his countryman Noel Cantwell at Old Trafford. Gracious and good-humoured no matter what the circumstances, the dark-haired Dubliner was transferred to Brighton but made little impact at the Goldstone Ground before bowing out of the English game.

Bill was United's bulwark, a definitive old-fashioned stopper who might have been carved out of solid rock.

1952/53–1969/70

682 **9**
GAMES GOALS

BORN	St Helens, Lancashire, 5.1.32.
HONOURS	European Cup 67/8. League Championship 55/6, 56/7, 64/5, 66/7. FA Cup 62/3. 1 England cap (54).
OTHER CLUBS	MANAGER: Chicago Sting (75–77), Tulsa Roughnecks (78–79), San Jose Earthquakes (80), all USA; Farstad, Stenjker (twice),Lillestrom, Viking Stavanger, all Norway (80–88); Mazda, Japan (88–91).

It wasn't often that Matt Busby selected a Manchester United side without Bill Foulkes. But on one of those rare occasions when the manager preferred another player – Ian Greaves towards the end of the 1955/56 Championship campaign, when Bill was stretched by National Service commitments – the indomitable Lancastrian's reaction summed up his personality and outlook better than any words.

Bill Foulkes

Always a fitness fanatic, he trained harder than ever so that he would be ready to step in when called back to first-team duty. No moans, no transfer requests, just dedication and a fierce, almost frightening determination to put himself back on top. And, of course, he succeeded. The next season Bill, then a full-back, was first choice again. He went on to hold down a place until the end of the next decade.

Amazingly, for the first few years of his Old Trafford tenure Bill continued with the mineworking job he had taken straight from school. His record is even more unusual in that he was still a part-time footballer when he was called up for England just 22 months after his United debut, then never made another international appearance despite completing an 18-season First Division career. Perhaps the truth was that as a full-back he was never outstanding. He was rather lacking in mobility and could best be described as a competent, workmanlike performer. But as a centre-half, which he became in the second season after surviving the Munich disaster, he was United's bulwark, a definitive old-fashioned stopper who might have been carved out of solid rock.

When faced with tough, bustling opponents, Bill was in his element. He relished the physical challenge and was particularly strong in the air. On the ground he kept it simple, knowing his ball-playing limitations and being careful not to expose them. His weakness was against trickier centre-forwards like Alex Young, Joe Baker and Ian St John, men who did not stand and battle it out but moved away from him, thus becoming difficult to dominate.

But year in, year out, Bill was a man who could be relied on, a hard, resilient, single-minded character who won more Championship medals – four – than any other United player of his era, held the club's appearance record until overtaken by Bobby Charlton and earned a European Cup medal at the age of 36. Somehow it was fitting that this most loyal of retainers, who later extended his Old Trafford tenure still further by holding coaching posts in the early 1970s, should set the club up for that greatest triumph.

When George Best danced down the right touchline and pulled the ball across the penalty area near the end of the semi-final against Real Madrid, the hearts of United supporters leapt. Here surely was a chance. Perhaps Charlton or Kidd, maybe Sadler, could get on the end of it. But no, it was Bill Foulkes, the man who managed only nine goals in nearly 700 games, side-footing the ball home. A proud moment for a proud man. No one could have deserved it more.

JOHNNY GILES

1959/60–1962/63

114 GAMES **13** GOALS

BORN	Dublin, 6.1.40.
HONOURS	FA Cup 62/3. 60 Republic of Ireland caps (59–79).
OTHER CLUBS	Home Farm, Republic of Ireland; Leeds United 63/4–74/5 (383, 86); West Bromwich Albion 75/6–76/7 (75, 3); Shamrock Rovers, Republic of Ireland.
MANAGER: West Bromwich Albion (75–77 and 84–85); Philadelphia Fury, USA (78); Shamrock Rovers (77–83); Republic of Ireland (77–80); Vancouver Whitecaps, USA (80–83).

Johnny Giles was that rarity, a Manchester United player of largely unrealised potential who moved on to become a world-class performer with another club.

He was always an inside-forward by choice but due to the competition for places at Old Trafford, at a time when he was yet to mature as a player, he was forced on to the wing to claim a place in the side. It was as a promising, efficient, but as yet far from outstanding flankman that Johnny earned an FA Cup winner's medal in 1963. Already he was demonstrating a delightful touch with both feet, though his game lacked the abrasive physical edge it was to attain at Leeds.

It was soon after that Cup triumph that he decided his future did not lie with Matt Busby's team. Johnny was part of the United side drubbed by Everton in the Charity Shield and as a result he was dropped. A strong character, he stood up for himself during discussions with the manager about team selection and the upshot was his departure from Manchester. Many at the club were saddened by the decision, being well aware of the curly-haired Dubliner's potential capabilities, but with so much talent at his disposal Matt could not promise a regular place and Johnny was not disposed to be patient.

Accordingly, a £37,500 transfer to Leeds was agreed, and his ultimate development into a play-maker of sublime skill and vision at Elland Road is now history. After retirement as a player, Johnny's management career saw him take charge of West Bromwich Albion (twice) and his country before he turned to journalism.

Albert Quixall was the golden boy who lost a little of his lustre at Old Trafford. He arrived from Sheffield Wednesday in September 1958 as the lad who had everything. The pundits of the day were in no doubt: he was an England international, he was in his prime, he could make a ball talk – surely there was nothing that Albert was not going to achieve.

He was food and drink to the media. On top of his undoubted credentials as a ball-playing inside-forward, he was blond, baby-faced and wore the shortest shorts ever seen on a football pitch to date. And to top it all he was changing clubs for a then-record fee of £45,000.

Matt Busby saw him as the man to restore a little of the class so cruelly ripped away from the club seven months earlier. After an initial stutter – United suffered seven League games without a win following the Yorkshireman's arrival – everything began to go according to the script. Despite the depredations of the Munich disaster, the side put together a run which saw only two defeats in 23 matches to become runners-up in the First Division.

Albert enjoyed several more moderately successful seasons, often demonstrating glorious skills, but then results slumped and pressure mounted. His confidence, ever fragile, suffered visibly. On his day, when United were going well, he could still look an outstanding player and produce a catalogue of crowd-pleasing tricks. But if the game turned into a battle his contribution diminished alarmingly.

Albert, a dressing-room joker with a distinctly nervous side to his character, bowed out of Old Trafford after being dropped following the 1964 Charity Shield debacle against Everton. He joined Oldham for £7,000, then served Stockport, before ending a career which was undeniably worthy, yet stopped frustratingly short of ultimate fulfilment.

ALBERT QUIXALL

1958/59–1963/64

183 GAMES **56** GOALS

BORN Sheffield, 9.8.33.
HONOURS FA Cup 62/3. 5 England caps (53–55).
OTHER CLUBS Sheffield Wednesday 50/1–58/9 (241, 63); Oldham Athletic 64/5–65/6 (37, 11); Stockport County 66/7 (13, 0).

SAMMY McMILLAN ▼

1961/62–1962/63

15	6
GAMES	GOALS

BORN • Belfast, 20.9.41.
HONOURS • 2 Northern Ireland caps (62).
OTHER CLUBS • Wrexham 63/4–67/8 (149, 52); Southend United 67/8–69/70 (77, 5); Chester 69/70 (18, 0); Stockport County 70/1–71/2 (74, 29).

He was never more than a fringe player at Old Trafford, but Sammy McMillan can be proud of his achievements during one of the club's transitional periods. An honest, strong-running left-winger or centre-forward, he netted six times in 11 outings during 1961/62, when Matt Busby was still rebuilding in the aftermath of Munich.

The amiable Ulsterman was handed a few more senior opportunities during the following campaign, then scored the goal that won a friendly against Juventus in Turin in May 1963. But just when his star appeared to be in the ascendancy, Sammy suffered two serious groin injuries which hindered his progress and, with new players being recruited as United prepared for a title assault, he was sold to Wrexham for £8,000 on Christmas Eve 1963.

In fact, the manager was reluctant to let him go, even offering another year's contract, but Sammy was desperate for first-team football and bade what he felt later to be a premature farewell to Old Trafford. Though he never added to the two Northern Ireland caps he gained during 1962, he went on to noteworthy service in the lower divisions.

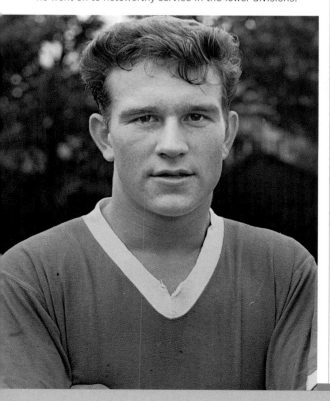

NOBBY LAWTON ▲

1959/60–1962/63

44	6
GAMES	GOALS

BORN • Manchester, 25.3.40.
OTHER CLUBS • Preston North End 62/3–67/8 (143, 22); Brighton and Hove Albion 67/8–70/1 (112, 14); Lincoln City 70/1–71/2 (20, 0).

The best thing that Nobby Lawton ever did for his career was to leave Manchester United. An intelligent, creative wing-half cum inside-forward, his only extended runs in the side came in the early 1960s when Matt Busby was assembling the components of his next great team. A lot of players, including expensive new arrivals, were being tried and it was a testing, unsettling time for youngsters trying to break through.

Although Nobby acquitted himself reasonably well, he never imposed himself enough to establish a regular place and the appearance on the scene of Paddy Crerand made his departure inevitable.

He took his subtle skills to Deepdale where he had the security of permanent first-team football. This gave him the space to develop his game that was not afforded him in the more competitive atmosphere of Old Trafford. With Preston North End, Nobby became a performer of some stature and richly deserved the honour of captaining his side in the 1964 FA Cup Final. Later he put in a creditable spell with Brighton before ending his playing days with Lincoln City.

Jimmy Nicholson kicked off his Manchester United career carrying a destructive and ludicrous millstone around his neck. Here, said various pundits who should have known better, was the new Duncan Edwards. Immediately, anything the young Irishman did was examined in a different light and he suffered accordingly. The fact that this creative, hard-working wing-half rose above such a fatuous comparison is a testimony to the ability which he had in abundance.

Jimmy made his United debut at the age of 17 and before his next birthday he was a full international. But his first complete campaign at Old Trafford – 1960/61, in which he played nearly 40 games in all competitions – proved to be his most effective.

Like so many promising youngsters he did not make the expected progress, due at least in part to ill luck with injuries, but also he had to contend with formidable competition from the likes of Nobby Stiles, Maurice Setters, Nobby Lawton and – the final straw – Paddy Crerand. As a result, sorely frustrated by the situation, he moved on in December 1964.

With his new club, Huddersfield Town, who secured his services for a paltry £7,500, he achieved the consistency which had previously eluded him. Jimmy, who ended his Football League days at Bury, developed into an accomplished all-round footballer who combined fluent passing with strong tackling and he blossomed into a bastion of the Northern Ireland side for more than a decade. It's just possible that he left Old Trafford too soon.

JIMMY NICHOLSON

1960/61–1962/63

 68 **6**

GAMES   GOALS

BORN ● Belfast, 27.2.43.
HONOURS ● 41 Northern Ireland caps (60–71).
OTHER CLUBS ● Huddersfield Town 64/5–73/4 (281, 26); Bury 73/4–75/6 (83, 0).

NOEL CANTWELL

1960/61–1966/67

144 **8**
GAMES GOALS

BORN	Cork, 28.12.32.
HONOURS	FA Cup 62/3. 36 Republic of Ireland caps (53–67).
OTHER CLUBS	Cork Athletic, Republic of Ireland; West Ham United 52/3–60/1 (248, 11).
	MANAGER: Coventry City (67–72); Republic of Ireland (67–68); New England Tea Men, USA (72 and 78–82); Peterborough United (72–77 and 86–88).

During his six years with United, Noel Cantwell was unique in that his mere presence at the club was at least as important as his performances on the field.

He arrived from West Ham United for £29,500 in late 1960, an experienced full-back cum centre-half cum occasional centre-forward who was already an established Republic of Ireland international. By that time Matt Busby had done with short-term measures after Munich and was looking to build a team for the next decade. He needed Noel to provide stability, character and knowledge, to inspire and cajole the younger players along what the manager realised could be a tortuous trail back to the top.

That's not to say that the versatile Irishman was not a splendid performer in his own right. He had fine control, was a precise passer and was dominant in the air, even though he was perhaps a sluggish mover, especially on the turn.

But above all he was a great thinker about the game and possessed the ability to pass on his wisdom. Intelligent, articulate, personable and a man of integrity, Noel was mooted at one time as a possible successor to Matt Busby, and there is no shortage of close observers, both inside and outside the club, who maintain that if Cantwell had been handed United's reins then the demoralising decline of the early 1970s might have been avoided.

So why didn't it happen? After all, the two men liked and respected each other, they shared an all-consuming love of the game and both had a compelling vision of how it should be played. However, though both espoused entertaining football, there was a fundamental chasm in their preferred methods. By and large the Busby creed was based on untramelled adventure, while Cantwell believed passionately in the benefits of coaching, which he felt was crucial to success in the modern game.

Still, though he was to take charge of Coventry City rather than Manchester United, Noel could look back on a distinguished Old Trafford record which included skippering the side to FA Cup triumph in 1963 and serving as an influential club captain – despite playing only four games – during the 1966/67 title campaign.

One or two affectionate expletives may have been deleted, but what follows is the essence of a telling tribute from Jimmy Greaves, uttered after a 1964 United-Spurs clash which Maurice Setters had watched from the trainer's bench. 'I can't understand why such a fine wing-half as Maurice should be out of any first team. I'd certainly rather have him with me than against me. He is fair but I know, from painful experience, all about his power.' Although Spurs had lost heavily, Jimmy still felt a measure of relief at having avoided a confrontation with the bone-crunching West Countryman.

In truth, no one relished an on-the-field clash with Maurice Setters. He was a ruthlessly fearsome tackler to whom most of the cliches used about performers of his ilk could be justifiably applied, and for his height he was as good a header as could be found.

Maurice was bought from West Bromwich Albion for £30,000 in January 1960 to bring stability to United's defence at a crucial time, and this he achieved to a substantial degree. Primarily a destroyer and forager, he was not outstandingly skilful, and it was when he played the game simply, just winning the ball and laying it off, that he was at his most effective. Flaws began to appear only when he attempted 40-yard passes in the manner of Paddy Crerand or Bobby Charlton.

Unquestionably Maurice played a major role in the development of the mid-1960s title-winning side but, sadly for him, his only reward was to be an FA Cup-winner's medal in 1963. Though he boasted sufficient overall quality, it was his ill fortune to disappear during Matt Busby's relentless search for the right blend, Nobby Stiles proving too hard an act to overcome.

Thus, in November 1964, another £30,000 fee took Maurice to Stoke City, where he became a great favourite, as he did subsequently with Coventry City.

Later, after various coaching stints, he excelled as number two to Jack Charlton with the Republic of Ireland.

MAURICE SETTERS

1959/60–1964/65

193 **14**
GAMES GOALS

BORN ● Honiton, Devon, 16.12.36.
HONOURS ● FA Cup 62/3.
OTHER CLUBS ● Exeter City 53/4–54/5 (10, 0); West Bromwich Albion 55/6–59/60 (120, 10); Stoke City 64/5–67/8 (87, 5); Coventry City 67/8–69/70 (51, 3); Charlton Athletic 69/70 (8, 1).
MANAGER: Doncaster Rovers (71–74).

David was a credit to the club and to himself, and it was a sad day when that shattered leg effectively ended his United career.

1961/62–1967/68

263 **144**
GAMES GOALS

BORN • Hamilton, Lanarkshire, 15.4.34.
HONOURS • League Championship 64/5, 66/7. FA Cup 62/3. 5 Scotland caps (58–61).
OTHER CLUBS • Stockport County 50/1–53/4 (16, 6); Arsenal 54/5–60/1 (166, 97); Stoke City 68/9–69/70 (44, 11); Waterford, Republic of Ireland, 70/1. MANAGER: Lincoln City (71–72).

Let there be no doubt about it; David Herd was no ordinary performer. In 263 senior games for Manchester United he scored 144 goals, a record which might have been expected to place him on one of those lofty pedestals reserved for Old Trafford idols. Yet often, particularly before the 1964/65 Championship campaign, he was the butt of brainless barrackers who saw him as something of an unskilled journeyman alongside the extravagant talents of Denis Law, Bobby Charlton and, George Best. In fact, he was one of Matt Busby's most inspired buys, a classic case of acquiring just the right man for the job.

David Herd

David arrived from Arsenal for £37,000 in the 1961 close season, already a Scottish international and a proven goalscorer, yet somehow not a star. He assumed the leadership of the United front line, demonstrating an ability, honesty and enthusiasm that swiftly endeared him to the more discerning among the Red Devils' disciples. But it was the arrival of Law a year later that seemed to lift him into a different class. Instantly they struck up a deadly partnership which produced an avalanche of goals crucial to United's transformation from First Division strugglers into one of British soccer's dominant powers for the rest of the decade.

Yet there was a time when David might have missed out on that glory surge. After his two goals at Wembley helped to lift the FA Cup in 1963, he took part in a dreadful Charity Shield display against Everton and was axed along with Johnny Giles and Albert Quixall. But while Giles and Quixall were not slow to signal their disaffection and soon moved on, David knuckled down to win back his place, a task he accomplished to thrilling effect. That season he notched 20 League goals, another 20 the next and a further 24 the one after. He was down to 16 as United took the title in 1966/67 although he was absent, after breaking his leg in the act of scoring against Leicester, for a third of the games.

David, as clean a striker of the ball as Old Trafford has seen, was at his best when charging on to long passes from Charlton or Paddy Crerand. He was a strong runner, hard to shake off the ball, and was equipped with a rasping shot. His accuracy, too, could be stunning and he could net from astonishing angles. Weaknesses? Well, for such a powerful man he was, perhaps, not outstanding in the air, and there were times when his confidence needed boosting by team-mates.

Overall though, David was a credit to the club and to himself, and it was a sad day when that shattered leg effectively ended his United career. His professional playing days – which had begun in the same Stockport County side as his father, Alec, in 1951 – continued with two seasons at Stoke City and ended with three months under his old pal, Shay Brennan, at Waterford.

DAVID GASKELL

1957/58–1966/67

118	0
GAMES	GOALS

BORN	Wigan, Lancashire, 5.10.40.
HONOURS	FA Cup 62/3.
OTHER CLUBS	Wrexham 69/70–71/2 (95, 0).

When 16-year-old goalkeeper David Gaskell walked on to the Maine Road pitch to represent United in the 1956 Charity Shield against Manchester City, he could have been forgiven for presuming that soccer stardom was there for the taking.

Admittedly he was coming on only as a substitute – for Ray Wood – but it was a prestigious game, his was a precocious talent and time was on his side.

Yet when he played his last game for United a decade later, the Old Trafford career he looked back on had been as much frustrating as fulfilling. Despite making more than 100 appearances he had never made the custodian's job emphatically his own, due substantially to being a contemporary of the brilliant Harry Gregg but also in significant part to a succession of injuries, both grievous and niggling. Indeed, frequently he played in severe discomfort, his enormous courage disguising the extent of his disability.

David was a flamboyant performer, a spectacular shot-stopper whose natural athleticism enabled him to thrill the crowds with his acrobatics and his aggressive sense of adventure. He was not always impressive when dealing with crosses, however, and there was doubt in influential quarters about the suitability of his temperament for long-term success at the top level.

He picked up an FA Cup winner's medal in 1963, being preferred rather controversially to Harry, who was just back from one of his own protracted absences. Afterwards, David's chances were limited and he experienced a rift with the United management, going on to play rugby union for Orrell while still on the club's books before drifting into non-League football with his hometown club, Wigan Athletic.

There followed a successful comeback with Wrexham which was ended, seemingly inevitably, by injury.

PHIL CHISNALL ▼

1961/62–1963/64

47 GAMES **10** GOALS

BORN Manchester, 27.10.42.
OTHER CLUBS Liverpool 64/5 (6, 1);
Southend United 67/8–70/1 (142, 28);
Stockport County 71/2 (30, 2).

Few United players in modern history have flattered to deceive as much as Phil Chisnall. Here was a richly skilled inside-forward who made his debut while the team was in a state of flux and a regular place was up for grabs. All he had to do, it seemed, was to use the gifts at his disposal.

But other crucial ingredients proved to be missing from the footballing make-up of this England schoolboy and under-23 international. In the heat of First Division battle a lack of determination and toughness – both physical and mental – became evident and, at that exalted level, he proved a little short of pace. His confidence suffered and Phil was duly transferred to Liverpool, where he also failed to make his mark, before carving a worthy niche for himself at Southend United.

IAN MOIR ▲

1960/61–1964/65

45 GAMES **5** GOALS

BORN Aberdeen, 30.6.43.
OTHER CLUBS Blackpool 64/5–66/7 (61, 12); Chester 67/8 (25, 3); Wrexham 67/8–71/2 (150, 20); Shrewsbury Town 71/2–72/3 (25, 2); Wrexham 73/4–74/5 (15, 0).

The margin between a top player and an average one can be frustratingly narrow, a truism illustrated perfectly by Ian Moir. In training this gifted little Scottish wingman could perform feats with a ball that only the likes of George Best could hope to equal, yet he never had the necessary application to go with that rich vein of natural talent.

Ian's longest run in the side came at the start of the 1963/64 season when Matt Busby shook up his front line after a woeful Charity Shield performance against Everton. With his pace and his skill in both feet he should have been on the threshold of a golden future as the team which was to win two Championships and the European Cup took shape. But Ian's play lacked insight and this proved fatal for his aspirations at Old Trafford, although he went on to see worthy service with Blackpool and Wrexham, among others.

JOHN CONNELLY

1964/65–1966/67

113	35
GAMES	GOALS

BORN St Helens, Lancashire, 18.7.38.

HONOURS League Championship 64/5. 20 England caps (59–66).

OTHER CLUBS Burnley 56/7–63/4 (216, 85); Blackburn Rovers 66/7–69/70 (149, 36); Bury 70/1–72/3 (128, 37).

In the pop-dominated culture of the 1960s, John Connelly always seemed an unfashionable sort of player. With his slicked-back hair and perpetual grimace he was like a refugee from the pages of the dear old Book of Football Champions, in which the heroes of the day were invariably pictured straining every sinew.

John was, in fact, an old-fashioned winger and none the worse for that. He was fast, equally effective on either flank, a precise crosser and a splendid finisher. As an ever-present in his first season at Old Trafford John scored 15 goals, an outstanding tally for a wingman, to help take the title.

But his contribution did not end there. He was a sturdy customer and not averse to tackling back as he proved forcibly in the crucial clash with Leeds at Elland Road near the end of the 1964/65 season. That blustery April afternoon saw him demonstrate the commitment of a midfield workhorse as he harried and frustrated the likes of Leeds play-maker Bobby Collins. And John's goal, the sole strike in one of those grim, end-of-season encounters in which the big prizes are won and lost, sealed the match – some would say the Championship.

When Matt Busby paid Burnley £56,000 for his services in April 1964, there were those who wondered why the United manager wanted a seemingly rather stale and stereotyped player who had dropped out of the international reckoning and whose best days were probably gone.

In fact, the move renewed the Connelly impetus. Soon he was restored to England duty and he played in the opening game of the 1966 World Cup Finals, bringing brief excitement to a drab goalless draw by hitting the Uruguay woodwork twice and being unlucky to lose his place afterwards.

That summer, however, there was a difference of opinion with his Old Trafford boss and John was sold unexpectedly to Blackburn Rovers, United recouping £40,000 in the process.

Commendably, the experienced flankman refused to let his career merely peter out and three good years at Ewood Park were followed by a praiseworthy spell at Bury.

PAT DUNNE ▲

1964/65–1965/66

66	0
GAMES	GOALS

BORN	Dublin, 9.2.43.
HONOURS	League Championship 64/5. 5 Republic of Ireland caps (65–66).
OTHER CLUBS	Shamrock Rovers, Republic of Ireland (twice); Plymouth Argyle 66/7–70/1(152, 0). MANAGER: Shelbourne.

No one can ever take away from Pat Dunne the fact that he won a League Championship medal in 1964/65. The £10,000 recruit from Shamrock Rovers played 37 games that term and clearly possessed merit or Matt Busby would not have persevered with him. But, without wishing to understate the attributes of a man who played for his country, the Republic of Ireland, it must be said that he will go down as one of the more fortunate goalkeepers to carry off the top domestic club prize.

Pat, whose chance came because of injuries to Harry Gregg, was brave at forwards' feet and a fine, occasionally brilliant shot-stopper on his line, but when it came to crosses and commanding his area he was not in the front rank. One costly example of his weakness in the air came near the end of a bitter mid-1960s confrontation with Leeds United when he flapped at a ball his defenders expected him to claim and allowed Billy Bremner to steal the winner. In February 1967 Pat joined Plymouth Argyle in a £5,000 deal and quickly became something of a local hero at Home Park. Subsequently he returned to Shamrock, later sampling management and continuing to play at various levels until the grand old age of 55.

GRAHAM MOORE ▼

1963/64

19	5
GAMES	GOALS

BORN	Hengoed, Glamorgan, 7.3.41.
HONOURS	21 Wales caps (59–70).
OTHER CLUBS	Cardiff City 58/9–61/2 (85, 23); Chelsea 61/2–63/4 (68, 13); Northampton Town 65/6–66/7 (54, 10); Charlton Athletic 67/8–70/1 (110, 8); Doncaster Rovers 71/2–73/4 (69, 3).

After one of the most impressive debuts any United newcomer ever had, it was all downhill for Graham Moore at Old Trafford. The tall Welsh international inside-forward sparkled in the 4–1 home thrashing of Spurs in November 1963, displaying delightful touch and vision that promised much for the future. The Stretford Enders lapped up his skills, licking their lips at the prospect of future feasts. Sadly all that awaited them was a famine.

Graham, who joined United from Chelsea for £35,000, had problems with his weight – not of his own making, being of a naturally heavy build – and soon he was struggling. Far too ponderous for a place in Matt Busby's rebuilding plans, he moved to Northampton Town before going on to perform classily for Charlton Athletic.

Those who saw him play witnessed a glorious combination of silk and dynamite which took the breath away.

1956/57–1972/73

754 247

GAMES GOALS

BORN • Ashington, Northumberland, 11.10.37.
HONOURS • European Cup 67/8. League Championship 56/7, 64/5, 66/7. FA Cup 62/3. 106 England caps (58–70).
OTHER CLUBS • Preston North End 74/5 (38, 8).
MANAGER: Preston North End (73–75); Wigan (acting, 83).

Football history abounds with heroes, but there has never been another like Bobby Charlton. The miner's son from Northumberland was a player with a sublime and unique talent, a soccer idol without the proverbial feet of clay, and he remains the British game's finest living international ambassador.

Bobby Charlton

Those who saw him play were privileged. They will bear witness to a glorious combination of silk and dynamite which took the breath away. As Paddy Crerand, for so long his midfield partner, put it: 'You never saw a more graceful sight on a football pitch. Bobby was pure poetry.'

Paeans of praise have been sung to his most spectacular attributes – the pulverising shot, the uncannily accurate long-distance pass and the devastating body swerve – but the most precious of his gifts, and the one which made the rest so deadly, was his instinct. Bobby possessed a natural feel for his work which amounted to genius, a term not to be used lightly but the only one which will serve here. That is not to say he didn't work at his game. In the early days he could be found kicking a ball against a wall for two hours at a time in an effort to improve a particular skill.

Before Munich, while beginning to make his mark, Bobby played with a carefree exuberance which was to vanish forever as he took on extra responsibility in the wake of the tragedy. He was both a forager and goal-scorer and there are some respected judges who cherish memories of this phase of his career more than any other.

Then, for four seasons in the early 1960s, he became a left-winger, and there are those who maintain that was his best position. Certainly, when he received the ball early, he was a thrilling sight as he surged along the touchline before cutting in for one of those awesome strikes.

But most agree that Bobby was not seen in his true pomp until he became the deep-lying play-maker, a more demanding role which used his ability to the full. From midfield, in concert with Crerand, he orchestrated some of the most scintillating play in British soccer history. The fruits were two Championships and the European Cup. Meanwhile there was the little matter of helping England take the 1966 World Cup.

Was there, though, a price to pay for such excellence? Was this a player without a flaw? The answers, of course, are 'yes' to the first question, 'no' to the second. There were times when Bobby, taking his own intuitive path, strayed out of position, which could mean extra work for covering team-mates. And deep, tactical plans were not his forte, nor were desperate, neck-or-nothing tackles.

But what of it? A successful team needs a blend of different talents. And no one who played alongside Bobby would have had him any other way. He was a match-winner extraordinary and a gentleman supreme who became a national institution. Since his retirement he has overcome a native shyness which many mistook for aloofness, yet has retained the modesty that was always part of his public appeal. Now a director at Old Trafford, his beloved 'theatre of dreams', Bobby Charlton will be remembered as long as football itself. The knighthood which arrived in 1994 was a fitting tribute, though to his legions of long-time admirers it was barely necessary. To them, he has always been Sir Bobby.

Usually he was not a man to dive in with a biting tackle; the Brennan way was more composed and full of guile.

1957/58–1969/70

356 **6**
GAMES GOALS

BORN ● Manchester, 6.5.37.
HONOURS ● European Cup 67/8. League Championship 64/5, 66/7. 19 Republic of Ireland caps (65–70).
OTHER CLUBS ● MANAGER: Waterford, Republic of Ireland (70–74).

'To know Shay Brennan is to like him. Anyone who meets this lovely, laughing fellow is richer for the experience.' So goes a tribute to the easy-going, Manchester-born Republic of Ireland international from a long-time United colleague, and it typifies the affection and esteem in which he is still held.

Seamus Brennan

Tales of Shay's charming, selfless nature abound, but less is said of his attributes as a player, and this does not do justice to a man who played more than 350 games for one of the great club sides.

He was a steady, rather than brilliant full-back whose main strengths were quickness of recovery, good positioning and unflappability. Usually he was not a man to dive in with a biting tackle; the Brennan way was more composed and full of guile. His winger tended to be ushered into what seemed like acres of inviting space before, suddenly and unexpectedly, he would find himself in a corner. Then, with the minimum of fuss, the ball would be nicked from the unsuspecting flankman's foot and be on its way either to safety or into the creative custody of Bobby Charlton or Paddy Crerand.

Shay was not dominant in the air but was deceptively skilful on the ball, a talent he nurtured during his early days as an inside-forward. His initial impact came as a makeshift winger in the patchwork United side which faced Sheffield Wednesday a few days after Munich. He emerged an unlikely hero, scoring twice in a 3–0 win, yet characteristically playing down his part in the triumph.

But his future was not be in attack. When Matt Busby revamped his rearguard in 1961, Shay took on the right-back job he was to retain for most of the decade. There were pundits who predicted that, while he might manage regularly to outwit domestic opponents, he would be destroyed by the cuter wiles of European adversaries. But the Irish-Mancunian made nonsense of that, holding his own through a succession of Continental campaigns and claimed his reward with a European Cup winner's medal in 1968.

On the international front, Shay was one of the first men to take advantage of a new FIFA ruling allowing players to represent the country of their parents' birth, and in 1965 he won the first of 19 caps for the Republic of Ireland. Earlier, there had been hopes of an England career when he was selected for a 40-man squad to prepare for the 1966 World Cup, but he was discarded before selection of the final party.

After retiring as a player, Shay proved that nice guys can succeed in management by guiding League of Ireland club Waterford to a series of trophies.

If Bobby Charlton left a gap then it was a racing certainty that Nobby Stiles would fill it.

1960/61–1970/71

392 **19**
GAMES GOALS

BORN	Manchester, 18.5.42.
HONOURS	European Cup 67/8. League Championship 64/5, 66/7. 28 England caps (65–70).
OTHER CLUBS	Middlesbrough 71/2–72/3 (57, 2); Preston North End 73/4–74/5 (46, 1). MANAGER: Preston North End (77–81); Vancouver Whitecaps, USA (81–84); West Bromwich Albion (85–86).

Everyone is familiar with the Nobby Stiles school of football, or are they? In fact, those who dismissed him as nothing more than an effective hatchet man – 'every team must have one' is a frequent sententious comment from the very folk who shout loudest when their own favourites are kicked up in the air – are a long way from the mark.

Nobby Stiles

It would be fatuous to assert that hardness was not a key facet of his game, witness those famous mantrap tackles. But mere physical presence was not the half of it. Nobby Stiles was one of the most tactically aware of players, his intelligent, instant assessments of dangerous situations and his capacity to act decisively combining to make him a priceless asset to Manchester United.

Nobby, who was no passing master yet had more skill than most people gave him credit for, was ideally equipped to be a sweeper. In this role he was the perfect foil for Bill Foulkes who, at least in his latter years, was most effective alongside a nippy and resourceful teammate. Bobby Charlton also owed plenty to the little Mancunian, especially when the pair operated together in midfield for their country. Nobby's unobtrusive but astute covering allowed his more gifted clubmate the freedom to roam and gave full range to Charlton's lethal but sometimes unpredictable talents. If Bobby left a gap then it was a racing certainty that Nobby would fill it.

Evaluated in isolation, Stiles was not the most gifted of footballers. But viewed in the context of the United and England set-ups of the mid-1960s he was as close to being indispensable as an individual can be. Of course, the mechanics of his game were not the extent of his worth. Equally important was his unquenchable will to win. Nobby was an inspirational organiser and an inveterate shouter, an image so glaringly incompatible with his mild, almost meek demeanour off the pitch.

In the early part of his career, Stiles had problems with his eyesight. At one point he was set to man-mark the elusive John White of Tottenham Hotspur, only to find himself running with the wrong fellow because he couldn't identify his quarry. Harry Gregg noticed Nobby's plight and mentioned it to Matt Busby, who had been puzzled for some time because his promising wing-half had been misreading the flight of the ball and making too many off-beam challenges. Accordingly the manager ordered an eye test and Nobby was fitted with contact lenses. After a difficult period of adjustment, during which he found himself bumping into opponents purely by accident, he seemed a new player, his judgement and timing improved beyond recognition.

One of Nobby's keenest disappointments came in 1963 when, despite having played in 31 League matches and missed only one FA Cup tie, he was omitted from the side which beat Leicester City at Wembley. But his manager convinced him that he was needed and no transfer request was forthcoming.

After being in and out the following season, Nobby claimed a regular place in 1964/65 and exerted huge influence throughout the Reds' subsequent successful sequence. And he still found time to endear himself to the nation with that toothless grin and clumsy jig at the climax of England's 1966 World Cup campaign.

Towards the end of the decade he was laid low by injury and, after two frustrating seasons, was allowed to join Middlesbrough for £20,000. There followed a spell at Preston under Bobby Charlton before Nobby took up management, first at Deepdale, then later at West Bromwich, where he served initially under brother-in-law Johnny Giles. Later he became involved with the youth set-up at Old Trafford before he left to hone his burgeoning reputation as an after-dinner speaker. It seemed that Nobby's entertainment value was touching new peaks, though certain retired strikers were finding his reminiscences a trifle painful …

The legend of Law will pass into posterity as an example of sport at its most blindingly brilliant.

1962/63–1972/73

399	236
GAMES	GOALS

BORN • Aberdeen, 24.2.40.
HONOURS • League Championship 64/5, 66/7. FA Cup: 62/3.
55 Scotland caps (58–74).
OTHER CLUBS • Huddersfield Town 56/7–59/60 (81, 16);
Manchester City 59/60–60/1 (44, 21), Torino,
Italy, 61/2 (27, 10); Manchester City 73/4 (24, 9).

When old pros get together to talk about great footballers, one name above all gets them bubbling. They recall with reverence the wizardry of Best, the glory of Charlton and the superhuman deeds of Edwards, but it is the memory of Denis Law that really sets their pulses racing.

Denis Law

Denis belonged to the fans – after all, he was 'The King' wasn't he? – but somehow, beyond that, he was the players' player. It wasn't just his phenomenal strike rate, or even those dazzling flashes of genius which could swing a game in an instant. It was something deeper, more fundamental; a quality that was indefinable and yet had a lot to do with the size of his heart.

Law's fairytale future could hardly have been predicted by Huddersfield Town supporters when a spindly, pallid teenager ran out for his debut in 1956. But soon Manchester City were impressed and took him to Maine Road for a short spell before dispatching him to the Italian club, Torino. An unhappy sojourn in the sun followed before Matt Busby stepped in with a new British record transfer fee of £115,000 in August 1962.

United made up for a poor League season by winning the FA Cup in 1963 and it was Denis who set them on the way with a typical piece of sorcery. He received the ball from Paddy Crerand, spun on the spot like a scarlet top and scored with a devastating cross-shot before the nonplussed Leicester defence could move.

This was but a taste of the feast to come in the next few years. A golden river of goals followed, 160 of them in just 222 games over his first five seasons. Many of them were spectacular, some seemingly impossible, and everything was done with a cocky panache the fans found irresistible.

His record owed much to sharpness of reflex and inspired control; awesome aerial ability for one of such slight stature and a downright refusal to give up any cause; toughness that would have done credit to rawhide and bravery that would have shamed a Roman gladiator.

But Denis Law's most precious gifts were awareness and anticipation. He seemed to see the action several frames ahead of everyone else and knew how to capitalise instantly on that advantage. At times it was uncanny, as though he could read the minds of defenders and colleagues alike. With such a knack he had to play up front, but what a midfield man Denis could have made! Lauded though he was, he was never given full credit for his all-round skill. His tackling and passing were exemplary and as for dribbling, how about the shoulder-dropping dash which set up Bobby Charlton's explosive strike in the 1967 Charity Shield?

But there are two abiding sadnesses about his Old Trafford years. First he was cheated by knee trouble of a role in the 1968 European Cup victory; then he endured a few seasons of anti-climax during which the club was unsettled and the knee was not improving. Eventually, and controversially, he was given a free transfer by Tommy Docherty and went on to enjoy an Indian summer with Manchester City and Scotland.

Two criticisms levelled at Denis are that he was hot-tempered and injury-prone. Well, the former was an unchangeable part of his make-up, an aspect of the lethal Law cocktail. And the latter, apart from his final years, is a fallacy. Given the physical punishment he received, his overall appearance record was excellent. He ranks, undeniably, with the all-time greats and his achievements will stand forever. The legend of Law will pass into posterity as an example of sport at its most blindingly brilliant.

Paddy's vision, anticipation and sublime passing skills rendered lack of pace irrelevant. Crerand was able to play, and often dictate proceedings, in his own time.

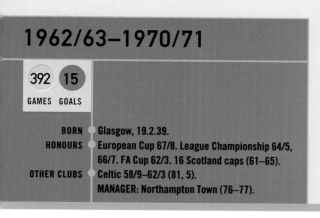

1962/63–1970/71

392 **15**
GAMES GOALS

BORN Glasgow, 19.2.39.
HONOURS European Cup 67/8. League Championship 64/5, 66/7. FA Cup 62/3. 16 Scotland caps (61–65).
OTHER CLUBS Celtic 58/9–62/3 (81, 5).
MANAGER: Northampton Town (76–77).

If ever a man made a mockery of the traditional standards by which great footballers are judged it was Paddy Crerand. Indeed, the Scottish international wing-half – variously described as slow, ungainly, a bad header and a poor goal-scorer – veritably ridiculed the rulebook and wrote his own rich volume of Old Trafford folklore.

Paddy Crerand

It's true he was not the most rapid of Red Devils; he didn't need to be. His vision, anticipation and sublime passing skills rendered lack of pace irrelevant. Paddy was able to play, and often dictate proceedings, in his own time.

His movement on the field was hardly reminiscent of a gazelle, but fans and team-mates could live with that, rating it, perhaps, on a par with George Best's failure to make the half-time tea. As for his ability in the air, well, it's true he occasionally dumbfounded his colleagues by heading the ball twice in a match . . .

And goals? He didn't often supply the finishing touch but, in his heyday, the majority of United's successful strikes were due in some measure to his remarkable talents.

Paddy, who was to have a brief spell as assistant manager at Old Trafford under Tommy Docherty in 1974, thought deeply about his game. He made it his business to know the opposition and was more aware than most about what was going on around him. An apt illustration is an incident in the 1963 FA Cup Final against Leicester City, the game which signalled the Reds' return as a major power after Munich.

Though still allegedly adjusting to English football, United's recent £53,000 signing from Celtic had done enough homework to know that Gordon Banks liked to throw the ball to Scottish schemer Davie Gibson, the springboard of so many attacks. Seeing Banks in possession and noting that Gibson was free, Paddy pounced while others idled. He beat his countryman to the ball, threaded a pass through a crowded penalty area and Denis Law did the rest. It was a vivid cameo that captured the very essence of vintage Crerand. Of course, there were days when inspiration deserted him, but in such games he would never hide from the ball and would always continue to probe.

An extrovert Glaswegian, raised in the Gorbals, Paddy allowed his fervour to get the better of him at times and occasionally he landed in trouble with referees. Indeed, it's been said that he never moved so fast as when headed for a melee 40 yards away! But his fiery nature was as much a part of Crerand the player as Crerand the man. It would be hard to find a United follower who would have wanted him any other way.

And if part of that huge heart will be forever at his beloved Parkhead – the home of Celtic, his first club – it would be a rare Stretford Ender who wouldn't forgive him.

His loyalty to Old Trafford was never in doubt, his contribution to the club's cause colossal. It was a red-letter day, indeed, when Matt Busby crossed the border to claim him for Manchester United.

BOBBY NOBLE

1965/66–1966/67

33 **0**
GAMES GOALS

BORN • Manchester, 18.12.45.
HONOURS • League Championship 66/7.

If it were possible to design and build the ideal full-back then there could hardly have been a more perfect model than Bobby Noble. He was quick, his tackling was granite-hard and immaculately timed, he used the ball well and he read the game with astonishing maturity.

Indeed, in the spring of 1967 the stocky blond Mancunian was, by common consent, the most accomplished young left-back in the land and there seemed to be no clouds on his horizon. He was newly married and super-fit, excelling yet still improving in a vibrant team. But then, after playing 29 consecutive games as United stormed towards their second title in three seasons, Bobby was snatched from football at the age of 21.

Disaster struck on the way home from a goalless draw at Sunderland, when he suffered hideous head, chest and leg injuries in a car crash near his home in Sale. For a time his life hung in the balance and the recovery, when it came, was frustratingly tortuous.

In May 1968 – ironically during the week of the Reds' European Cup triumph – Bobby underwent an operation to restore his sight for the purposes of everyday life but not, as it transpired, for top-flight football. Later he made gallant and harrowing attempts at a comeback, turning out for the club's junior teams, but it became poignantly obvious that he was not going to make it.

He trained as hard as he knew how, but always felt in his heart that he would never return to first-team action. His timing and sharpness had gone, and he could no longer judge the flight of the ball, a hopeless situation for a defender who had prided himself on his anticipation. When the truth sank in it dealt Bobby a devastating blow, one that left him overwhelmingly depressed.

Certainly it was a savage reversal of fortune for the feisty youngster who had captained a side including George Best, David Sadler and John Aston to FA Youth Cup success in 1964. Now his career was over almost before it had begun.

Thereafter he went on a coaching course at Lilleshall but didn't take to it. In time he was to regret his lack of patience, but by then it was too late, and he looked to a new life outside the game.

Everyone who saw Bobby Noble play was in agreement: not only was he sure to play for England, but there was nothing to stop him being a fixture at left-back for club and country for the next decade.

Beyond the ability and the hardness there was an almost unnerving certainty about his play which marked him out as something special. His accident was a personal catastrophe for a gifted young athlete and a body blow to Manchester United and England.

WILLIE ANDERSON

1963/4–1966/67

WINGER

 12
GAMES **0**
GOALS

BORN:
Liverpool, 24.1.47.

OTHER CLUBS:
Aston Villa 66/7–72/3 (231, 36); Cardiff City 72/3–76/7 (126, 12); Portland
Timbers, USA.

FRANK HAYDOCK

1960/61–1962/63

CENTRE-HALF

 6
GAMES **0**
GOALS

BORN:
Eccles, Lancashire, 29.11.40.

OTHER CLUBS:
Charlton Athletic 63/4–65/6 (84, 4); Portsmouth 65/6–68/9 (72, 1);
Southend United 68/9–69/70 (33, 4).

ALBERT KINSEY

1964/65

INSIDE-FORWARD

 1
GAMES **1**
GOALS

BORN:
Liverpool, 19.9.45.

OTHER CLUBS:
Wrexham 65/6–72/3 (253, 80); Crewe Alexandra 72/3–74/5 (32, 1).

WILF TRANTER

1963/64

HALF-BACK

 1
GAMES **0**
GOALS

BORN:
Pendlebury, Lancashire, 5.3.45.

OTHER CLUBS:
Brighton and Hove Albion 65/6–67/8 (47, 1); Baltimore Bays, USA;
Fulham 68/9–71/2 (22, 0).

DENNIS WALKER

1962/63

WING-HALF

 1
GAMES **0**
GOALS

BORN:
Northwich, Cheshire, 26.10.44.

OTHER CLUBS:
York City 64/5–67/8 (153, 49); Cambridge United 70/1–72/3 (56, 4).

David was at his best alongside the stopper, where his fine touch, cultured passing and intelligence came into their own.

1963/64–1973/74

333 GAMES **27** GOALS

BORN ● Yalding, Kent, 5.2.46.
HONOURS ● European Cup 67/8. League Championship 66/7.
4 England caps (67–70).
OTHER CLUBS ● Preston North End 73/4–76/7 (105, 3).

For a popular man, David Sadler had an unexpected knack of perplexing some of his Old Trafford team-mates. There was no doubting his ability or commitment. But a few of the more demonstrative characters to play for United during David's decade at the club never ceased to be astonished by a coolness in the face of any provocation which at times bordered on serenity – and that's a quality rarely evident in the highly competitive world of big-time football.

David Sadler

In fact David, certainly a model professional in deed and attitude, was also blessed with the most commendable attributes of the archetypal amateur sportsman. Hardly surprising, perhaps, as he was an England amateur international centre-forward in his pre-United days.

His first spell in the side was when he took over briefly from David Herd at the start of the 1963/64 season. He performed adequately but if he had remained a number nine his Old Trafford career would probably have been a short one. Instead he made the centre of defence his premier position, while his versatility – he could also perform in midfield – added to his value.

David played for England at centre-half but he was at his best alongside the stopper, where his fine touch, cultured passing and intelligence came into their own. His greatest club honour was a 1968 European Cup winner's medal, a fitting addition to his Championship gong of the previous season.

An often overlooked contribution to the European triumph was the tall Kentishman's goal in the second leg of the semi-final against Real Madrid. It came deep inside the second half with the Reds 3–1 down on aggregate and with hope evaporating fast; George Best nodded on a Bobby Charlton free-kick, the Spanish defenders remained leaden-footed, but David, by now committed to attack in a bid to break Real's stranglehold, read the situation to perfection, striding forward to bundle the ball over the line from close range. Not brilliant, not spectacular, but it gave the Reds new life and six minutes later the comeback was complete.

It was a typically low-key but invaluable contribution from a thoroughbred footballer who, possibly, was prevented from reaching the very top class by a certain lack of ruthlessness. Nevertheless, he went on to play more than 300 senior games for United before being allowed to join Preston for £25,000 in November 1973. Ironically at a time when Old Trafford was short of quality performers, it was at Deepdale that David played some of his most accomplished football.

FRANCIS BURNS

1967/68–1971/72

155	7
GAMES	GOALS

BORN Glenboig, Lanarkshire, 17.10.48.
HONOURS 1 Scotland cap (69).
OTHER CLUBS Southampton 72/3 (21, 0); Preston North End 73/4–80/81(273, 9); Shamrock Rovers, Republic of Ireland, 81/2.

If Denis Law thought he was unlucky to miss the 1968 European Cup Final, at least he could blame the callous fate that had put him on the injured list. Poor Francis Burns had no such scapegoat.

Francis, a polished full-back enjoying an impressive first season in the team, had played 36 League matches and seven out of the eight European encounters leading up to that historic clash with Benfica. But, come the appointment with glory, he found himself dropped. In fact, he had been omitted for the semi-final second leg against Real Madrid at the Bernabeu Stadium because Matt Busby had felt the vastly experienced Shay Brennan would cope better with the great Gento. Shay did well and retained his place for the final, leaving Francis to rue his ill fortune, a sadly familiar situation as it turned out.

The young Scot was a cultured, competitive performer with an exemplary attitude who was perhaps just half a yard of pace short of being truly outstanding. He was dedicated to fitness, but it was that, or the lack of it, which was to scupper his United future. He needed three cartilage operations in 18 months and his Old Trafford career lost impetus, though he fought back to win a Scottish cap in November 1969.

There followed a £50,000 transfer to Southampton in 1973 but he experienced further injury problems at The Dell and went on to settle with Preston, for whom he played frequently in midfield, for seven successful years.

JIM RYAN ▼

1965/66–1969/70

27	4
GAMES	GOALS

BORN	Stirling, 12.5.45.
OTHER CLUBS	Luton Town 70/1–76/7 (184, 21); Dallas Tornadoes, USA, 76–79.
	MANAGER: Luton Town (90–91).

Jim Ryan never did himself justice the first time around at Old Trafford. Here was a player who on the training ground could give one of the best full-backs in Europe, Tony Dunne, an almighty chasing. But somehow, come match day, that confidence would have evaporated. Gone was the wizard of the dribble, to be replaced by a nervous-looking individual who never seemed likely to make a first-team berth his own. That was a shameful waste of this clever Scot, who also boasted speed and wiry strength among his attributes.

His United path having taken a similar course to that of Ian Moir a few years earlier, Jim was transferred to Luton Town in 1970, one of four Reds who moved to Kenilworth Road in a £35,000 package. At last, he became a more consistent performer, carving out a useful career with the Hatters, whom he was later to manage. In 1991 Jim returned to Old Trafford to coach the reserves, with marked success, and he stood in as Alex Ferguson's assistant in the interregnum between Brian Kidd and Steve McClaren in 1998/99.

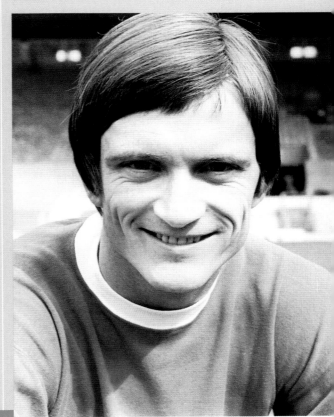

JOHN FITZPATRICK ▲

1964/65–1972/73

147	10
GAMES	GOALS

BORN	Aberdeen, 18.8.46.

Opinions differ sharply over the merits of Scottish wing-half cum full-back John Fitzpatrick. Some say the combative Aberdonian was impetuous, foolhardy even, in his tackles, that his timing was often awry and that he was not really of the class required of a Manchester United player. Others maintain that he was a canny battler with more ability than was generally realised, whose career was sabotaged by injury. There is certainly no doubting the latter fact. John's knee problems cost him dearly, ultimately forcing him out of the game, after several operations, at the age of 26.

In his early days in first-team contention he was viewed as a stand-in for Nobby Stiles, a player whose fierce commitment he matched without having the same tactical awareness. But John's most effective spell was towards the turn of the decade when he had an extended run at right-back as Shay Brennan's distinguished service neared an end.

Despite playing nearly 150 games over a generally successful period for the club, 'Fitz' left with no medals to show for his efforts.

He was a natural ball-player with sublime control, packed a thumping shot and possessed a sweet body-swerve.

1967/68–1973/74

264 **70**
GAMES GOALS

BORN	Manchester, 29.5.49.
HONOURS	European Cup 67/8. 2 England caps (70).
OTHER CLUBS	Arsenal 74/5–75/6 (77, 30); Manchester City 76/7–78/9 (98, 44); Everton 78/9–79/80 (40,11); Bolton Wanderers 80/1–81/2 (43, 14); Atlanta Chiefs, USA, 81; Fort Lauderdale Strikers, USA, 82–84; Minnesota Kicks, USA, 84. MANAGER: Preston North End (86); Blackburn Rovers (98-99).

The rise and fall of Brian Kidd as a Manchester United player remains one of the most frustrating episodes in the club's modern history. At the age of 18 he catapulted himself into the first team with spectacular performances on the 1967 Australian tour and a precocious display in the Charity Shield against Spurs. As the season progressed it was apparent that here was a potential world-beater.

Brian Kidd

In terms of ability, there was little that Brian lacked. He was a natural ball-player with sublime control, packed a thumping shot and possessed a sweet body-swerve. He was strong and gave as good as he got in his confrontations with battle-hardened First Division defenders. And he was left-sided, which brought balance to the forward line and was seen as another huge plus.

That first season was an unqualified success for the youngster, culminating with the comic-strip-hero experience of scoring in the Reds' historic European Cup triumph on his 19th birthday. The goal – United's third and the one which effectively put the trophy beyond Benfica's reach – was an unusual one, Brian's first six-yard header being parried, his second floating almost gently into the net over the heads of the stranded defenders. To this observer, at least, it seemed to happen in slow motion; to the travelling Stretford Enders, it confirmed the callow Mancunian as a hero of the front rank. 'Kiddo' had arrived.

After such a meteoric rise it was not surprising that his progress should slow down, but he did well enough to line up twice for England in 1970. Then, imperceptibly, the slide started. United were no longer such an impressive side, Brian did not mature tactically as fast as he did physically and, in a troubled team environment, his game suffered.

One theory is that he had grown too accustomed to playing alongside world-class stars, and that when, one by one, the likes of Crerand, Law, Charlton and Best declined in influence, he was unable to respond by raising his own level of contribution.

Certainly Tommy Docherty, whose hopes that Brian would forge a lethal striking partnership with Lou Macari were to be emphatically dashed, was unable to revive the former hero's flagging fortunes and in August 1974 a £110,000 deal took him to Arsenal.

For the Gunners, also experiencing a period of transition, he did well in difficult circumstances, before going on to creditable spells with Manchester City and Everton. Meanwhile the Stretford Enders were left to rue what might have been if 'Kiddo' had been granted the luxury of a few more seasons in a successful side.

Later he returned to Old Trafford, first as a youth coach, than as a forthright and enterprising assistant to Alex Ferguson. As all who witnessed his exuberant mini pitch invasion following Steve Bruce's late winner at home to Sheffield Wednesday in spring 1993 will have realised, Brian's enthusiasm for the cause had not waned one jot! Clearly his talents were worthy of a top job and in 1998 he accepted the challenge offered by struggling Blackburn Rovers, only to be dismissed within a year after presiding over relegation and a poor start in the lower flight.

As a footballer, he was practically flawless. He had the assets to be outstanding in any position.

1963/64–1973/74

466 **178**
GAMES GOALS

BORN	Belfast, 22.5.46.
HONOURS	European Cup 67/8. League Championship 64/5, 66/7. 37 Northern Ireland caps (64–77).
OTHER CLUBS	Stockport County 75/6 (3, 2); Cork Celtic, Republic of Ireland, 75/6 (3, 0); Los Angeles Aztecs, USA, 76–78 (54, 27); Fulham 76/7–77/8 (42, 8); Hibernian 79/80–80/1 (17, 3); Fort Lauderdale Strikers, USA, 79 (19, 2); San Jose Earthquakes, USA, 80 (26, 8); Golden Bay, USA; Bournemouth 82/3 (5, 0).

There are two ways to remember George Best. One will lead to anger, frustration and, unless you're blessed with a mightily strong constitution, mounting blood pressure. The other will bring joy, gratitude and, above all, a sense of wonder. So really there should be no contest, should there? Of course, it would be a rare Manchester United fan who did not feel the odd pang of remorse that the Belfast boy, for most people's money the most naturally gifted British footballer of modern times, did not grace Old Trafford for, say, another decade. But greed is a particularly unsavoury sin. George spent 11 seasons with United and for perhaps seven or eight of them gave so much pleasure, created so much that was beautiful and left so many undying memories that, certainly at this distance, it is churlish to cavil about short rations.

George Best

From his first days in England it was evident that the shy, homesick wisp of a lad was special. The talent he paraded in training, goading the likes of Harry Gregg with his trickery, assured George of rapid promotion to the first team. He remained there for that vintage side's most dazzling years, an era that effectively ended in 1968 with the European Cup triumph in which he played such an inspirational part.

Throughout the mid-1960s George, while still maturing as a player, shone as brightly as any star in Matt Busby's extravagant firmament. One jewel of a performance followed another as immortality beckoned. Two that stood out were the tormenting of poor Chelsea full-back Ken Shellito at Stamford Bridge in 1964 and the demolition of Benfica, including two goals in the first 12 minutes, at the Stadium of Light in 1966.

By 1968 he was at his most irresistible. He was European and English Footballer of the Year and topped the First Division scoring charts with 28 goals. But also he was part of a side which, imperceptibly at first, started to slide. George remained magnificent and inevitably shouldered more on-field responsibility, an extra burden to add to the increasing outside pressure created by his racy lifestyle.

Come 1971/72 United were facing steady criticism but temporarily silenced the snipers by topping the League in the autumn. One goal George scored during this run, involving a spellbinding dribble against Sheffield United, was made in heaven. But results fell away, his personal problems piled up and the rest is now distressing history. Despite various comebacks, notably with Fulham, he was lost to the game.

What made him different from the rest? Well, as a footballer, he was practically flawless. He had the assets to be outstanding in any position. Aside from his legendary skill and speed George was also deceptively tough, could tackle like a full-back and was naturally fit. Sometimes he held the ball too long – this could infuriate teammates while perhaps offering them a handy breather – but the habit was wholly paid for by the sinuous sorties on which he destroyed defences single-handedly.

In the end he was unable to handle the goldfish-bowl existence which was thrust upon him. Even in retrospect it is difficult to see, given his personal make-up, what could have been done to change the outcome. But let's not pine for what might have been. Let's wish George Best well and thank the gods that sent him to thrill us.

Alex was a good 'talker' who expected – and usually got – the final say in his penalty box.

1966/67–1977/78

535 **2**
GAMES GOALS

BORN Mitcham, Surrey, 18.9.44.
HONOURS European Cup 67/8. League Championship 66/7.
FA Cup 76/7. Second Division Championship
74/5. 1 England cap (68).
OTHER CLUBS Millwall 63/4–65/6 (137, 0); Chelsea 66/7 (1, 0);
Dallas Tornadoes, USA.

Alex Stepney assured himself of Old Trafford immortality in one moment of explosive action on a balmy May night at Wembley in 1968. Matt Busby's men were locked at one-apiece with Benfica in the European Cup Final. Extra time loomed as Eusebio outstripped the United defence and found only the 'keeper between himself and glory.

Alex Stepney

The brilliant Portuguese shot hard and with an extravagantly flamboyant flourish, rather than attempting to slot the ball safely into a corner of the net; Alex reacted magnificently, grabbing the ball to his midriff – or did it merely hit him? Anyway, it stuck, United were reprieved and went on to reach the end of their rainbow. After that most Red Devils fans would have forgiven Alex anything. As it turned out they had little to pardon as, with only the odd hiccup, he built a reputation as one of the club's greatest custodians.

He was acquired for £55,000 – then a world record fee for a 'keeper – from Chelsea soon after the start of the 1966/67 term which was to end with the Championship pennant flying at Old Trafford. With Harry Gregg's career virtually ended by injury, the manager opted for Alex after deciding that neither Pat Dunne nor the injury-prone David Gaskell was the right man for the job. The breezy Londoner, who had performed marvels for Millwall before his one-match stay at Stamford Bridge, vindicated Matt's judgement with a series of accomplished displays which made him a first-team fixture until his form dipped at the turn of the decade.

For half a season he was replaced by Jimmy Rimmer and reacted by asking for a transfer, which was refused. Thereafter he won back his place and reigned supreme – apart from a brief troubled interlude when Tommy Docherty preferred Paddy Roche – until 1977/78, his last campaign. Spells in America and with non-league Altrincham led up to retirement as a player, after which he sampled several occupations before returning to the Manchester soccer scene as a coach with City in 1995.

Throughout most of his time at United, Alex was ranked among the leading British 'keepers, though he won only one England cap and never attained the stature of the likes of Jennings, Clemence and Shilton. He was never a flashy performer and perhaps his most impressive quality was his positioning, though he could also demonstrate agility when required. Alex was a good 'talker' who expected – and usually got – the final say in his penalty box, and he was a constructive user of the ball who would never hoof it upfield when he could throw to a well-placed colleague.

In his early years at Old Trafford he was subject to occasional short spells when confidence on crosses appeared to desert him. As his game matured such aberrations became fewer and he was at his best towards the end of his career.

Alex was the one constant figure throughout an incident-packed, often turbulent 12 years in which he played for five managers and which saw United take the game's most glittering prizes, plunge into the pit of relegation and emerge transformed to record new triumphs. A dressing-room joker and a lethal five-a-side striker – who could forget that he headed the Reds' scoring list halfway through one season, courtesy of two penalties? – Alex Stepney was one of the club's most influential and entertaining characters. His part in the Old Trafford story is truly an honoured one.

When he moved he was still the best full-back at the club and there was no comparable replacement on the horizon.

1960/61–1972/73

530 **2**

GAMES GOALS

BORN	Dublin, 24.7.41.
HONOURS	European Cup 67/8. League Championship 64/5, 66/7. FA Cup 62/3.
	33 Republic of Ireland caps (62–76).
OTHER CLUBS	Shelbourne, Republic of Ireland; Bolton Wanderers 73/4–78/9 (170, 0); Detroit Express, USA.

Before the advent of Paul Parker and Denis Irwin, there was no vestige of doubt that Tony Dunne was United's most accomplished full-back since the Munich disaster. Indeed, even taking generous account of Alex Ferguson's marvellous modern pairing, and of the Neville brothers subsequently, there is a persuasive argument that the diminutive Irishman remains the finest to wear the red shirt on either defensive flank since the incomparable Roger Byrne.

Tony Dunne

The very fact that Tony is mentioned in tandem with the venerated ex-skipper illustrates his standing more eloquently than pages of the purplest prose. Furthermore, casting the net wider than Old Trafford, it's fair to say that at the zenith of the dapper Dunne's career – the middle 1960s – only Ray Wilson among British left-backs was a more complete footballer.

Plucked by the far-sighted Matt Busby from the virtual obscurity of the League of Ireland club, Shelbourne, for a mere £5,000, the 18-year-old who crossed the water in the spring of 1960 was a waspish whippersnapper blessed with the precious gift of speed. He could make a sliding tackle, see his winger waltz away with the ball and yet recover and win it back within five or six yards. Then, once in possession, it was rare that Tony would waste it. Instead of trying fancy tricks he would always take the simple option, usually a gentle side-foot to Paddy Crerand or Bobby Charlton. This consistency, allied to bravery and that unnerving pace, made him a bastion of United's defence for more than a decade. But could he have contributed more?

Some critics would have it that any man who could sprint like Tony should have been more prominent in attack. Well, it's true that he was hardly the bane of opposition defences – although he did, at times, overlap effectively – but in a team of such gifted creators that was not his priority. It was more important that he concentrated on defence and thus created a solid base for the makers of magic. Then later, as the glory days began to drift away, he was more than adequately occupied at the back.

Often United have been accused of letting top players go on for much too long, but in the case of Tony Dunne the reverse is palpably true. When he was allowed to move to Bolton in 1973 he was still the best full-back at the club and there was no comparable replacement on the horizon.

At Burnden Park he added a further 166 League games to his tally of 414 with United and maintained an impeccable standard to the end. And ironically, finding himself in the company of less illustrious colleagues, he blossomed as an all-round performer, taking responsibility on the pitch in a way that, presumably, he had never deemed necessary before. Under the management of another former United full-back, Ian Greaves, he emerged as a moulding defensive influence on the Trotters' younger players, and sometimes even a creator of attacking opportunities with distribution more ambitious than he had attempted previously.

Thus, assuredly, whatever the rights or wrongs of his departure from Old Trafford during the early days of Tommy Docherty's reign, Tony can be proud of a magnificent career.

PAUL EDWARDS ▼

1969/70–1972/73

68 GAMES **1** GOALS

BORN ○ Crompton, Lancashire, 7.10.47.
OTHER CLUBS ○ Oldham Athletic, first on loan 72/3–77/8 (112, 7);
Stockport County on loan 76/7 (2, 0);
Stockport County 78/9–79/80 (67, 2).

Despite making almost 70 appearances for Manchester United and winning three England under-23 caps, Paul Edwards was a moderate performer. The lanky defender enjoyed two first-team runs – one at full-back and the other in the centre – without ever looking completely at home in the top flight.

Paul, a modest, amiable man, was blessed with an unflappable temperament but his all-round ability, particularly his distribution, let him down. Most of his games were played under Wilf McGuinness, and after Frank O'Farrell took over his opportunities were strictly limited. In March 1973 he was transferred to Oldham for £15,000, going on to help the Latics lift the Third Division title in 1974 before finishing his Football League days at Stockport.

CARLO SARTORI ▲

1968/69–1971/72

55 GAMES **6** GOALS

BORN ○ Calderzone, Italy, 10.2.48.
OTHER CLUBS ○ Bologna, Italy.

If Carlo Sartori had happened along a few years earlier – or later come to that – the chances are that he would never have got near the United first team. The truth is that this popular, red-haired midfielder was not out of the top drawer and never looked likely to carve a long-term niche for himself at Old Trafford.

His chance came during a period of change, as the great side of the 1960s was being dismantled. After making his senior debut as a substitute for Francis Burns at White Hart Lane in October 1968, he worked prodigiously and cheerfully, but was short of pace and devoid of class. He contributed several important goals, though, notably winners at home to Arsenal in 1969/70 and at Nottingham Forest a season later.

Carlo, who was born in Italy but moved to England when he was very young, joined Bologna on leaving the Reds in 1972.

After six weeks the signing of Ian Ure, the only player bought by United during the reign of Wilf McGuinness, bore the hallmark of inspiration. The arrival of the rugged Scottish international centre-half from Arsenal, for £80,000 in August 1969, coincided with the end of a chronic run which culminated in the dropping of Bobby Charlton and Denis Law; dire straits indeed.

Ian, who stood out like a beacon with his flopping mop of blond hair, played eight League games before tasting defeat and he had apparently stabilised a shaky defence. Sadly the improvement was not maintained and by the following season he was fighting a losing battle to stay in the side, unable to overcome the relatively modest opposition of first Steve James and then Paul Edwards.

To be fair to Ian, his best days were behind him when he arrived at Old Trafford. In his time at Dundee and, to a lesser extent, at Highbury he was a far more effective performer. With United he retained his characteristic aggression but seemed to have lost his poise, being easily dragged out of position and lured into wild challenges which often left the Reds' rearguard woefully exposed.

Eventually Ian departed to join St Mirren, where briefly he replaced a promising young man, name of Gordon McQueen . . .

IAN URE

1969/70–1970/71

65 **1**

GAMES GOALS

BORN   Ayr, 7.12.39.
HONOURS   11 Scotland caps (61–67).
OTHER CLUBS   Dundee 58/9–62/3 (106, 0); Arsenal 63/4–69/70 (168, 2); St Mirren 72/3 (3, 0).

JIMMY RIMMER ▼

1967/68–1972/73

46 GAMES **0** GOALS

BORN Southport, Lancashire, 10.2.48.
HONOURS European Cup 67/8 (non-playing sub). 1 England cap (76).
OTHER CLUBS Swansea City on loan 73/4 (17, 0); Arsenal 73/4–76/7 (124, 0); Aston Villa 77/8–82/3 (229, 0); Swansea City 83/4–85/6 (66, 0).
MANAGER: Swansea City (caretaker, 95–96).

In many ways Jimmy Rimmer was the equal of Alex Stepney, the man who denied him a lengthy career with Manchester United. Indeed in some respects, such as dealing with crosses, Jimmy was superior, at least in Alex's early days at Old Trafford. But in one crucial department the Londoner was in a different league. When it came to confidence, so vital for any footballer but particularly a goalkeeper, Jimmy lagged well behind.

The only sustained first-team spell for the 1964 FA Youth Cup winner came in 1970/71, during the trouble-torn reign of Wilf McGuinness, and many thought he was unlucky to lose his place when he did.

When it became clear there was no future with the Reds, Jimmy moved to Arsenal – and did well – before reaching his peak with Aston Villa, with whom he bagged a European Cup winners medal to go with the one he received as a United substitute in 1968. While at Villa Park he won one England cap before finishing his career with Swansea.

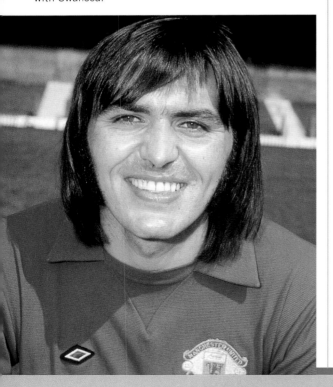

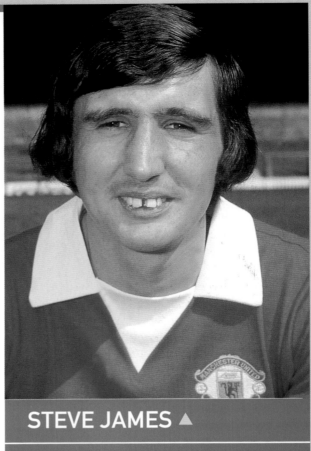

STEVE JAMES ▲

1968/69–1974/75

161 GAMES **4** GOALS

BORN Coseley, Staffordshire, 29.11.49.
OTHER CLUBS York City 75/6–79/80 (105, 1).

A chronic lack of self-belief stood between Steve James and a real tilt at the top with Manchester United. After demonstrating huge potential in the club's junior sides, he took over Bill Foulkes' centre-half role midway through 1968/69 but failed to make the position his own and lost it to Ian Ure the following season. After another year of being in and out, Steve was back in regular possession in 1971/72, a campaign in which United flattered to deceive and frittered away a substantial Championship lead.

Thereafter life was something of a battle for Steve at Old Trafford, and it became a losing battle the moment Tommy Docherty signed Jim Holton to shore up the centre of his defence. The big Scot quickly became a fixture and Steve was suddenly a perpetual reserve. A handful of games followed after Jim broke his leg, but even after the tall Midlander helped to clinch the Second Division title in the spring of 1975 there was no future for him, and he moved on to York City.

A hard-working, conscientious player, he was a competent tackler and good in the air but his game lacked that competitive edge needed for survival in the First Division.

John Aston was not the most fortunate of footballers, his Old Trafford years being bedevilled by two problems not of his own making. One, following in the footsteps of a famous father, he came to terms with. The other, becoming an aunt sally to sections of his home crowd, haunted him until the day he left.

John – son of John Aston Snr, a United hero of the 1940s and 1950s – was a fast, direct winger but one who boasted few frills to his game. As such he found himself an innocent victim of the spectacular success of Best, Law and Charlton. When United played badly, he was often unfairly singled out for persecution by fans who were reluctant to lash their idols. If a scapegoat was needed, usually John fitted the bill.

But he battled on philosophically, revealing ever more of the resolute spirit that had been evident from his earliest days on the Red Devils' groundstaff in 1962.

Back then, his situation had been awkward in the extreme, his father being not only a crowd favourite of days gone by, but also the club's youth coach. Thus John Snr was effectively John Jnr's boss, with all the inevitable strains such a dual relationship can cause. As a result, the youngster understood that if there were to be 50-50 decisions made then they would probably go against him, but he refused to buckle and eventually he reaped due rewards.

The first of these was a place in the team which lifted the FA Youth Cup in 1964, shoulder to shoulder with the likes of Best, Sadler and Noble. Then came a hard-won Championship medal in 1966/67 before a broken leg, suffered against Manchester City at Maine Road in August 1968, signalled the beginning of the end of his tenure at Old Trafford. However, drawing yet further on that seemingly bottomless well of determination, he went on to do well elsewhere, notably at Luton Town.

And whatever other memories John holds of United, both the painful and the pleasurable, he can always cherish his performance in the most important match in the club's history – the 1968 European Cup Final.

That night at Wembley he truly walked with the gods as he lacerated the Benfica defence with pure pace. Fans may drool over the goals of Charlton and Best, the fairytale birthday celebration of Kidd and the miraculous save of Stepney; but, in truth, no one made a more mammoth contribution to that golden triumph than John Aston. What an occasion to come up with the show of a lifetime!

JOHN ASTON

1964/65–1971/72

185 **27**

GAMES GOALS

BORN	Manchester, 28.6.47.
HONOURS	European Cup 67/8. League Championship 66/7.
OTHER CLUBS	Luton Town 72/3–77/8 (174, 31); Mansfield Town 77/8 (31, 4); Blackburn Rovers 78/9–79/80 (15, 2).

ALAN GOWLING

1967/68–1971/72

87 **21**
GAMES GOALS

BORN	Stockport, Cheshire, 16.3.49.
OTHER CLUBS	Huddersfield Town 72/3–74/5 (128, 58); Newcastle United 75/6–77/8 (92, 30); Bolton Wanderers 77/8–81/2 (149, 28); Preston North End 82/3 (40, 5).

Alan Gowling was not a pretty sight on the football field. He bounded about energetically, with all the grace of a gangling crab. But this lack of poetry in his motion belied the fact that he could be an effective, occasionally devastating performer.

For four seasons the England amateur international, a supremely fit front-runner capable of prodigious amounts of honest endeavour, hovered on the fringe of the first team, having shrugged off earlier strain imposed on his soccer development by simultaneous university studies. The highlight of that period, achieved at home to Southampton in February 1971, was scoring four goals in a game, something no United man was to equal at senior level until Andy Cole's beanfeast against Ipswich nearly a quarter of a century later.

However, it was the 1971/72 campaign that was to prove the most eventful during the Gowling tenure at Old Trafford. New manager Frank O'Farrell converted him into a foraging wing-half and it seemed Alan had found his most productive niche. He helped United take an early lead in the title race and captained the England under-23 side.

Unhappily this new-found stature was not to last, at least not at Old Trafford. The team's fortunes tumbled and at the end of the season Alan, still only 23, was sold to Huddersfield for £65,000. He reverted to a striking role and enjoyed a subsequent career of much merit, particularly in spells at Newcastle and Bolton.

A dedicated individual of even temperament who, in his time, has chaired both the Professional Footballers Association and the United Former Players Association, he will go down as a player who made the absolute most of rather limited natural ability.

Intelligent and articulate, Alan was blessed with richer gifts in other fields, going on to make full use of his economics degree in the world of business.

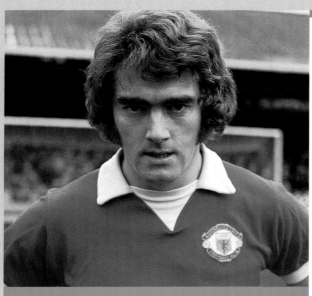

TED MᴀᴄDOUGALL ▲

1972/73

18 **5**
GAMES GOALS

BORN   Inverness, 8.1.47.
HONOURS   7 Scotland caps (75).
OTHER CLUBS   York City 67/8–68/9 (84, 34); Bournemouth 69/70–72/3 (146, 103); West Ham United 72/3–73/4 (24, 5); Norwich City 73/4–76/7 (112, 51); Southampton 76/7–78/9 (86, 42); Bournemouth 78/9–79/80 (52, 16); Blackpool 79/80–80/1 (13, 0).

Ted MacDougall may be excused if his memories of Old Trafford are not of the charitable variety. He arrived from Bournemouth with a prodigious strike rate to live up to – he netted 103 times in 146 games for the Dean Court club – and a fee of £200,000 on his head. His task: to score the goals to haul United away from the foot of the First Division.

Whether he was good enough to do that we shall never know; for just 18 games and five goals later, Ted MacDougall was on his way to West Ham. Frank O'Farrell, the man who bought him and who surely would have given him the extended run needed to prove himself capable or otherwise, was sacked. Tommy Docherty was appointed as the new manager and from that moment Ted's fate was sealed. The Doc quickly made it obvious that his countryman played no part in his plans and Ted departed a frustrated man.

Many respected critics assert that the nippy opportunist, sometimes so devastating with his head, did not have the class to be a success for Manchester United. But the fact remains that, after briefly experiencing further lean times at Upton Park, he went on to put in prolific scoring stints with Norwich and Southampton. At Old Trafford he was simply not given the chance.

WYN DAVIES ▼

1972/73

17 **4**
GAMES GOALS

BORN   Caernarvon, 20.3.42.
HONOURS   34 Wales caps (63–73).
OTHER CLUBS   Wrexham 60/1–61/2 (55, 22); Bolton Wanderers 61/2–66/7 (155, 66); Newcastle United 66/7–70/1 (180, 40); Manchester City 71/2–72/3 (45, 8); Blackpool 73/4–74/5 (36, 5); Crystal Palace on loan 74/5 (3, 0); Stockport County 75/6 (30, 7); Crewe Alexandra 76/7–77/8 (55, 13).

Just an old jumper well past his best, or a battle-hardened campaigner whose experience would have been invaluable to United had he been given the opportunity? Those who recall Wyn's brief contribution to the Old Trafford cause are divided in their opinion. But the one man whose opinion mattered, manager Tommy Docherty, was in no doubt. After taking over the club, he allowed the Welsh international centre-forward only one more senior game before packing him off to Blackpool.

A season earlier many Manchester City fans had felt that 'Wyn the Leap' – he earned the epithet through stirring deeds during his prime with Bolton Wanderers and Newcastle United – should never have been replaced by Rodney Marsh and were aghast when he was allowed to join the old enemy.

As events turned out Wyn, whose ball skills had never approached his aerial ability, was made to look more limited than ever with the Reds, probably because he was playing for a struggling team and alongside another non-established striker in Ted MacDougall. Any hope he had of an Indian summer at Old Trafford disappeared with Frank O'Farrell.

TONY YOUNG ▼

1970/71–1975/76

97 GAMES | **1 GOALS**

BORN ● Urmston, Lancashire, 24.12.52.
HONOURS ● Second Division Championship 74/5.
OTHER CLUBS ● Charlton Athletic 75/6–76/7 (20, 1); York City 76/7–78/9 (78, 2).

Tony Young was an aggressive utility player who was not good enough to hold his own in the First Division. His first, limited chances came during the regimes of Wilf McGuinness and Frank O'Farrell but it was not until Tommy Docherty took over that he enjoyed an extended run. That was in 1972/73 when he replaced Tommy O'Neil at right-back in a highly indifferent team.

He retained a place, either at full-back or in midfield, for most of the subsequent campaign but lost out as the Doc shifted the accent from defence to offence in an unsuccessful bid to avoid relegation.

Tony remained mainly in the Old Trafford shadows for another two seasons, winning a Second Division Championship medal mostly on substitute appearances, before joining Charlton Athletic. Soon afterwards he linked up again with McGuinness at York City before going non-League.

TOMMY O'NEIL ▲

1970/71–1972/73

68 GAMES | **0 GOALS**

BORN ● St Helens, Lancashire, 25.10.52.
OTHER CLUBS ● Blackpool on loan 72/3 (7, 0); Southport 73/4–77/8 (197,16); Tranmere Rovers 78/9–79/80 (74, 10); Halifax Town 80/1–81/2 (40, 2).

Most players with more than half a century of appearances for Manchester United to their credit had more elan than Tommy O'Neil. The diminutive defender had what it took for a lengthy Football League career – he proved that with spells at Southport, Tranmere Rovers and Halifax Town – but he was not cut out for the top flight. Tommy was always a trier and he demonstrated his tenacity, as well as the lack of genuine competitors for the right-back position, by hanging on to a first-team place throughout Frank O'Farrell's only full season at Old Trafford.

Indeed, there was a time when it looked as if he might pick up a Championship medal as the Reds led the table in the autumn. Sadly that honour eluded him, as it continued to elude United for another two decades.

PAUL BIELBY
1973/74

WINGER

4 GAMES **0** GOALS

BORN:
Darlington, County Durham, 24.11.56.

OTHER CLUBS:
Hartlepool United 75/6–77/8 (93, 8); Huddersfield Town 78/9 (31, 5).

IAN DONALD
1972/73

FULL-BACK

6 GAMES **0** GOALS

BORN:
Aberdeen, 28.11.51.

OTHER CLUBS:
Patrick Thistle 72/3 (1,0); Arbroath 73/4-74/5 (4,0).

CLIVE GRIFFITHS
1973/74

DEFENDER

7 GAMES **0** GOALS

BORN:
Pontypridd, Glamorgan, 22.1.55.

OTHER CLUBS:
Plymouth Argyle on loan 74/5 (11, 1); Tranmere Rovers 75/6–76/7 (59, 0).

GEORGE BUCHAN
1973/74

FORWARD

4 GAMES **0** GOALS

BORN:
Aberdeen, 2.5.50.

OTHER CLUBS:
Aberdeen 68/9–72/3 (29, 2); Bury 74/5–75/6 (65, 6).

PETER FLETCHER
1972/73–1973/74

FORWARD

7 GAMES **0** GOALS

BORN:
Manchester, 2.12.53.

OTHER CLUBS:
Hull City 74/5–75/6 (36, 5); Stockport County 76/7–77/8 (51, 13); Huddersfield Town 78/9–81/2 (99, 37).

FRANK KOPEL
1967/68–1968/69

FULL-BACK

12 GAMES **0** GOALS

BORN:
Falkirk, Stirlingshire, 28.3.49.

OTHER CLUBS:
Blackburn Rovers 68/9–71/2 (25, 0); Dundee United 71/2–81/2 (284, 7); Arbroath 81/2–83/4 (62, 1).

JOHN CONNAUGHTON
1971/72

GOALKEEPER

3 GAMES **0** GOALS

BORN:
Wigan, Lancashire, 23.9.49.

OTHER CLUBS:
Halifax Town on loan 69/70 (3, 0); Torquay United on loan 71/2 (22, 0); Sheffield United 73/4 (12, 0); Port Vale 74/5–79/80 (191, 0).

DON GIVENS
1969/70

FORWARD

9 GAMES **1** GOALS

BORN:
Limerick, Republic of Ireland, 9.8.49.

HONOURS: 56 Republic of Ireland caps (69–82).

OTHER CLUBS:
Luton Town 70/1–71/2 (83, 19); Queen's Park Rangers 72/3–77/8 (242, 76); Birmingham City 78/9–80/1 (59, 10); Bournemouth on loan 79/80 (5, 4); Sheffield United 80/1 (11, 3); Neuchatel Xamax, Switzerland.

WILLIE WATSON
1970/71–1972/73

FULL-BACK

14 GAMES **0** GOALS

BORN:
Motherwell, Lanarkshire, 4.12.49.

OTHER CLUBS:
Miami Toros 73; Motherwell 73/4-77/8 (127,2).

JIM McCALLIOG ▼

1973/74–1974/75

38 GAMES **7** GOALS

BORN ● Glasgow, 23.9.46.
HONOURS ● Second Division Championship 74/5. 5 Scotland caps (67–71).
OTHER CLUBS ● Chelsea 64/5–65/6 (7, 2); Sheffield Wednesday 65/6–68/9 (150, 19); Wolverhampton Wanderers 69/70–73/4 (163, 34); Southampton 74/5–76/7 (72, 8); Chicago Sting, USA, 77; Lincoln City 78/9 (99, 0).
MANAGER: Halifax Town (90–91).

Jim McCalliog and Manchester United should have been good for each other. Sadly they parted after 11 months, the relationship seemingly stale before it had the chance to flourish.

The Scottish international midfielder – who had also played up front in a career taking in Chelsea, Sheffield Wednesday (where he was outstanding) and Wolves – arrived at Old Trafford from Molineux for £60,000 in March 1974 as Tommy Docherty made his last desperate bid to avoid relegation. The trap-door to Division Two was already half open but Jim, after sharing in two defeats, sparked hopes of salvation as United went six games without defeat. This included a 3–0 drubbing of Everton in which he scored twice. The Stretford End sensed a new messiah, but it all proved an illusion and the Reds went down.

Jim played a full part in the first half of the Second Division resurgence, his silky, unhurried style and cultured passing blending successfully with the whirlwind approach of the team as a whole. But he could not hold his place, joined Southampton for £40,000, and, a season later, had the last laugh on United. It was Jim who provided the pass for Bobby Stokes to snatch away the FA Cup in one of the great Wembley upsets.

TREVOR ANDERSON ▲

1972/73–1973/74

19 GAMES **2** GOALS

BORN ● Belfast, 3.3.51.
HONOURS ● 22 Northern Ireland caps (73–78).
OTHER CLUBS ● Portadown, Northern Ireland; Swindon Town 74/5–77/8 (131, 34); Peterborough United 77/8–78/9 (49, 6); Linfield, Northern Ireland.

Trevor Anderson was one of those frustrating players with all the ability needed to become a star, yet who lacked some vital, unspecified, magical something.

It was Frank O'Farrell who bought the slightly-built, Belfast-born forward from Portadown to prepare for a future of which he, as an about-to-be-sacked manager, was not destined to be part. So it was Tommy Docherty who drafted him into the relegation battle in that same season and the move paid dividends, Trevor scoring the only goal in a win at Leeds which did much to keep the Reds temporarily in the top flight.

At this stage the skilful, elegant striker looked to be headed for the top and within weeks of his United debut he was playing for Northern Ireland. But the side made a bad start to the next campaign and Trevor was one of many players discarded by the Doc. There followed three successful years at Swindon and a short spell at Peterborough before he returned to Ireland, his full potential sadly unfulfilled.

The George Graham affair was one of the more eccentric episodes during the tumultuous reign of Tommy Docherty at Old Trafford. As one of his first acts on taking over, the Doc paid Arsenal £120,000 for George and described him thus: 'He's a midfield player of the highest class. I rate him alongside Gunter Netzer. I like his skill and control but most of all I like the confidence he brings to everything he does.'

Quite an introduction, and 'Stroller' duly helped United beat the drop to Division Two in 1972/73. He seemed an ideal stabilising influence and it was no shock when he was made captain on Bobby Charlton's retirement.

But there was strife in store. As the Reds slumped again he could do nothing right for the crowd, even when he played well. In fact, the 29-year-old play-maker's best days were behind him – at Highbury, where he had helped Arsenal to win the double – and his relaxed style probably gave the (false) impression that he was coasting. Still, it was appalling that the majority of the criticism he received was more hysterical than constructive.

The Doc jettisoned him from the team in January 1974 and ten months later swapped him for Portsmouth's once-great but then ageing striker Ron Davies, who was never to start a game for the Reds; it seemed a somewhat bizarre deal.

Eventually George became a manager, doing well with Millwall, then hitting fabulous heights with Arsenal until his record was tarnished by the 'bung' scandal. Meanwhile his Old Trafford fall from being 'another Netzer' to the wilderness remains as a perplexing slice of United history.

GEORGE GRAHAM

1972/73–1974/75

46 GAMES **2** GOALS

BORN	Bargeddie, Lanarkshire, 30.11.44.
HONOURS	12 Scotland caps (71–73).
OTHER CLUBS	Aston Villa 62/3–63/4 (8, 2); Chelsea 64/5–66/7 (72, 35); Arsenal 66/7–72/3 (227, 60); Portsmouth 74/5–76/7 (61, 5); Crystal Palace 76/7–77/8 (44, 2); California Surf USA, 78. MANAGER: Millwall (82–86); Arsenal (86–95); Leeds United (96–98); Tottenham Hotspur (98-).

As United struggled unavailingly to avoid relegation, Willie was one of the most effective and consistent performers.

1968/69–1974/75

294 GAMES | **33** GOALS

BORN ● Sauchie, Stirlingshire, 2.10.44.
HONOURS ● Second Division Championship 74/5. 21 Scotland caps (67–74).
OTHER CLUBS ● Burnley 62/3–67/8 (183, 19) and 75/6 (13, 0); Bolton Wanderers 75/6–79/80 (155, 10); Chicago Sting, Minnesota Kicks, both USA, Vancouver Whitecaps, Canada; Blackpool 80/1–81/2 (42, 4).

Willie Morgan was a tremendous footballer – and if only he could have forgotten about George Best he would have been even better. There were times when Willie, a gifted winger who later became equally effective in midfield, seemed obsessed with the Irish genius. He wasted no opportunity to assert that he was in the same class as George, a standpoint ludicrous to anyone who had seen them both play. But it would be wrong if this apparent blind spot was to obscure the commendable contribution Willie made to Manchester United.

Willie Morgan

The Scottish international arrived from Burnley, where he was very much the star, for £117,000 soon after the 1968 European Cup triumph. It was an unsettling time for a young man who had fallen out with the Turf Moor regime to the extent that he had been training alone, and he seemed short of both fitness and confidence in his early outings as a Red Devil. Before long, Willie was dropped, but he fought back and, as such giants as Law, Charlton and Crerand began to age, his on-field influence grew, despite differences with new manager Wilf McGuinness.

A turning point in the Morgan career came when Wilf's successor, Frank O'Farrell, moved him from the flank to midfield. In both positions Willie's instant control and dazzling dribbling skills took the eye, but in the deep-lying role a huge capacity for work and a willingness to bite into tackles gave his game an extra dimension. On the debit side were a poor goal-scoring record – he was a rather weak striker of the ball – and, on too many occasions for it to be overlooked, a disturbing tendency to make a disappointing final pass.

However, as United struggled unavailingly to avoid relegation, Willie was one of the most effective and consistent performers, succeeding George Graham as captain and forging an apparently close bond with Tommy Docherty, yet another new boss. Indeed the Doc, who as Scotland manager had recalled Morgan to his country's colours, once went so far as to dub his skipper the best right-winger in the world! After a major eye operation during the summer of 1974, Willie began the Second Division campaign in fine fettle, but late autumn brought disagreement with Docherty, a rift that was to flare again in the spring when the 29-year-old was replaced by young Steve Coppell. That summer, despite a petition from some of the popular Morgan's fans, he was allowed to rejoin Burnley. After a short second stay at Turf Moor he went on to a successful spell with Bolton, a sojourn in America and a final fling with Blackpool.

What a shame that acrimony had soured his latter days at Old Trafford and that it should boil over into a court confrontation in 1978, when Tommy accused his former favourite of libel. The case collapsed and Willie was cleared after the Doc admitted lying under oath.

IAN MOORE

1971/72–1973/74

43 **12**
GAMES GOALS

BORN	Ipswich, Suffolk, 17.1.45.
HONOURS	1 England cap (70) .
OTHER CLUBS	Nottingham Forest 63/4–71/2 (236,105).

Big, powerful, goal-scoring wingers who can excite crowds and win matches out of nothing are rare and valuable beings. One such was Ian Moore. Here was a man who possessed the potential for huge achievement and his premature retirement due to injury was arguably a major factor in United's subsequent slide into the Second Division.

The loss of such a performer – who finished top scorer for Nottingham Forest in five of his last six seasons at the City Ground – would be hard for any club to take. For United, struggling manfully but without much inspiration to stay in the top flight, it was a body blow.

Ian had been plagued by lack of fitness during his time at Forest, a sad circumstance which had limited him to only one England cap by the time he arrived at Old Trafford in March 1972. He sustained several more injuries during his all-too-brief days as a Red Devil, the final damage being an accident to his ankle in the gym. Yet in one way United fans were lucky to have had the chance to savour his talents at all. Ian was the subject of a transfer saga which reached a peak of absurdity when Derby County paraded him in front of the Baseball Ground fans, believing him to be their player. In fact, Forest had not signed the transfer forms and Frank O'Farrell stepped in with a £200,000 cheque.

Ian went on to total fewer than 50 games for the Reds but he will not be forgotten by those who saw him in his pomp. He scored on each of his first three outings, the third a stunning effort against Coventry at Highfield Road which saw him pick the ball up wide, surge past several defenders and finish with a firm shot.

Eventually Ian, who preferred not to use his full surname of Storey-Moore, was fit enough for a non-League comeback but that was scant consolation for a man whose career was shattered at its peak.

MICK MARTIN ▲

1972/73–1974/75

43 **2**
GAMES GOALS

BORN Dublin, 9.7.51.
HONOURS 51 Republic of Ireland caps (72–83).
OTHER CLUBS Home Farm and Bohemians, both Republic of Ireland; West Bromwich Albion 75/6–78/9 (89, 11); Newcastle United 78/9–82/3 (147, 5); Vancouver Whitecaps, Canada; Cardiff City 84/5 (7, 0); Peterborough United 84/5 (12, 0); Rotherham United 85/6 (5, 0); Preston North End 85/6 (35, 0).

Mick Martin was a willing midfield workhorse who didn't have the quality to make the grade at Old Trafford. A rather one-paced player, the Republic of Ireland international would trundle manfully, and that wasn't enough for the sometimes hyper-critical United crowd. Most of his games were played for a struggling side and often he was singled out as a convenient scapegoat.

Yet it's possible that he was never given a chance in what might have proved to be his most effective position. During his early years with Bohemians and subsequently, on odd occasions, for his country he turned out in the centre of defence and acquitted himself admirably. In one game against England at Wembley in 1976 he managed to subdue former United colleague Stuart Pearson, although 'Pancho' did snatch his side's goal in a 1–1 draw.

One man who thought highly of Mick was another ex-United player, Johnny Giles, who took him from Old Trafford to West Bromwich Albion. And there were times when Johnny, in his capacity as Eire boss, preferred the solid attributes of Mick – whose father, Con, also wore the green shirt – to the more mercurial talents of Gerry Daly.

On leaving the Hawthorns, Martin Jnr gave yeoman service to Newcastle before a period in Vancouver. A brief tour of lower division clubs preceded retirement and a return to St James' Park as a coach.

ARNOLD SIDEBOTTOM ▼

1972/73–1974/75

20 **0**
GAMES GOALS

BORN Barnsley, Yorkshire, 1.4.54.
HONOURS Second Division Championship 74/5.
OTHER CLUBS Huddersfield Town 75/6–77/8 (61, 5); Halifax Town 78/9 (21, 2).

When Arnie Sidebottom gave up soccer to concentrate on cricket he made the wisest decision of his professional life. As a pace bowler he enjoyed a creditable career with Yorkshire and went on to play in a Test match for England against Australia in 1985. Had he soldiered on as a centre-half in the lower reaches of the Football League – he served both Huddersfield Town and Halifax Town after leaving Old Trafford – he would not have stood the slightest chance of international recognition.

Not that long, lean Arnie was a particularly bad footballer. Although rather spindly for a central defender, he was reasonably effective in the air and, if he was a tad ponderous over the first five yards, he could move quickly enough when he got into his stride.

But he was never a dominant figure at the rearguard's core and his stint as deputy for the injured Jim Holton during the 1974/75 Second Division Championship campaign demonstrated clearly that he would never be better than an average performer.

For Arnie that must have been a mortifying circumstance, but in the long run it was a situation for which Yorkshire cricket had ample cause to be grateful.

At times he was vilified for his rumbustious approach. In fact, there wasn't an ounce of malice in him.

1972/73–1974/75

69	5
GAMES	GOALS

BORN ● Lesmahagow, Lanarkshire, 11.4.51.
HONOURS ● Second Division Championship 74/5. 15 Scotland caps (73–74).
OTHER CLUBS ● Shrewsbury Town 71/2–72/3 (67, 4); Sunderland 76/7 (15, 0); Coventry City 76/7–79/80 (91, 0).

No one was more surprised than Jim Holton to find himself a folk hero within weeks of joining Manchester United from Shrewsbury Town. There he was, a mammoth, sometimes clumsy centre-half at a club where superstar forwards were the rule and defenders, in general, were out of the limelight.

Jim Holton

But at Old Trafford in January 1973 unusual circumstances prevailed. The Reds were at the foot of the table with a leaky defence and the fans were not happy. Then along came Jim and immediately gave them what they wanted – dominance, commitment and a hint that First Division survival might, after all, be just around the corner. All this was wrapped up in a rugged, warm, man-on-the-street package that supporters took to their hearts. More cultured, calculating players such as Martin Buchan they could respect; Jim Holton they could love.

Within a few months United had avoided the drop and their new centre-half was playing for Scotland in the World Cup Finals, a fairytale if ever there was one. But like so many football fantasies it was not to have a happy ending. The following season, despite Jim's ever increasing effectiveness, the Reds were relegated. Then, after making 14 appearances in the Second Division campaign, he broke his leg in a 4–4 thriller at Sheffield Wednesday and was never again to return to first-team duty. A comeback in the reserves ended with another break and by the time he was ready for action once more, Brian Greenhoff had made the position his own. So Jim moved on to Sunderland, then Coventry City, then Sheffield Wednesday, but he was rarely fit and quit the professional game in 1981.

He will be remembered as a superb header and tackler who was rarely drawn out of position, though occasionally he could be caught for pace. At times he was vilified for his rumbustious approach. In fact, there wasn't an ounce of malice in him, even if it was not for nothing that the Stretford End sang: 'Six foot two, eyes of blue, Big Jim Holton's after you!'

News of his sudden death, at the age of 42 in October 1993, shocked the entire soccer community. Having overcome two major disappointments in his time – failure to make the grade as a teenager with Celtic, then injury-induced early retirement – Jim had carved out a happy niche as a pub landlord in Coventry. For a while life was good, but tragedy was lying in wait for one of the game's more engaging cult heroes.

ALEX FORSYTH

1972/73–1977/78

119 **5**
GAMES GOALS

BORN	Swinton, Berwickshire, 5.2.52.
HONOURS	Second Division Championship 74/5. 10 Scotland caps (72–75).
OTHER CLUBS	Partick Thistle 70/1–72/3 (52, 5); Glasgow Rangers 78/9–80/1 (25, 5); Motherwell 82/3 (19, 0); Hamilton Academical 83/4–84/5 (63, 9).

When Tommy Docherty took over an ailing Manchester United towards the end of 1972 one of his first moves was to sign Alex Forsyth. It was perhaps not surprising that the new manager should go to Partick Thistle with a £100,000 cheque for the up-and-coming full-back, as it was he who had first picked Alex for the Scottish international side. And although it was not one of the Doc's most widely hailed forays into the transfer market, Alex never let club or colleagues down and he shared in the glory of promotion from the Second Division as well as the despair of the big drop the previous season.

'Bruce,' as he inevitably became known, was a strong tackler and a supremely clean striker of the ball, but he was too slow for a berth among the elite. Despite his determination and excellent positional play he could be shown up against a tricky winger and it was no surprise when, ultimately, he lost his place to the more mobile Jimmy Nicholl.

Much loved by the crowd, particularly the Stretford End, Alex was extremely effective going forward and possessed a thunderous shot. This was never better demonstrated than in a League match with Wolves in 1975, when he crashed the ball against the post from fully 30 yards and it rebounded almost to the centre circle. The crispness and timing of his kicking were also apparent in his characteristically massive clearances, which were a delight to the likes of Stuart Pearson and Sammy McIlroy up front.

When it became clear that he had no future at Old Trafford, Alex left for Glasgow Rangers, then served Motherwell and Hamilton Academical before quitting the game.

When Stewart Houston arrived at Old Trafford from Brentford in December 1973 he was something of a surprise recruit. United were struggling to avoid relegation, the defence was shaky and most observers were expecting an expensive buy to help tighten it up. Instead Tommy Docherty paid just £55,000 for Stewart, who had played under him at Chelsea, failed to make the grade and moved on to Griffin Park, apparently destined for a career in the League's lower reaches.

The next five years proved the Doc's judgement, in this case, to be impeccable. Stewart matured into one of the most consistent left-backs in the country and went on to play for Scotland. A magnificent all-round athlete, he was tall for a full-back, which was invaluable in United's somewhat under-sized rearguard of that time. He made his height count in both penalty areas, being especially useful on the opposition's far post at set pieces.

But Stewart's greatest asset was the accuracy of his left foot. His speciality was the long ball along the touchline, usually to Gordon Hill or the wide-ranging Stuart Pearson, a manoeuvre which set up countless attacks. The lack of comparable ability on his right side was offset by his mobility and reading of the game, which also made little of a slight lack of pace.

Stewart picked up a loser's medal in the 1976 FA Cup Final and was cheated of compensation the following year when he broke a leg at Bristol City shortly before the Wembley clash with Liverpool. Thereafter he was never the same and lost his place to Arthur Albiston. In July 1980 he moved to Sheffield United on a free transfer, later assisting Colchester before shining as a coach and joining Arsenal in that capacity. He went on to manage Queen's Park Rangers, then returned to coaching with Tottenham Hotspur.

STEWART HOUSTON

1973/74–1979/80

250 **16**

GAMES GOALS

BORN ● Dunoon, Argyllshire, 20.8.49.

HONOURS ● Second Division Championship 74/5. 1 Scotland cap (75).

OTHER CLUBS ● Chelsea 67/8–69/70 (9, 0); Brentford 71/2–73/4 (77, 9); Sheffield United 80/1–82/3 (94, 1); Colchester United 83/4–85/6 (107, 5). MANAGER: Arsenal (caretaker, 95 and 96); Queen's Park Rangers (97).

The Macari method combined frenetic energy and raw courage with subtle skills, a rare blend.

1972/73–1983/84

400 **97**

GAMES GOALS

BORN ● Aberdeen, 4.6.49.
HONOURS ● FA Cup 76/7. Second Division Championship 74/5. 24 Scotland caps (72–78).
OTHER CLUBS ● Celtic 68/9–72/3 (58, 26); Swindon Town 84/5–85/6 (36, 3).
MANAGER: Swindon Town (84–89); West Ham United (89–90); Birmingham City (91); Stoke City (91–93); Celtic (93–94); Stoke City (94–97).

'I always like to give value for money' said Lou Macari in a TV interview after scoring on his debut for Manchester United. When he departed to become player-manager of Swindon Town 11 years later, he had done that, and then some.

Lou Macari

At the time of joining the Reds, the 23-year-old Aberdonian – who had incurred the scorn of Bill Shankly for spurning Anfield in favour of Old Trafford – was fresh from several seasons of success as a striker with Celtic, and it was in this role that he started his stay south of the border. But the stint up front for United turned out to be a traumatic experience for the tiny Scottish international. He failed to make an impact and looked set to be branded a £200,000 misfit.

Then Tommy Docherty shuffled his pack and gave Lou a midfield position that afforded him the freedom to roam. As a result he was transformed from a liability into one of the most effective players in the land throughout the second half of the 1970s. The new Lou Macari was an inspirational footballer, a key member of the Doc's lovely attacking side which won promotion in 1974/75 and made an exhilarating return to the top flight the next season.

Though never a heavy scorer in his Red Devil days, he chipped in with his share of strikes; however, the most priceless he had a hand in was an outrageous fluke with which he was not even credited. The goal which beat Liverpool in the 1977 FA Cup Final came when the wee fellow hit a wildly off-beam shot which rebounded from the chest of Jimmy Greenhoff, then caromed in a crazy arc beyond stranded 'keeper Ray Clemence and into the net. Of course, he claimed cheekily that it was the product of much hard work on the training ground, but listeners that gullible were hard to find!

That was a freak occurrence, but the basics of Lou's game owed nothing to fortune. A teetotaller and non-smoker, he was so fit that he didn't seem tired even after hustling his way through the most hectic of encounters. The Macari method combined frenetic energy and raw courage with subtle skills, a rare blend which got both crowds and colleagues buzzing. One of his most spectacular attributes, despite standing just 5ft 5in, was his ability in the air, where he was especially lethal at the near post.

Few players had more influence on their eras at Old Trafford than Lou Macari. He would have won more honours at Liverpool, but he couldn't have created a more indelible impression.

As a boss, too, he cut a considerable, often controversial dash – he faced the possibility of prison before his name was cleared in a scandal over illegal payments at Swindon – and his reigns tended not to be boring. The ultimate judgement on Macari the manager seemed likely to depend on the outcome of the massive challenge he accepted in November 1993, that of restoring the glory days to Celtic. However, eight months later he was sacked before bouncing back in typically indestructible manner to commence a second sparky spell at Stoke.

BRIAN GREENHOFF

1973/74–1978/79

270 **17**
GAMES GOALS

BORN ● Barnsley, Yorkshire, 28.4.53.
HONOURS ● FA Cup 76/7. Division Two Championship 74/5. 18 England caps (76–80).
OTHER CLUBS ● Leeds United 79/80–81/2 (72, 1); Hong Kong football; Rochdale 82/3–83/4 (16, 0).

There has probably never been a Manchester United player who made more of relatively limited natural talent than Brian Greenhoff. But that is not to belittle the achievements of a man whose career was punctuated by serious injuries, who played a vital role in one of the most exciting club sides of the 1970s and who won 18 England caps.

Brian, who was to be joined later at Old Trafford by brother Jimmy, broke into the first team as an industrious midfielder early in the ill-fated 1973/74 season. He was one of the few players to enhance his reputation during the unsuccessful bid to stave off relegation and his star rose further during the promotion year that followed.

With Jim Holton sidelined by a broken leg, Brian found himself in the centre of defence alongside Martin Buchan at the start of the 1975/76 campaign and it was there that he enjoyed his most successful spell. For two and a half years, until the arrival of Gordon McQueen, he did a sturdy, dependable job. Brave, determined and never flashy, he lacked dominance in the air and was not as fast as his partner but generally he held his own against the country's top strikers.

After a run at right-back in the early part of 1978/79 Brian, who was so versatile he was occasionally pressed into service as emergency front-man or even goalkeeper, struggled to hold his place in the senior line-up and the next summer moved to Leeds United for £350,000.

But injury continued to plague him and his time at Elland Road was not productive. A brief spell at Rochdale followed before Brian called it a day. He could congratulate himself on a career in which not a single shred of ability was wasted.

One of Tommy Docherty's shrewdest moves was the signing of Gerry Daly – and one of his most questionable was allowing the gifted Republic of Ireland midfielder to slip away following a difference of opinion. Gerry was bought from Bohemians for just £20,000 and dispatched to Derby County for £180,000 four years later. The profit was undeniably handsome but most Reds fans were left with the feeling that a potentially outstanding player had been unnecessarily lost.

When he arrived at Old Trafford as a pale, thin youngster he looked as though a puff of wind would blow him away; but there was more to Gerry Daly than met the eye. Light he may have been but the young Irishman was deceptively wiry and, after he had built up his stamina with a new and strenuous training regime, he lost little time in demonstrating his abundant talent.

Gerry made his debut in the 1973 Anglo-Italian tournament and was in and out of the relegation side. But the Second Division campaign proved the making of him and he became an integral part of the promotion combination with his precise passing, tireless running and fierce shooting.

Back in the First Division he became an increasingly influential member of the team, notably from the penalty spot, where he succeeded with 16 out of 17 efforts during his Old Trafford career. But then, in late 1976, he was dropped and replaced by converted striker Sammy McIlroy following the reshuffle precipitated by the arrival of Jimmy Greenhoff.

Easy-going Gerry clashed with the Doc and departed for the Baseball Ground where, ironically, the two were to be reunited. Despite numerous later moves in this country and America he never quite recaptured the early form which may, arguably, have flowered more luxuriantly in the headier atmosphere of Old Trafford to which he was best suited.

GERRY DALY

1973/74–1976/77

 142 32

GAMES GOALS

BORN	Dublin, 30.4.54.
HONOURS	Second Division Championship 74/5. 48 Republic of Ireland caps (73–86).
OTHER CLUBS	Bohemians, Republic of Ireland; Derby County 76/7–79/80 (112, 31); Coventry City 80/1–83/4 (84, 15); Leicester City on loan 82/3 (17, 1); Birmingham City 84/5–85/6 (32, 1); Shrewsbury Town 85/6–86/7 (55, 8); Stoke City 86/7–87/8 (22,1); Doncaster Rovers 88/9 (39, 4).

His first touch was usually immaculate, either a subtle first-time lay-off or a deft piece of control.

1974/75–1978/79

179 **66**
GAMES GOALS

BORN	Hull, Yorkshire, 21.6.49.
HONOURS	FA Cup 76/7. Second Division Championship 74/5. 15 England caps (76–78).
OTHER CLUBS	Hull City 69/70–73/74 (129, 44); West Ham United 79/80–81/2 (34, 6).

The upraised fist, the infectious, boyish grin; they said it all. Stuart Pearson had struck again. There was no more joyful sight for Manchester United fans in the second half of the 1970s when 'Pancho' – so named after an earlier Old Trafford Pearson, Mark – was in his swashbuckling pomp.

Stuart Pearson

Stuart arrived from Hull City in a £200,000 deal after United were relegated in 1973/74. His first task was to inject punch into a hitherto rather feeble attack and this he did to the tune of 17 goals as the Red Devils surged to the Second Division title. Many of his strikes during that helter-skelter campaign – notably a superbly placed drive in the crucial home clash with promotion rivals Sunderland – remain vivid in the memory.

But there was much more to his game than scoring. He was primarily a target man and every team-mate, from Alex Stepney through to Gordon Hill, knew that Stuart was always available to receive a pass. When he did get the ball his first touch was usually immaculate, either a subtle first-time lay-off or a deft piece of control. Then, belying that characteristic knock-kneed gait, there was searing pace to take him past defenders, and, although his finishing could be unreliable, his fierce shot brought many a spectacular goal. The England man's quicksilver mobility made him difficult to mark and, together with the equally elusive Jimmy Greenhoff, he presented a confusing, ever-changing set of problems which stretched most defenders.

He has been called injury-prone and that has always rankled. He did miss almost all of 1978/79 after a knee operation, but for four years before that it was unusual for his name to be absent from the team sheet. Stuart regained fitness but was not satisfied with the one-year contract offered by Tommy Docherty and in September 1979 he moved to West Ham for £220,000. Within eight months he had pocketed an FA Cup winner's medal to add to the one he had gained with United against Liverpool in 1977, when he had embellished a bright personal performance with a sharply-taken opening goal.

In 1986 Stuart became boss of non-League Northwich Victoria, then proved he could still muster a clean pair of heels with a spell on the wing for Sale Rugby Club. Thereafter he returned to the Football League, coaching with West Bromwich Albion before serving as Frank Stapleton's assistant manager at Bradford City. Until the pair of them were dismissed, rather surprisingly, in the spring of 1994, aspiring young strikers at the Valley Parade could hardly have asked for more eminent role models.

But it is with the Red Devils that the name of Stuart Pearson will remain most closely associated. When he bade farewell to Old Trafford, 'Pancho' left behind him the lasting affection of the fans and exhilarating memories of a centre-forward who played the game with dash.

CHRIS McGRATH ▼

1976/77–1980/81

34 **1**
GAMES GOALS

BORN Belfast, 29.11.54. GAMES: 15 (19). GOALS: 1.
HONOURS 21 Northern Ireland caps (74–79).
OTHER CLUBS Tottenham Hotspur 73/4–75/6 (38, 5); Millwall
on loan 75/6 (15, 3); Tulsa Roughnecks, USA,
81–82.

Chris McGrath represented a £30,000 gamble by United which didn't pay off. There was never any doubt about the natural ability of the Irish international winger, but after a spell with Tottenham Hotspur had begun with rich promise only to fizzle out in frustration, and a loan period with Millwall had also ended in failure, he did not look a good bet.

However, Tommy Cavanagh, then training the Reds, thought otherwise and his enthusiasm convinced manager Tommy Docherty to offer Chris the chance to salvage his career.

Sadly it was not to be. Chris could look brilliant on the ball but all too often he would beat three defenders only to be robbed by the fourth when colleagues were better placed. When his Old Trafford contract was cancelled he spent two seasons in America but was never given another chance in the Football League.

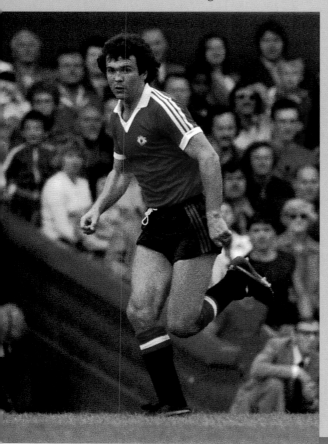

TOMMY JACKSON ▲

1975/76–1976/77

23 **0**
GAMES GOALS

BORN Belfast, 3.11.46.
HONOURS 35 Northern Ireland caps (68–77).
OTHER CLUBS Glentoran, Northern Ireland; Everton 67/8–70/1
(32, 0); Nottingham Forest 70/1–74/5 (81, 6).

When Tommy Jackson joined newly-promoted Manchester United in the summer of 1975 it was on the express understanding that his job would be to captain the reserves. But watching the experienced Irish midfielder in action during pre-season training gave manager Tommy Docherty other ideas.

The Reds at that time were an exciting, but also excitable, young side. Someone was needed during the initial months in the First Division to calm things down, hold the midfield, while the likes of Steve Coppell, Gerry Daly and company buzzed effervescently in all directions.

Tommy, an ex-Evertonian who joined United on a free transfer from Nottingham Forest, was the surprise choice and he carried out the task in a workmanlike, unspectacular fashion until the arrival of Gordon Hill changed the pattern of play. He stayed to make just two appearances the following season before getting a free transfer and leaving the League.

David McCreery shared a dubious distinction with David Fairclough of Liverpool: they were both dubbed 'Supersub.' Both players invariably wore the number-12 shirt for their clubs and both were frequently called to arms. And while Fairclough's contributions were usually more dramatic, little David McCreery – who was brought on to replace Gordon Hill in the 1976 and 1977 FA Cup Finals – offered at least equal value in terms of effort and consistency.

His earliest flirtations with the first team were as understudy to striker Stuart Pearson, but although he worked like a slave and was probably the fastest man at the club – he was known as 'Roadrunner' – David lacked the necessary physical presence for that role. He progressed to become stand-in for all the forwards and midfielders and soon it became obvious that he was best used in the latter position.

David, who was picked for Northern Ireland after starting just a dozen League games for United, was a tireless forager endowed with infectious enthusiasm but, at that stage, he lacked the polish and creativity to become a Reds regular. With so many outstanding players at Old Trafford, it was difficult to see him making that final breakthrough, and it was no surprise in August 1979 when he left to link up again with Tommy Docherty at Queen's Park Rangers, the Reds banking a £200,000 cheque.

But it wasn't until he had played in America and moved to Newcastle that he served up the most compelling football of his career, relishing the responsibility that had never been vested in him at Old Trafford. Come 1993/94, there were few blades of Brunton Park not being covered by the 36-year-old David in his role as Carlisle United's player-manager, and no one greeted his success and longevity with more pleasure than his old United team-mates. They recall him fondly as an irrepressible trier and a smashing lad.

DAVID McCREERY

1974/75–1978/79

108 **8**
GAMES GOALS

BORN Belfast, 16.9.57.
HONOURS FA Cup 76/7. 67 Northern Ireland caps (76–90).
OTHER CLUBS Queen's Park Rangers 79/80–80/1(57, 4); Tulsa Roughnecks, USA, 81–82; Newcastle United 82/3–88/9 (243, 2); Heart of Midlothian 89/90–90/1 (29, 0); Hartlepool United 91/2 (30, 0); Carlisle United 92/3–93/4 (35, 0); Hartlepool United 94/5 (9, 0).
MANAGER: Carlisle United (92–93); Hartlepool United (94–95).

The new Steve Coppell was certainly a valuable team member, but he never pleased the crowds like the old one.

1974/75–1982/83

395	70
GAMES	GOALS

BORN ● Liverpool, 9.7.55.
HONOURS ● FA Cup 76/7. 42 England caps (77–83).
OTHER CLUBS ● Tranmere Rovers 73/4–74/5 (38, 10).
MANAGER: Crystal Palace (84–93 and, as technical director, 95–96); Manchester City (96); Crystal Palace (97–98 and 99-).

The Manchester United career of Steve Coppell divides neatly – if, to many observers, frustratingly – into two parts. First came the exciting young performer of the Docherty days, knocking the ball past full-backs, running them ragged and slinging over centres with a style and accuracy reminiscent of that glorious age before Alf Ramsey made wingers unfashionable.

Steve Coppell

Then came the Sexton reign and with it a marked change in the role of the intelligent young Liverpudlian. Those buccaneering surges, which so personified the reborn Red Devils on their emergence from their Second Division nightmare, were largely replaced by tidy, thoughtful play wide on the right of midfield. The new Steve Coppell was certainly a valuable member of Dave Sexton's side, which came so close to League and FA Cup triumph without lifting a trophy, but he never pleased crowds like the old one.

It was always going to be difficult to live up to his early years with United. In fact, his arrival reads like a Boys' Own adventure. The rookie wingman – just signed from Tranmere for £40,000 with another £20,000 to follow if he made 20 appearances! – was pulled on to replace Willie Morgan during an Old Trafford encounter with Cardiff City, 11 games from the end of the Division Two campaign. The Reds had been expected to win comfortably but after an hour there was no score and the supporters were getting restless. Thirty minutes later United ran off 4–0 winners with the new boy having made two of the goals.

Steve retained his place for the rest of the season and henceforth was an automatic choice until a knee injury, picked up playing for England in November 1981, ultimately forced him to quit at the age of 28, after three operations and much heartache, in September 1983.

Perhaps one reason why his exhilarating football of 1975/76 and 1976/77, when he formed such a thrilling wing tandem with Gordon Hill, became more subdued was that in later years some defenders worked out how to combat his direct running. They would lay off him, which made it harder to pass them, and thus they could reduce his effectiveness. In fairness to Sexton, that factor may have had a lot to do with the change in Steve's approach.

In the new role he enjoyed four seasons as an ever-present, during which his work rate, determination and overall contribution to the team effort were immense. And even if the old panache was less evident there were still moments of attacking brilliance and vital goals to savour.

Steve's international career blossomed correspondingly and, deservedly, he attained a Bobby Charlton-type image for integrity and sportsmanship. Combined with an astute brain, these qualities enabled Steve, at one time chairman of the Professional Footballers Association, to move smoothly into management and he achieved impressive early success with Crystal Palace.

Inevitably this inspired forecasts that one day he might occupy the boss's seat at Old Trafford, and even his resignation from the Selhurst Park job following relegation in 1993 did not scupper the thought altogether. However his subsequent inability to cope with the stress of running Manchester City – he walked out of Maine Road after only 33 days in charge – made the chances of Steve Coppell managing Manchester United, even in the distant future, seem exceedingly slim.

Gordon's left-flank flair took the eye as United played their most captivating football for nearly a decade.

1975/76–1977/78

133 **51**

GAMES GOALS

BORN ● Sunbury-on-Thames, Middlesex, 1.4.54.
HONOURS ● FA Cup 76/7. 6 England caps (76–77).
OTHER CLUBS ● Millwall 72/3–75/6 (86, 20); Derby County 77/8–79/80 (24, 5); Queen's Park Rangers 79/80–80/1 (14, 1); Chicago Sting and Montreal Manic, both USA.

Gordon Hill was the final piece in Tommy Docherty's jigsaw who found himself surplus to Dave Sexton's requirements. And his departure from Old Trafford, to rejoin the Doc at Derby, somehow summed up the vastly different attitudes of the two managers.

Gordon Hill

Undoubtedly Gordon was blessed with sumptuous gifts. At Millwall his wing sorcery earned him the nickname of 'Merlin', and he purveyed a brand of magic for which Docherty was delighted to pay £80,000 in November 1975. That boldest of bosses believed the confident Londoner could put a spell on First Division defences and bring a swaggering new dimension to the newly-promoted Reds; and so, to a large degree, it proved.

Gordon's left-flank flair was a major factor in United's glittering form as they played their most captivating football for nearly a decade. There were few full-backs he couldn't skin as he belted for the byline or cut in towards goal. And that finishing! There were times when it was nothing less than world-class, as in the 1976 FA Cup semi-final against Derby when two 20-yarders – one a delicate curler, the other a fearsome drive – saw his side through to Wembley. The Hill strike rate, too, was awesome for a winger, culminating in a record very close to a goal every two games in his final season.

But despite all that instinctive ability there was another side to Gordon, one which some colleagues could tolerate but which infuriated others. When the Reds were defending he did not seem interested. Chasing and tackling were alien to him and when he was pressurised into doing so his cocky attempts to dribble out of trouble often angered his own defence. Indeed, Martin Buchan was once moved to box his ears during a match.

A parting between Gordon and Sexton, for whom individual skill came second to teamwork, was inevitable, and in April 1978 a £275,000 deal took the England man to Derby and the Doc. At the Baseball Ground, his displays alternated between the exasperating and the enchanting and soon he was off to Queen's Park Rangers, where his new boss was . . . Tommy Docherty. But Loftus Road didn't see the best of the mercurial flankman, either, and before long he had crossed the Atlantic to try his luck in the North American League.

Meanwhile the more romantic United fans continued to mourn his departure from Old Trafford. Gordon may have been a soccer eccentric, but on his day he took the breath away.

He expected those around him to meet his own high standards and could be formidable when they didn't.

1971/72–1982/83

455 **4**
GAMES GOALS

BORN ● Aberdeen, 6.3.49.
HONOURS ● FA Cup 76/7. Second Division Championship 74/5. 34 Scotland caps (71–78).
OTHER CLUBS ● Aberdeen 66/7–71/2 (136, 9); Oldham Athletic 83/4–84/5 (28, 0). MANAGER: Burnley (85).

For a decade Martin Buchan stood alone as Manchester United's most influential player. There were few observers who didn't hail the Scottish international central defender as world-class, although a handful reckoned his use of the ball did not merit such a lofty accolade. But wherever Martin is placed on the global scale, none could seriously deny the immense contribution he made to the Reds after Frank O'Farrell brought him south from Aberdeen in March 1972 as the first major step in rebuilding a defence that was beginning to creak alarmingly.

Martin Buchan

By then, though still only 23, Martin had played for his country, captained his club, won a Scottish Cup medal and been voted Scottish player of the year. For a man of this calibre and maturity United willingly parted with £125,000, and rarely have they struck a better bargain.

A supremely self-confident and disciplined individual, he settled quickly and began turning in the cool, classy displays which became his hallmark. By now United were a poor side, though, and after two seasons of travail they were relegated. Martin, by this time skipper, led them back up at the first attempt, setting an exemplary personal example.

But it was during the next five seasons that he reached his zenith, forming two effective partnerships, first with Brian Greenhoff and then Gordon McQueen. Martin was a firm rather than ferocious tackler and could read the game well, but his prime asset was his speed. If he made a mistake, which was not common, usually he could change gear and rectify it before opponents could take advantage. Perhaps his quality of passing didn't always equal other facets of the Buchan game, but this rarely mattered as he tended to limit his distribution to the simple variety. Occasionally, when feeling more ambitious, he might give the ball away but there was always the insurance of that scorching acceleration.

A man of strong principles, Martin upset some people with an uncompromising attitude which could border on the eccentric. He expected those around him to meet his own high standards and could be formidable when they didn't – ask Gordon Hill, whose ears he once boxed in public.

But above all Martin Buchan will be remembered as one of those United players the fans could not bear to see missing from the line-up, in much the same way as Bryan Robson's absence was dreaded in later years. When he looked likely to miss the 1977 FA Cup Final against Liverpool, the prophets of doom were out in force. On that occasion, though not fully fit, he played – majestically – and largely snuffed out the threat of Kevin Keegan as the Red Devils took the trophy.

As the 1980s dawned, Martin faced increasing fitness problems and in August 1983 he bowed out of Old Trafford. There followed a short spell as a player at Oldham and an even shorter one as boss of Burnley, a task for which he had the sense to realise he was not cut out. The final word, if one is needed, on Martin's prowess at his peak can rest with the managers. They voted him First Division player of the year in 1977; and they should know.

Perhaps the enduring sadness about Jimmy's association with United is that it didn't begin earlier.

1976/77–1980/81

122 GAMES **36** GOALS

BORN — Barnsley, Yorkshire, 19.6.46.
HONOURS — FA Cup 76/7.
OTHER CLUBS — Leeds United 62/3–68/9 (96, 19); Birmingham City 68/9 (31, 14); Stoke City 69/70–76/7 (274, 76); Crewe Alexandra 80/1 (11, 4); Toronto Blizzard, USA, 81; Port Vale 81/2–82/3 (48, 5); Rochdale 82/3–83/4 (16, 0). MANAGER: Rochdale (83–84).

Jimmy Greenhoff was born to be a footballer, and he didn't need flashy tricks to prove it. Just a glimpse of the blond Yorkshireman doing something simple – say, taking a pass and laying it off – was enough to demonstrate that the man had style, pure and simple.

Jimmy Greenhoff

He was introduced by Tommy Docherty into an essentially buoyant United side which had lost a little of its characteristic zest. A new face was needed and when financial pressure forced Stoke City to put Jimmy up for sale at a mere £120,000 in November 1976, the Doc saw him as the ideal tonic.

By turns subtle and explosive, the mobile front-man soon forged a formidable link with Stuart Pearson and both scored in the 1977 FA Cup Final triumph over Liverpool. In fairness to the Merseysiders, though, it should be admitted that Jimmy's winner was an utter fluke, as he unwittingly deflected a wayward shot from Lou Macari into the goal. Injury to 'Pancho' split the seemingly telepathic partnership which had so delighted connoisseurs of first-touch football, but Jimmy proved an equally fine foil to Joe Jordan and maintained his productive form until he, too, fell prey to fitness problems. Then, half-way through his 35th year and with the expensive Garry Birtles having arrived on the scene, Greenhoff Snr accepted a move to Crewe Alexandra in December 1980.

Though he was a brilliant volleyer, the former Leeds United and Birmingham City favourite's finishing lacked that consistently clinical quality possessed by the most prolific of goal-scorers. But he could claim some spectacular and vital strikes. A typical stroke of inspiration came against Liverpool in the 1979 FA Cup semi-final replay on an emotional night at Goodison Park, when he adroitly headed Mickey Thomas's awkwardly bouncing cross past Ray Clemence to book the Reds' passage to Wembley. This time the men from Anfield could not blame Dame Fortune, having fallen victim to a masterly piece of opportunism.

Perhaps the enduring sadness about Jimmy's association with Manchester United is that it didn't begin earlier. Often he is dubbed the best player never to be capped by England, and if his peak years had been spent at Old Trafford rather than in the Potteries – with all due respect to Stoke, who had to make the most of limited resources – surely he would not have been condemned to the international wilderness, apart from five appearances at under-23 level. Nevertheless, the deeds of 'Jimmy the One', whose delicious elan was matched only by his engaging modesty, will linger long in the memories of all who relished his four years as a Red Devil.

JIMMY NICHOLL

1974/75–1981/82

247 GAMES **6** GOALS

BORN Hamilton, Canada, 28.2.56,
HONOURS FA Cup 76/7. 73 Northern Ireland caps (76–86).
OTHER CLUBS Sunderland on loan 81/2 (3, 0); Toronto Blizzard, Canada, 82–83; Sunderland 82/3 (29, 0); Glasgow Rangers 83/4 (17, 0); West Bromwich Albion 84/5–85/6 (56, 0); Glasgow Rangers 86/7–88/9 (65, 0); Dunfermline Athletic 89/90–90/1(24, 0); Raith Rovers 90/1–95/6 (128, 7). MANAGER: Raith Rovers (90–96); Millwall (96–97); Raith Rovers (97–99).

The experience of Jimmy Nicholl illustrates vividly how a change of manager can devastate a player's career. There was Jimmy, aged 25, at the height of his powers, a United regular and a bastion of the Northern Ireland back four, when Dave Sexton was sacked and Ron Atkinson appointed.

But Ron had always admired John Gidman, saw that the Everton right-back was available and made him one of his first signings. And that, effectively, was the end of Jimmy's days at Old Trafford. When the axe fell, the flame-haired, Canadian-born defender had already amassed more than 200 appearances and seemed set for a marathon stint with the Reds.

Jimmy was a much-lauded youth star who made his senior bow during United's brief Second Division sojourn. Then came an impressive run during the next campaign and soon it was apparent that he would quickly oust Alex Forsyth for keeps. So it proved and, far from being over-awed at replacing such a crowd favourite, Jimmy grew rapidly in confidence.

Perhaps his outstanding passing ability, natural ball control and mature reading of the game masked a lack of speed, occasional rashness in the tackle and a slight deficiency in the air, but he formed an effective and promising full-back partnership with Arthur Albiston.

His detractors accused him of being too casual but his apparently relaxed approach belied a deep-seated will to win and, ironically, pace and aggression became more apparent in his game during his last full season with the Reds. Some reckoned he would have made a better sweeper, but he never excelled in that position when given the chance for his country.

On leaving Old Trafford, he served Sunderland, West Bromwich Albion and Glasgow Rangers among others, before making a nonsense of the evidence on his birth certificate by continuing to turn in sterling performances as player-manager of Raith Rovers into his 40th year.

PADDY ROCHE ▲

1974/75–1981/82

53 GAMES   **0** GOALS

BORN ● Dublin, 4.1.51. GAMES: 53. GOALS: 0.
HONOURS ● 8 Republic of Ireland caps (72–75).
OTHER CLUBS ● Shelbourne, Republic of Ireland;
Brentford 82/3–83/4 (71, 0);
Halifax Town 84/5–88/9 (184, 0).

Paddy Roche was an accomplished goalkeeper whose only real flaw was lack of self-belief – now there's a statement to surprise many a loyal Reds fan. The frightening, some would say sinister, truth is that after one round of bad press, at the time he was picked to replace Alex Stepney for four games in 1975/76, he was labelled for life as a bungler and the public was largely brainwashed into believing it. Not so his team-mates. They never doubted that he was good enough.

The self-effacing, slender Irishman's reputation was founded on an incident in a top-of-the-table clash with Liverpool when he appeared to drop the ball for a soft goal. It looked bad and he was pilloried, but later Brian Greenhoff admitted colliding with the custodian, causing him to fumble. But the damage was done and a destructive myth was born.

The problem was that the United defenders were used to playing in front of Alex, a line 'keeper. Paddy, who throughout six years as understudy to Stepney and Gary Bailey got only three brief runs as first choice, liked to command his area and at first his colleagues would get in his way. In fact, the agile Eire international, who later served Brentford before a marvellous spell with Halifax, possessed the safest hands of any United custodian – barring Harry Gregg and Peter Schmeichel – since the war. What a shame that he didn't have the confidence to go with them.

NIKOLA JOVANOVIC ▼

1979/80–1980/81

26 GAMES   **4** GOALS

BORN ● Cetinje, Yugoslavia, 18.9.52.
HONOURS ● Yugoslavia caps.
OTHER CLUBS ● Red Star Belgrade and Buducnost, both Yugoslavia.

Nikola Jovanovic had all the class and talent to become a resounding success at Old Trafford.
The lanky Yugoslav international central defender cum midfielder was blessed with skill and intelligence in abundance, was elegant on the ball and had an eye for goal, as he demonstrated with an impressive brace against Leicester City in the autumn of 1980.

So why did the £350,000 signing from Red Star Belgrade, who had nursed a lifelong ambition to be a Red Devil and who turned down a more lucrative offer from Bayern Munich to come to Old Trafford, return so soon to his own country, his potential unfulfilled?

Probably it boiled down to a lack of instinctive communication with his colleagues on the pitch. Nikki could speak English well enough but perhaps he could not think in English, and when split-second decisions are made in the heat of battle it is vital for players – particularly defenders – to have instant understanding of their team-mates' intentions.

Nikki also struggled to adjust to the pace of the English game, being used to the more deliberate build-up of Yugoslav soccer. His move to United was a gamble that failed, but it was an imaginative experiment by Dave Sexton and one that deserved praise for its boldness.

TOMMY BALDWIN

1974/75

FORWARD

2
GAMES

0
GOALS

(On loan from Chelsea)

BORN:
Gateshead, County Durham;
10.6.45.

OTHER CLUBS:
Arsenal 64/5–66/7 (17, 7);
Chelsea 66/7–74/5 (187,
74); Millwall on loan 74/5
(6, 1); Brentford 77/8 (4, 1).

RON DAVIES

1974/75

CENTRE-FORWARD

10
GAMES

0
GOALS

BORN:
Holywell, Flintshire, 25.5.42.

HONOURS:
29 Wales caps (64–74).

OTHER CLUBS:
Chester 59/60–62/3 (94, 44); Luton Town 62/3–63/4 (32, 21); Norwich City 63/4–65/6
(113, 58); Southampton 66/7–72/3 (240, 134); Portsmouth 73/4–74/5 (59, 18); Millwall
75/6 (3, 0).

JONATHAN CLARK

1976/77

MIDFIELDER

1
GAMES

0
GOALS

BORN:
Swansea, Glamorgan, 12.11.58.

OTHER CLUBS:
Derby County 78/9–80/1(53, 3); Preston North End
81/2–86/7 (110, 10); Bury 86/7 (14, 1); Carlisle
United 87/8–88/9 (49, 2).

PETER COYNE

1975/76

FORWARD

2
GAMES

1
GOALS

BORN:
Hartlepool, County Durham,
13.11.58.

OTHER CLUBS:
Crewe Alexandra 77/8–80/1
(134, 47); Swindon Town
84/5–88/9 (110, 30); Aldershot
on loan 89/90 (3, 0).

TOM CONNELL

1978/79

DEFENDER

2
GAMES

0
GOALS

BORN:
Newry, Northern Ireland,
25.11.57.

OTHER CLUBS:
Coleraine, Northern Ireland.

ALAN FOGGON

1976/77

WINGER

3 GAMES **0** GOALS

BORN:
Chester-le-Street, County Durham, 23.2.50.

OTHER CLUBS:
Newcastle United 67/8–70/1 (61, 14); Cardiff City 71/2–72/3 (17, 1); Middlesbrough 72/3–75/6 (115, 45); Sunderland 76/7 (8, 0); Southend United 77/8 (22, 0); Hartlepool United on loan 77/8 (18, 2).

STEVE PATERSON

1976/76–1979/80

DEFENDER

10 GAMES **0** GOALS

BORN:
Elgin, Morayshire, 8.4.58.

OTHER CLUBS:
MANAGER: Inverness Caledonian Thistle (95–).

COLIN WALDRON

1976/77

CENTRE-HALF

4 GAMES **0** GOALS

BORN:
Bristol, 22.6.48.

OTHER CLUBS:
Bury 66/7 (20, 1); Chelsea 67/8 (9, 0); Burnley 67/8–75/6 (308, 16); Sunderland 76/7–77/8 (20, 1); Atlanta Chiefs, USA; Rochdale 79/80 (19, 1); Tulsa Roughnecks, USA.

TONY GRIMSHAW

1975/76

MIDFIELDER

2 GAMES **0** GOALS

BORN:
Manchester, 8.12.57.

ANTO WHELAN

1980/81

FULL-BACK

1 GAMES **0** GOALS

BORN:
Dublin, 23.11.59.

OTHER CLUBS:
Bohemians, Shamrock Rovers (twice), Cork, all Republic of Ireland.

JIMMY KELLY

1975/76

MIDFIELDER

1 GAMES **0** GOALS

BORN:
Carlisle, Cumberland, 2.5.57.

OTHER CLUBS:
Chicago Sting, USA, 76.

MARTYN ROGERS

1977/78

FULL-BACK

1 GAMES **0** GOALS

BORN:
Nottingham, 26.1.60.

OTHER CLUBS:
Queen's Park Rangers 79/80 (2, 0). Died 1992.

TOM SLOAN

1978/79–1980/81

FORWARD

12 GAMES **0** GOALS

BORN:
Ballymena, Northern Ireland, 10.7.59.

HONOURS:
3 Northern Ireland caps (79).

OTHER CLUBS:
Ballymena United, Northern Ireland; Chester 82/3 (44, 3).

Sammy's twinkling feet could take him dancing past challenges that would floor less gifted operators.

1971/72–1981/82

418 **71**
GAMES GOALS

BORN ● Belfast, 2.8.54.
HONOURS ● FA Cup 76/7. Second Division Championship 74/5. 88 Northern Ireland caps (72–86).
OTHER CLUBS ● Stoke City 81/2–84/5 (133, 14); Manchester City 85/6 (12, 1); Orgryte, Sweden 86; Manchester City 86/7 (1, 0); Bury 86/7–87/8 (43, 6); FC Moedling, Austria 88; Bury 88/9–89/90 (57, 2); Preston North End 89/90 (20, 0). MANAGER: Macclesfield Town (93–2000); Northern Ireland (2000–).

Sammy McIlroy was Irish, had bags of talent and, when only 17, he scored a fine goal against Manchester City on his debut for the Reds. So there was never any doubt with whom the media would compare him. It is to Sammy's eternal credit that he rose above the fatuous headlines about 'the new George Best' and, in commendably level-headed manner, went on to build his own immensely successful United career.

Sammy McIlroy

The slim Ulsterman started first-team life as a striker but the fanfares following his dramatic Maine Road entrance did not win him a regular place and for a season and a half he remained on the fringe. Then a car accident sidelined him for several months and, with United desperately blooding new men in an unavailing bid to find a winning blend, his future looked rocky. He battled back into contention but it wasn't until the Second Division campaign of 1974/75 that he hit convincing form.

Though never a prolific marksman, he formed an effective partnership with Stuart Pearson which lasted for two and a half years until Jimmy Greenhoff arrived. Then Sammy moved to midfield, at the expense of Gerry Daly, and played the best football of his life. He was given a free role on the left where, despite being right-footed, he prospered for four years.

Sammy, who won nearly 90 caps, had tremendous instinctive ability and his twinkling feet could take him dancing past challenges that would floor less gifted operators. This natural nimbleness was revealed to sparkling effect two minutes from the end of the 1979 FA Cup Final. With United a goal down to Arsenal, he scurried into the area, squirmed past one defender, then nutmegged another before squeezing the ball past Pat Jennings for the equaliser. Because of the Gunners' heart-stopping response a minute later, Sammy never garnered the full credit for an inspired effort and it remains a neglected gem.

On the negative side there is little to report, though the hyper-critical might point out that he was poor in the air, not a great tackler and lacked the strength and toughness that would have made him a still more formidable all-round performer.

Sammy's character, though, was never in doubt and it spoke volumes for his approach that he retained his enthusiasm after the colossal disappointment of being discarded by Ron Atkinson when he was only 27 and barely at his peak. That was in February 1982, when he was sold to Stoke City for £350,000. Thereafter he beavered on through spells at Manchester City, Bury and Preston before managing several non-League clubs, notably Macclesfield Town, whom he led into the Third and then the Second Division.

But for all that mature endeavour, which was capped by his appointment as Northern Ireland boss as the century turned, it was as a Red Devil in his youth and early prime that Sammy McIlroy knew his finest footballing hours.

When a knee injury halted Gary's career, it probably deprived him of his best years.

1978/79–1986/87

373	0
GAMES	GOALS

BORN ● Ipswich, Suffolk, 9.8.58.
HONOURS ● FA Cup 82/3, 84/5. 2 England caps (85).

Big, blond and full of self-belief, Gary Bailey somehow conveyed the impression that here was a man born to keep goal. But if the image was perfect, did the performance match up to it? In fact, Gary's career was something of a paradox. On the one hand he was often vilified, particularly for his handling of crosses; on the other he became a full England international and was the last line of defence for one of Britain's leading clubs for nearly a decade.

Gary Bailey

The son of former Ipswich custodian Roy Bailey, Gary was sent to Old Trafford for a trial by ex-United man Eddie Lewis, who discovered him in South Africa. The precocious youngster made a quick impression, survived a scare when – prophetically as it was to prove – his knee locked in training, and was offered an early first-team breakthrough when a deal for Coventry's Jim Blyth fell through at the 11th hour.

With characteristic confidence he made the most of his chance. He kept a clean sheet on his debut against Ipswich, despite having to peer through curtains of rain, and thereafter made the position his own. His rapid progress was confirmed when, just three months later, he played for England at under-21 level.

That first season ended on a traumatic note when United were beaten by a late Arsenal goal in the FA Cup Final, and some commentators blamed the rookie 'keeper for not cutting out the cross from which Alan Sunderland netted his dramatic winner. Having said that, it should be noted that the build-up from an inspired Liam Brady and the delivery from Graham Rix were sheer perfection.

Come 1983 Gary repaid any real or imaginary debt by making the last-minute point-blank save from Brighton's Gordon Smith that enabled the Reds to earn a Wembley replay, then go on to lift the trophy. Two years later, he kept a clean sheet and earned a second FA Cup winner's medal as United beat the favourites, Everton.

By then Gary, who gained a physics degree during his Manchester years, had developed into a top-notch shot-stopper who faltered occasionally when he left his line, though rarely with catastrophic results. He was a good talker on the pitch and benefited hugely from the coaching of Harry Gregg.

So where does all this leave him? Always just behind the very front rank, certainly; but equally without doubt he had the edge on most of his First Division peers. When a knee injury halted Gary's career at the age of 29, it probably deprived him of his best years.

Despite the fangs and the frequent frowns, Jordan was an intelligent, thoughtful player.

1977/78–1980/81

126 GAMES | 41 GOALS

BORN — Carluke, Lanarkshire, 15.12.51.
HONOURS — 52 Scotland caps (72–82).
OTHER CLUBS — Morton 68/9–70/1 (12, 2); Leeds United 71/2–77/8 (169, 35); AC Milan 81/2–82/3 (52, 12);Verona 83/4 (12, 1); Southampton 84/5–86/7 (48, 12); Bristol City 86/7–89/90 (57, 8). MANAGER: Bristol City (88–90); Heart of Midlothian (90–93); Stoke City (93–94); Bristol City (94–97).

When Joe Jordan crossed the Pennines from Elland Road he carried with him a villainous reputation of the darkest hue. He was the big bad wolf, the snarling warrior who devoured defenders and cleaned those famous fangs on the corner flag.

Joe Jordan

True to form, his introductory days at Old Trafford did little to dispel the lurid image. Before Joe could pull on the red shirt in earnest he had to serve a suspension for mis-deeds at Leeds, and when he did take the field as Dave Sexton's first signing he was booked in two of his earliest games. United fans who revelled in the subtle delights of the Pearson-Greenhoff tandem squirmed in apprehension at the prospect of the £350,000 battering ram replacing one of their trusty rapiers.

As it turned out, Joe did not prove to be the destructive ogre they had feared and by the end of his third full campaign for the Reds, most supporters were sorry to see him leave. Indeed the Stretford Enders, who had loved to hate the glowering striker during his days as an idol of Elland Road, now took him to their hearts, revelling in his Attila-like reputation and warming to that famous gap-toothed grin (or grimace, as the fancy took him).

In fact, despite the fangs and the frequent frowns, the Scottish international was an intelligent, thoughtful player whose control, finishing and overall contribution to the team effort improved radically under Sexton, though his fearsome penalty-area presence, especially in the air, remained his forte.

Perhaps Joe, never a heavy scorer himself, would have been even more effective if the manager had persisted with the briefly prolific Andy Ritchie as his new partner after the departure of Greenhoff, instead of introducing the newcomer Garry Birtles. As it was, Jordan's last season with the Reds was his best, with 15 goals from 33 matches, a fine return for a target man.

Then it was off to Italy and AC Milan, who signed him for a mere £175,000, thanks to European transfer-fee restrictions. Next stop was Verona before he returned to England to serve first Southampton and then Bristol City, whom he went on to manage. His stints in the hot seats at Ashton Gate and elsewhere, while not wildly successful overall, were characterised by a mixture of acumen and integrity which suggested that Joe Jordan remained a man to watch. Although his second departure from Bristol appeared to cast doubt on his long-term future as a soccer boss, he returned to the game at international level, assisting Lawrie McMenemy with Northern Ireland before beginning a third stint with the Robins, this time as director of football.

McQueen, who supplemented his aerial dominance with a deceptive turn of speed, was an impressive performer.

1977/78–1984/85

228 **26**
GAMES GOALS

BORN ● Kilbirnie, Ayrshire, 26.6.52.
HONOURS ● FA Cup 82/3. 30 Scotland caps (73–81).
OTHER CLUBS ● St Mirren 70/1–72/3 (57, 5); Leeds United 72/3–77/8 (140, 15). MANAGER: Airdrieonians (87–89).

Gordon McQueen may not have been the greatest centre-half Manchester United ever had, but he was certainly one of the most entertaining. The blond giant provided a gloriously exciting spectacle as he soared above the opposition, whether to clear his own lines or to launch one of those murderous attacking headers that became his trademark.

Gordon McQueen

Then there were those mazy, lolloping left-wing dribbles past three or four defenders, an added and very occasional delight indulged in only when his side were a few goals to the good. Such adventurous sorties, on which somehow he brought to mind a lovably clumsy, overgrown puppy, further endeared him to most Reds fans, who had taken him to their hearts from the moment of his arguably overpriced £500,000 transfer from Leeds in February 1978.

Yet these very antics were symptomatic of the 6ft 3in Scottish international's one weakness: he was drawn out of position too easily. If the centre-forward he was marking fell back into midfield or roamed to the wing, Gordon would often chase him, sometimes leaving a yawning gap. It was this unpredictable element in his game, which Don Revie tried so hard to curb at Leeds, that prevented him from attaining the very highest standard.

The imperturbable Martin Buchan, an immaculate covering player, did much to limit the consequences of his countryman's penchant for roving and the two formed a formidable partnership. But when Gordon was paired with less organised individuals the alarm bells would ring.

For all that the popular centre-half, who supplemented his aerial dominance with a deceptive turn of speed, was an impressive performer for the Reds and he was much missed when injuries curtailed his appearances, allowing Kevin Moran and Paul McGrath to cement their claims to the central defensive positions.

Gordon – whose father Tommy kept goal for Hibernian and Accrington Stanley, among others – was freed at the end of 1984/85 and could look back on an eventful Old Trafford sojourn after taking the trans-Pennine trail blazed a month before him by his pal, Joe Jordan. His most memorable form came in 1979/80, when he netted nine times and toiled mightily at the back as United finished as League runners-up to Liverpool. More tangible reward came in 1983 when he gained an FA Cup winner's medal against Brighton, making up for his Wembley disappointment of four years earlier when his late goal against Arsenal signalled a rousing fightback that ended in gallant failure.

Gordon ended his playing days in Japan, where he survived a serious illness, before moving into management with Airdrieonians. Later he coached with St Mirren, his first senior club, and then Middlesbrough.

MICKEY THOMAS

1978/79–1980/81

110 GAMES **15** GOALS

BORN	Mochdre, North Wales, 7.7.54.
HONOURS	51 Wales caps (77–86).
OTHER CLUBS	Wrexham 71/2–78/9 (230, 33); Everton 81/2 (10, 0); Brighton and Hove Albion 81/2 (20, 0); Stoke City 82/3–83/4 (57, 14); Chelsea 83/4–84/5 (44, 9); West Bromwich Albion 85/6 (20, 0); Derby County on loan 85/6 (9, 0); Wichita Wings, USA; Shrewsbury Town 88/9 (40, 1); Leeds United 89/90 (3, 0); Stoke City 89/90–90/1 (46, 7); Wrexham 91/2–92/3 (34, 2).

If the footballing merits of Gordon Hill personified the Tommy Docherty era – sometimes brilliant, occasionally awful, always mercurial – then those of little Mickey Thomas, the man bought to replace Gordon on the left wing, summed up the methodical, industrious approach of new manager Dave Sexton.

In reality Mickey was more midfielder than winger and he faced a well-nigh impossible task in replacing his crowd-pleasing predecessor in the affections of the Old Trafford faithful. The fact that he went so far towards doing so says much for the ability and application of the mop-haired Welsh international workhorse, who was bought from Wrexham for £300,000 in November 1978 to – in the words of Dave Sexton – bring more balance and shape to the team.

During his three seasons with the Reds, Mickey won himself a reputation for selfless running that was second to none, and the fans identified with him as a trier who was more skilful than many pundits reckoned. His left-foot crosses, rather erratic on his arrival, showed a marked improvement under the coaching attentions of Sexton and, as he began to throw off an apparent inferiority complex, Mickey started to score his quota of goals. His most prolific term was 1979/80 when United finished within two points of champions Liverpool, against whom he had played his greatest game in the previous year's drawn FA Cup semi-final.

But hopes of a long-term future with United were dashed by the demise of Dave Sexton and the advent of Ron Atkinson, who wasted no time in swapping him for Everton's John Gidman in August 1981. At times an awkward man to manage, Mickey didn't settle at Goodison and became a wanderer whose travels brought him but limited joy, while a misdemeanour off the field landed him a jail term.

ANDY RITCHIE ▲

1977/78–1980/81

42	13
GAMES	GOALS

BORN Manchester, 28.11.60.
OTHER CLUBS Brighton and Hove Albion 80/1–82/3 (89, 23); Leeds United 82/3–86/7 (136, 40); Oldham Athletic 87/8–94/5 (217, 82); Scarborough 95/6–96/97 (69, 17); Oldham Athletic 96/7–97/8 (25, 2). MANAGER: Oldham Athletic (98–).

Any teenage striker who started 26 League games and scored 13 goals for a top side might reasonably expect that club to nurture his talent with the hope that one day he might save his employers a hefty fee. But if such were the expectations of Andy Ritchie, then he was sorely disappointed by Dave Sexton and his assistant, Tommy Cavanagh.

After making his debut in 1977/78, he seemed to stake an undeniable claim during the following campaign when he netted ten times in 17 outings, including a hat-trick against Leeds – after which he was dropped! In 1979/80 he was offered just three starts and managed three goals, all in one thrilling display of opportunism against Tottenham.

The fans loved it. That day the youngster and Joe Jordan looked the ideal pair. Now surely, despite talk that Andy might leave, there would be a happy outcome. The manager was using psychology to get the best out of him, wasn't he? Then the unthinkable: in October 1980 Andy joined Brighton for £500,000.

What had United lost? A fine striker of the ball with both feet who was greedy for goals, strong, willing and with good control. All he lacked was true pace. In came Garry Birtles, a £1,250,000 recruit who was to represent no more than a sadly forlorn footnote in the Reds' history. True, United received a handsome sum for a teenager and Andy, while enjoying a worthy career, never hit real heights elsewhere. But in the heady environment of Old Trafford, where he had already tasted success, who knows what he might have achieved?

ASHLEY GRIMES ▼

1977/78–1982/83

107	11
GAMES	GOALS

BORN Dublin, 2.8.57.
HONOURS 17 Republic of Ireland caps (78–88).
OTHER CLUBS Bohemians, Republic of Ireland; Coventry City 83/4 (32,1); Luton Town 84/5–88/9 (87, 3), Osasuna, Spain; Stoke City 91/2 (10, 1).

Lean, loping Republic of Ireland international Ashley Grimes was one of Old Trafford's 'nearly men.' An immensely skilful and competitive left-sided utility player, he was hit by a double dose of misfortune at a crucial time for his long-term aspirations as a Red Devil.

In 1979/80, when United missed the title by only two points, Ashley – who was equally at home in midfield or at left-back – played in more than half the matches and just might have been on the verge of that vital break-through to become a first-team regular. But then came two seasons when first injury, then illness, destroyed his momentum and it became clear that the man who had cost £20,000 from Bohemians was destined to be no more than a fringe player.

This was confirmed in 1982/83, first by the arrival of Arnold Muhren, then by a case of Wembley heartache. When Steve Coppell was unfit to face Brighton in the FA Cup Final, the Irishman, an eternal substitute who had performed admirably in the semi-final against Arsenal, remained on the bench while Steve's place went to the inexperienced Alan Davies.

That summed up his time at United and Ashley – who was blessed with a precise left foot and limitless stamina – decided it was time to go. For a time he served Coventry before a more productive spell at Luton Town saw him come closer, but not close enough, to realising his potential.

Ray's passing could reach sublime heights and his reading of the game was exemplary.

1979/80–1983/84

193 **10**
GAMES GOALS

BORN ● Hillingdon, Middlesex, 14.9.56.
HONOURS ● FA Cup 82/3. 84 England caps (76–86).
OTHER CLUBS ● Chelsea 73/4–78/9 (179, 30); AC Milan 84/5–86/7 (73, 2); Paris St Germain 87/8; Glasgow Rangers 87/8–89/90 (70, 2); Queen's Park Rangers 89/90–93/4 (154, 7); Crystal Palace 94/5 (1, 0); Queen's Park Rangers 94/5–96/7 (21, 0); Wycombe Wanderers 96/7 (1, 0); Hibernian 96/7 (16, 0); Millwall 96/7 (3,0); Leyton Orient 96/7 (3, 0).
MANAGER: Queen's Park Rangers (94–96); Fulham as chief coach (97–98).

Ray Wilkins

When Dave Sexton paid Chelsea £825,000 for Ray Wilkins in August 1979 there was much rejoicing in the Old Trafford camp. There was a genuine feeling that England's 22-year-old midfield general would be the long-sought-after missing link, the man who held the key to United winning the title for the first time in more than a decade.

After all, Ray was a richly gifted play-maker possessed of maturity and experience unusual for one of his age. Both Liverpool and Arsenal had tried to sign him and failed. Now surely, his time was ripe and Old Trafford would witness the flowering of a great talent. Well, he was a fine footballer and he gave United five seasons of trusty service, yet he failed palpably to reach the lofty pinnacles predicted for him.

What was special about Ray? His touch was inspired; his passing could reach sublime heights; his reading of the game was exemplary and his temperament was impeccable. But often his play was flawed by an apparent lack of ambition, a propensity to play safe, which led to Ron Atkinson uncharitably christening him 'The Crab' – because he was always passing sideways – and to the fans becoming frustrated by his laid-back style.

At times, presumably, Ray's cautious approach reflected team tactics, but nevertheless it created a sadly unsympathetic image of a man who had the raw materials to become a Reds immortal.

To be fair, he did turn in many magnificent performances for United, and though his scoring rate was disappointingly negligible – something like one goal every 19

matches – occasionally he would come up with a classic, such as his 25-yard left-foot curler in the first instalment of the 1983 FA Cup Final against Brighton.

For a time, Ray was skipper of both club and country before he suffered a fractured cheekbone and lost both jobs to Bryan Robson. In the wake of that setback, his form dipped noticeably, but he recovered to deliver some of his most compelling displays in his farewell season before joining AC Milan for £1.5 million in the summer of 1984.

Should he have stayed? If he had it would certainly have been harder, for financial reasons, to keep Robson out of the Italians' clutches, so it could be argued that, by the mere acting of leaving, Ray did Manchester United a priceless service.

Of course, such a thoroughbred footballer and decent man deserves better than such a glib epitaph and for a moment in 1991 it seemed he might get the chance to write a new ending to his personal chapter of the Old Trafford story.

Alex Ferguson pondered deeply on the need for a top-quality schemer and was said to be on the verge of offering the job to Ray, whose game was improving with every passing year. But it never happened; the personable thirtysomething continued to pull the midfield strings for Queen's Park Rangers and Alex pursued other options. What might have transpired if Ray and the Reds had been reunited, we'll never know.

GARRY BIRTLES

1980/81–1981/82

64 GAMES   **12** GOALS

BORN	Nottingham, 27.7.56.
HONOURS	3 England caps (80).
OTHER CLUBS	Nottingham Forest 76/7 80/1 (87, 32) and 82/3–86/7 (125, 38); Notts County 87/8–88/9 (63, 9); Grimsby Town 89/90–91/2 (69, 9).

The name of Garry Birtles became a byword for failure during his troubled two years at Old Trafford, yet here was a fine player who had looked one of the most effective strikers in the country with Nottingham Forest. Just promoted to the England team, he had seemed ripe for the move to United in October 1980. Glory beckoned, but it was footballing disaster which overtook him.

Reds fans, who to their credit treated Garry with patience and good humour, had to wait 30 games before the £1,250,000 signing struck his first League goal, and when it finally came – a 25-yarder against Swansea City – it was greeted with a mixture of joy, relief and irony. But why such an interminable wait? Well, it's true that Garry didn't have the best of luck, hitting the woodwork in several early games after which his confidence took a dive. But that wasn't the whole story.

More relevant was the fact that he was not suited to partner Joe Jordan. Garry and Joe, although players of a different type, were both left-sided and both gravitated naturally to the inside-left channel. So, through no fault of their own, they were attacking the same area and getting in each other's way, a likely consequence which presumably did not worry Dave Sexton when he bought the Forest man. As a result Garry scored just once in the 26 games in which he played alongside the Scot. Yet with Frank Stapleton the following season he managed 11 in 33 matches; not outstanding, but certainly respectable.

Despite this improvement, he was still not the Birtles of old, whose dashing runs had made such an impact. In September 1982, new boss Ron Atkinson let him return to the City Ground for a mere £275,000 and he regained his form, later shining also for Notts County. For Garry an ordeal was over, though the chance of a lifetime had passed him by.

SCOTT McGARVEY ▲

1980/81–1982/83

25	3
GAMES	GOALS

BORN Glasgow, 22.4.63.
OTHER CLUBS Wolverhampton Wanderers on loan 83/4 (13, 2); Portsmouth 84/5–85/6 (23, 6); Carlisle United, first on loan 85/6–86/7 (35,11); Grimsby Town 86/7–87/8 (50, 7); Bristol City 88/9 (26, 9); Oldham Athletic 89/90 (4, 1); Wigan Athletic on loan 89/90 (3, 0); Mazda, Japan, 90.

Scott McGarvey was the archetypal golden boy who dazzled in youth football but whose light dimmed all too soon at the top level. In his mid-teens, startling claims were made for the ability of the blond Glaswegian striker. A glittering international future was predicted and, indeed, he did turn out for Scotland under-21s.

After making his debut in 1980/81, Scott was given a run of nine successive games towards the end of the following campaign. Admittedly there were moments of promise, such as the flashing header he netted against Spurs at Old Trafford, but in general he failed to convince.

Nevertheless Scott, undeniably skilful but rather willowy and easily brushed off the ball, impressed in the subsequent pre-season friendlies. But he soon found himself overlooked in favour of another emerging youngster, name of Norman Whiteside. He drifted off for loan service with Wolves followed by moderate spells elsewhere, all that potential just a wistful recollection.

PETER BEARDSLEY ▼

1982/83

1	0
GAMES	GOALS

BORN BORN: Newcastle, 18.1.61.
HONOURS 59 England caps (86-96).
OTHER CLUBS Carlisle United 79/80–81/2 (104, 22); Vancouver Whitecaps, Canada; Newcastle United 83/4–86/7 (147, 61); Liverpool 87/8–90/1 (131, 46); Everton 91/2–92/3 (81, 25); Newcastle United 93/4–96/7 (129, 47); Bolton Wanderers 97/8 (17, 2); Manchester City on loan 97/8 (6, 0); Fulham on loan 97/8 (8, 1); Hartlepool United 98/9 (22, 2).

Peter Beardsley merits inclusion in this section purely out of curiosity value. For the question will always be asked: if Liverpool were ready to pay Newcastle £1.9 million for the England man, why didn't United snap him up for £250,000 from Vancouver Whitecaps when they had the chance?

He had been recommended by an enthusiastic Jimmy Murphy, who was sure the youngster had the makings of a star striker, and when Ron Atkinson saw him he agreed that the former Carlisle player was worth a trial. But, despite demonstrating huge potential in training, Peter was only ever to get one first-team chance – in a Milk Cup tie against Bournemouth in October 1982 – before making the return trip to Canada.

In retrospect, with the Geordie looking a more complete footballer than ever in his mid thirties back at St James' Park, such judgement seemed calamitous. But at the time Ron was blessed with Frank Stapleton, an emerging Norman Whiteside and the promising Scott McGarvey; and there was a young man named Mark Hughes coming through the reserve sides.

Win some, lose some …

He was a majestic leader of the line, always acutely aware of what was going on around him.

1981/82–1986/87

286 **78**
GAMES GOALS

BORN	Dublin, 10.7.56.
HONOURS	FA Cup 82/3, 84/5. 70 Republic of Ireland caps (76–90).
OTHER CLUBS	Arsenal 74/5–80/1 (225, 75); Ajax, Holland, 87/8 (4, 0); Derby County on loan 87/8 (10,1); Le Havre, France; Blackburn Rovers 89/90–90/1 (81, 13); Aldershot on loan 91/2 (1, 0); Huddersfield Town 91/2 (5, 0); Bradford City 91/2–93/4 (68, 2).
	MANAGER: Bradford City (91–94).

When Ron Atkinson signed Frank Stapleton from Arsenal in August 1981 – after bitter negotiations which ended in the hands of a transfer tribunal – he described his £900,000 capture as the best centre-forward in Europe.

Frank Stapleton

Now Frank was not short of admirable attributes but, at least in retrospect, Ron's mountain of praise does seem a little steep. After all, in six years at Old Trafford the Republic of Ireland striker never exceeded 14 League goals in a season, although admittedly there was a great deal more to his game than supplying the finishing touch. He was a majestic leader of the line, always acutely aware of what was going on around him. This subtle talent, which involves pulling defenders out of position with selfless running and creating dangerous positions for team-mates with delicate deflections and flicks, is not a flashy one but – certainly to the degree of excellence attained by Frank – it is rare indeed.

His control was impeccable with both feet and he possessed a fierce shot, but it is probably his power and timing in the air for which he will be best remembered. Prolific he was not, but Frank's greatest goals – his simple yet exquisitely directed header in the away draw with Dukia Prague in 1983 is a cherished example – were to be savoured. Against all that, he lacked half a yard of pace and was not the deadliest snapper-up of the half, or sometimes even whole, chance.

A cool, self-possessed individual, never one to indulge overmuch in laddish bonhomie, Frank was utterly dedicated in his preparation and offered an impressive level of consistency.

That thoroughly professional approach had impressed United coaches as far back as the early 1970s, when the tall Dubliner had been on the club's books as a schoolboy, but he was allowed to slip away to Highbury and the Old Trafford bank balance suffered accordingly. In 1979 there had been a price to pay on the field, too, when Frank turned in one of his finest Arsenal performances in the FA Cup Final, scoring one of the goals that beat the Red Devils. Of course, four years later he redressed the balance, contributing a close-range equaliser in the first Wembley meeting with Brighton, thus becoming the first man to score for different clubs in two FA Cup Finals.

Towards the end of his United days there was speculation that he might be converted to a central defender – in emergencies he had performed creditably in that position in two finals – but it was perhaps an unrealistic thought, and in July 1987 he was freed to join Ajax of Amsterdam.

An uncomfortable, injury-stricken period followed, then service with four English clubs and one French before Frank moved into player-managership with Bradford City, only to be sacked after failing narrowly to reach the Second Division promotion play-offs in 1994.

ARNOLD MUHREN

1982/83–1984/85

97 **18**
GAMES GOALS

BORN Volendam, Holland, 2.6.51.
HONOURS FA Cup 82/3. HONOURS: Holland caps.
OTHER CLUBS Ajax of Amsterdam and Twente Enschede, both Holland; Ipswich Town 78/9–81/2 (161, 21); Ajax of Amsterdam.

Arnold Muhren arrived from Ipswich Town in the summer of 1982 to become, at that time, the most skilful Red Devil since George Best. Though his talents were of a contrasting variety to the Irish magician's – deliberate and delicate rather than overtly breathtaking – his command of the ball was similarly complete. And just as George bowed out when he had much more to offer, so did the subtly superb Dutch schemer, albeit in utterly different circumstances.

Not that Ron Atkinson, then the United boss, could be blamed for letting such a world-class performer slip through his fingers. After all, Arnold was 34, plagued by injury and had been unable to command a regular place in the side when he was allowed home to join Ajax of Amsterdam in June 1985.

New faces such as Gordon Strachan and Jesper Olsen were arriving to increase the competition for places, which was already on the warm side, and who was to know that the slightly-built, left-sided creator still had at least four years of top football in him, including a masterly contribution to Holland's European Championship victory in 1988?

Some critics even questioned Ron's judgement in bringing Arnold to Old Trafford in the first place. When the Dutchman became a free agent at the end of four years with Ipswich, there were those who claimed he was past his prime and, even though no fee was involved, not worth signing.

But his early form removed the doubts. He gave the Reds a new dimension with his immaculate, unhurried passing and all-round vision, so much so that Martin Buchan – not a man to give praise lightly – remarked that Arnold was the only man in English football he would pay to watch! Certainly in his first two United campaigns the side looked at its best only when he was playing, and in 1983/84 a hitherto confident Championship surge faltered in March when he was injured.

When Arnold left, his exit was scarcely mourned amid the euphoria of the 1985 Wembley triumph over Everton. In the light of title failures over the next few seasons, a period of wailing and gnashing of teeth might have been appropriate.

Somebody up there doesn't like Remi Moses. Ever after joining United, the club he followed as a boy, Remi was doomed to see soccer's glittering prizes dangled tantalisingly in front of him, only to be whisked away as he reached out to grab them.

In fact, the abrasive little midfielder could shoulder the blame himself for his first disappointment, that of missing the 1983 FA Cup Final through suspension after being sent off in a League game at Highbury. But it was not his fault that he was injured and absent from the Reds' next FA Cup triumph in 1985. And when he did make it to Wembley, for the 1983 Milk Cup Final, all he picked up was a loser's medal.

There was worse to endure. In 1984/85 Remi's form was so consistent that he was elevated to the England squad. Then came the big moment: he was selected for the national team. And the inevitable letdown: injury prevented him from playing.

But the ultimate heartache was still in store. After three seasons of sporadic appearances, Remi succumbed finally to an ankle problem and retired from the game in May 1988 while still only 27.

He had arrived at Old Trafford from West Bromwich Albion in September 1981 as a £650,000 makeweight in the £2.4 million package that also included Bryan Robson.

Thus reunited with his former boss, Ron Atkinson, Remi briefly faced terrace jibes that he was the manager's favourite. But his spirited ball-winning and honest approach won over most of the doubters and it's a fact that the Reds looked harder to beat when Remi was in the side.

His all-round game, especially his passing, was becoming more accomplished as his fitness deteriorated. It was yet another cruel irony for a man who had already suffered more than enough.

REMI MOSES

1981/82–1987/88

198 **12**
GAMES GOALS

BORN • Manchester, 14.11.60.
OTHER CLUBS • West Bromwich Albion 79/80–81/2 (63, 5).

Arthur was in the team for a decade. The reason was plain: he was good at his job.

1974/75–1987/88

482 **7**
GAMES GOALS

BORN	Edinburgh, 14.7.57.
HONOURS	FA Cup 76/7, 82/3, 84/5.
	14 Scotland caps (82–86).
OTHER CLUBS	West Bromwich Albion 88/9 (43, 2); Dundee
	89/90 (10, 0); Chesterfield 90/1(3, 1); Chester
	City 91/2–92/3 (68, 0)

Arthur Albiston was never lauded as a superstar, he never figured in a transfer saga and his name was never tainted by even the faintest whiff of controversy. But when it comes to the final reckoning, when all the media hype is cast aside for the meaningless pap it truly is, and when the player's real worth down the years is reviewed, there will be few names that stand comparison with that of the plucky little Scottish left-back.

Arthur Albiston

For a start, only five men – Bobby Charlton, Bill Foulkes, Alex Stepney, Tony Dunne and pre-war goal-scorer Joe Spence – have played more senior matches for the Reds. While statistics alone can mislead, such a record speaks volumes of a consistency and loyalty beyond reproach.

Arthur was only 19, with just handful of first-team appearances behind him, when injury to Stewart Houston presented him with his big chance. He came into the side towards the end of 1976/77 and was immediately pitched into the FA Cup Final against Liverpool. He confounded critics who predicted that he would be a weak link, that the Merseyside flyer Steve Heighway would cut him to ribbons, and he played an accomplished part in a stirring victory. As well as locking up the left flank of the Red Devils' rearguard, he found time to attack on the overlap, leaving England internationals Phil Neal and Tommy Smith staggering in his wake on one scintillating run that was marred only by a wayward cross.

After the game, amid the inevitable euphoria, Arthur remained commendably level-headed, and it was typical of the generous youngster that he offered his winner's medal to the unfortunate Houston. Though much touched by the gesture, Stewart declined with thanks.

Once in the team Arthur remained a fixture for a decade. The reason was plain: he was good at his job. He had speed, assured control with both feet, first-class distribution and a canny tackle. His only weakness was lack of height which occasionally left him exposed against big strikers, especially when defending deep crosses to the far post.

Arthur played for his country – though probably not as often as his unflashy ability merited – and pocketed three FA Cup winner's medals, a Red Devils record at the time, though it has been equalled since by Bryan Robson and Mark Hughes.

When he was allowed to join West Bromwich Albion on a free transfer in August 1988 at the age of 31, he was as fit and mobile as ever and, arguably, he was still the best left-back at the club. Manchester United, and football in general, need more men like Arthur Albiston.

JOHN GIDMAN

1981/82–1985/86

118 **4**
GAMES GOALS

BORN	Liverpool, 10.4.54.
HONOURS	FA Cup 84/5. 1 England cap (77).
OTHER CLUBS	Aston Villa 72/3–79/80 (197, 9); Everton 79/80–80/1 (64, 2); Manchester City 86/7–87/8 (53, 1); Stoke City 88/9 (10, 0); Darlington 88/9 (13, 1).

The memory of John Gidman galloping joyously down Manchester United's right flank is a precious one to all those Reds supporters who love their soccer with a smile on its face. John, so typical of the Ron Atkinson era, was a buccaneering full-back who was at his happiest, and most impressive, when surging into attack. Particularly beloved of the Stretford End, he had the flair and charisma to become something of a folk hero, but a succession of serious injuries prevented him from making the maximum impact.

He was Ron's first signing, coming to Old Trafford from Goodison Park in exchange for Mickey Thomas and £50,000 in August 1981. With Jimmy Nicholl already at the club, right-back was not a weak position but the manager – always an admirer of the Everton man – could not turn down the chance to sign him.

John, who made his name and played his sole game for England during a distinguished spell with Aston Villa, surely would have enjoyed an even more illustrious career but for two off-the-field accidents, one of which nearly cost him his sight and the other his life. He was also cursed with soccer maladies, being sidelined for most of his second and third campaigns at Old Trafford.

John regained fitness in time for the 1985 FA Cup triumph but was struck down again in the second match of the next term. On recovery he won back his place but soon it became obvious that he was surplus to requirements and he moved to Manchester City, then Stoke, before becoming player-coach at Darlington.

John had his critics, who reckoned he was not defensively sound, and at times that may have been true. But he was exciting and his presence brought an extra dimension to the team. In short, he was the stuff of which Red Devils are made and he will be remembered with pleasure.

What a pity that Mike Duxbury had departed the Old Trafford scene some 12 months before the infusion of a particularly precocious crop of bright young things into the United youth team. The likeable Lancastrian, who served the Reds nobly and unselfishly throughout the 1980s, would have been an impeccable role model for that multi-talented new wave. Mike's United career may have been overshadowed to a large extent by the comings and goings of expensive star performers, but few of them contributed more to the Red Devils' cause than this loyal, adaptable – and yes, talented – local lad.

He emerged first in 1980/81, Dave Sexton's final season in charge, wearing eight different numbers on his back in the course of 33 games, operating in midfield, at full-back and as sweeper. Many thought right-back was his niche and the arrival of John Gidman seemed to dent his prospects. But Mike was so versatile that throughout the reign of Ron Atkinson he was usually somewhere in the starting line-up.

Then, when injury forced John to take a lengthy lay-off, Mike grabbed his chance to such effect that he won ten England caps at right-back. Indeed, on several international occasions his precise distribution, well-timed tackles and fine anticipation made him look one of the most able performers on view.

Perversely it was Mike's exploits for his country which led to a setback in his career. He made several blunders for England which rocked his confidence, and his club form suffered accordingly. In typically resilient manner Mike battled on. He shrugged off the chance of a move to Everton and resurfaced as one of the most flexible weapons in new boss Alex Ferguson's armoury, undeterred even by the arrival in 1987 of England international right-back Viv Anderson.

Sadly, his efforts in 1988/89 and 1989/90 were marred by knee problems and in the summer of 1990, after making contributions in the first four ties of United's victorious FA Cup campaign, Mike was freed to join Blackburn Rovers. Later he served under Frank Stapleton at Bradford City.

MIKE DUXBURY

1980/81–1989/90

376	7
GAMES	GOALS

BORN ● Accrington, Lancashire, 1.9.59.
HONOURS ● FA Cup 82/3, 84/5. 10 England caps (83–84).
OTHER CLUBS ● Blackburn Rovers 90/1–91/2 (27, 0); Bradford City 91/2–93/4 (66, 0).

ALAN DAVIES ▼

1981/82–1983/84

10	1
GAMES	GOALS

BORN ● Manchester, 5.12.61.
HONOURS ● FA Cup 82/3. 11 Wales caps (83–90).
OTHER CLUBS ● Newcastle United 85/6–86/7 (21, 1); Charlton Athletic on loan 85/6 (1, 0); Carlisle United on loan 86/7 (4, 1); Swansea City 87/8–88/9 (84, 8); Bradford City 89/90 (26, 1); Swansea City 90/1–91/2 (43, 4). Died 1992.

For a month in 1983 Alan Davies had a tantalising taste of the big time. First the young Welshman, who had turned out in only four League games, played on United's left wing against Brighton in the FA Cup Final. A few days later he was a star turn in the Reds' 4–0 replay triumph, laying on the first goal for Bryan Robson.

Then came an international debut against Northern Ireland and, ten days on, another cap – this time against mighty Brazil! It was hard to believe that before injury had forced Steve Coppell out of the Wembley reckoning, Alan had been just another face in United's Central League line-up.

But, as quickly as the skilful flankman cum midfielder had rocketed to prominence, he disappeared from the limelight. A broken ankle cost him the chance of a first-team spot at the start of the following campaign and he never forced himself back into contention. An entertaining dribbler and fine passer who was perhaps lacking in drive, he joined Newcastle before dropping into the lower divisions.

Ahead, though, lay the kind of tragedy which reduces sporting setbacks to utter irrelevance. In February 1992 Alan Davies, a family man, was found dead in his car near his home in South Wales. He had committed suicide.

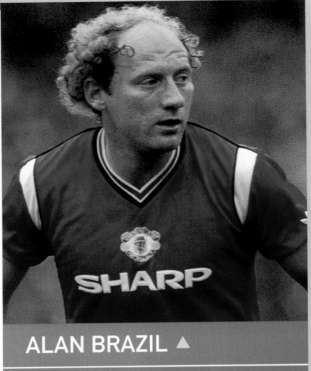

ALAN BRAZIL ▲

1984/85–1985/86

41	12
GAMES	GOALS

BORN ● Glasgow, 15.6.59.
HONOURS ● 13 Scotland caps (80–83).
OTHER CLUBS ● Ipswich Town 77/8–82/3 (154, 70); Tottenham Hotspur 82/3–83/4 (31, 9); Coventry City 85/6 (15, 2), Queen's Park Rangers 86/7 (4, 0). FC Baden, Switzerland, 88/9.

One moment in a crucial clash with Everton summed up the traumatic experience of Alan Brazil at Old Trafford. It was March 1985 and the Reds had to win to maintain their title challenge. Deep in the game the scores were level and stalemate loomed. Suddenly a chance fell to Alan. He struck it well, Neville Southall was beaten … and the ball hit the bar before bouncing away. Had he scored the Championship race may have been transformed and he would have been the hero. As it was he resumed the nightmare which had started not long after his £700,000 move from Spurs in June 1984.

It could all have been so different. Alan was a skilful, strong-running striker who had oozed quality and became a Scottish international while with Ipswich Town. The transfer to Spurs should have made him, but he failed to settle and United effectively got him out of jail.

Sadly, though his strike rate for the Reds was not at all bad, he could not overcome competition from Whiteside, Hughes and Stapleton. Alan never had a real run in the side and his United career withered. Attempts to revive his fortunes elsewhere were dogged by injury and came to nothing. A distressing fall from grace was complete.

GRAEME HOGG ▲

1983/84–1987/88

109	1
GAMES	GOALS

BORN	Aberdeen, 17.6.64.
OTHER CLUBS	West Bromwich Albion on loan 87/8 (7, 0); Portsmouth 88/9–90/1 (100, 2); Hearts 91/2–94/5 (58, 3); Notts County 94/5–97/8 (66, 0); Brentford 97/8 (17, 2).

Brave, willing and dependable but not quite good enough for the top level; somehow that always seemed likely to be the verdict on the Old Trafford career of Scotland under-21 centre-half Graeme Hogg.

A burly, rather cumbersome, left-footed stopper whose aerial power was not matched by his all-round game, Graeme enjoyed his most successful season in 1984/85 when he played in 29 First Division matches and missed just one tie as United reached the FA Cup Final. At the time, clearly, he had the edge on Gordon McQueen and Kevin Moran in the battle to become Paul McGrath's regular partner, even though injury robbed him of a Wembley place.

Still only 20, he must have been confident that there would be other chances of glory. But after sharing in United's exhilarating start to the following campaign, his fortunes declined with those of the team. Often he was fighting for fitness and slipped out of the reckoning.

Throughout the next two seasons the muscular Aberdonian performed with admirable commitment on his intermittent first-team outings. But when the arrival of Steve Bruce confirmed that he was not part of Alex Ferguson's long-term plans, Graeme, who impressed during a brief loan spell with West Bromwich Albion, accepted that his Red Devil days were over and joined Portsmouth in August 1988.

PETER BARNES ▼

1985/86–1986/87

25	4
GAMES	GOALS

BORN	Manchester, 10.6.57.
HONOURS	22 England caps (77–82).
OTHER CLUBS	Manchester City 74/5–78/9 (115, 15); West Bromwich Albion 79/80–80/1 (77, 23); Leeds United 81/2 (31, 1); Real Betis, Spain, 82/3; Leeds United 83/4 (27, 4); Coventry City 84/5 (18, 2); Manchester City 86/7 (8, 0); Bolton Wanderers on loan 87/8 (2, 0); Port Vale on loan 87/8 (3, 0); Hull City 87/8 (11, 0); Farense, Portugal 88/9; Bolton Wanderers 88/9 (3, 0); Sunderland 88/9 (1, 0); Tampa Bay Rowdies, USA, 90; Cliftonville, Northern Ireland, 92/3; Melbourne City, Australia.

Whatever the knockers say about Peter Barnes they would do well to remember one thing; he played a thrilling part in the most successful start to a season ever enjoyed by Manchester United. In 1985/86 the Red Devils won their first ten League games and didn't lose until their 16th. And the mercurial winger with the dancing feet was an integral component of a breathtaking side.

Of course, the euphoria in autumn gave way to hesitation in winter and dismay in spring, and the anti-Barnes brigade will claim that summed him up – immense promise followed by failure when it mattered. And there was a cruel truth in that. No one denied his talent, most evident in early Maine Road days, but, too often, application and spirit were lacking.

Ultimately Peter justified his reputation and faded away before rejoining City in January 1987. But Ron Atkinson's £50,000 gamble in taking him from Coventry 18 months earlier was not wholly in vain. The former England flankman left behind a small but precious fund of memories to cherish.

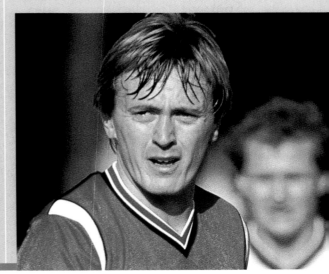

ARTHUR GRAHAM

1983/84–1984/85

51 **7**
GAMES GOALS

BORN ● Glasgow, 26.10.52.
HONOURS ● 10 Scotland caps (77–80).
OTHER CLUBS ● Aberdeen 69/70–76/7 (228, 34); Leeds United 77/8–82/3 (223, 37); Bradford City 85/6–86/7 (31, 2).

Chunky winger Arthur Graham was a budget-priced short-term success. Though nearing the end of his career, the diminutive but combative Scottish international was drafted in from Leeds United for around £30,000 in August 1983 after the premature retirement of Steve Coppell left the Reds without an experienced flankman.

Arthur, once a teenage prodigy with Aberdeen, made an immediate impact with an eye-catching performance in the Charity Shield defeat of Liverpool and he consolidated his position with a string of impressive displays. A strong, tricky runner and an accurate crosser of the ball, he possessed a rasping shot, could operate on either wing and was never loth to chase back and help out in defence.

Though he managed only five League goals himself – something of a disappointment in view of his three hat-tricks for Leeds – he laid on plenty for the likes of Norman Whiteside and Frank Stapleton, and it was a testimony to his outstanding form that Ron Atkinson was content to stick with him until Jesper Olsen arrived the following season.

Just three months short of his 31st birthday when he became a Red Devil, the scampering Scot was never going to be an investment for the future. But he proved such an admirable stopgap that, during one particularly heady interlude, there was even talk of an international recall.

Arthur departed for Bradford City in June 1985, his spirited spell at Old Trafford having proved a worthy sign-off from the top flight. At Valley Parade he went on to coach the youth and reserve teams, also serving a month-long stint as caretaker manager in 1989.

Few players have shed more of their own blood on a soccer pitch than Kevin Moran. The fearless, some might say reckless, central defender – surely the owner of the most stitched head in football – served the Red Devils with valiant distinction for an incident-packed decade before Alex Ferguson gave him a free transfer, in recognition of his splendid record, and the club doctor could take life a little more easily.

Kevin, a Republic of Ireland stalwart throughout the 1980s and well into the 1990s, arrived at Old Trafford from Gaelic football in Dublin and took a while to adjust to English soccer. He battled with characteristic commitment until Dave Sexton brought him into the first team, sometimes deploying him as a midfield strong man. But Kevin was more effective at the back, where gradually he became established as injuries began to take their toll of Gordon McQueen and Martin Buchan.

His distribution, poor at first, improved over the years though his forte was winning the ball, especially in the air where he made up for a comparative lack of height by his neck-or-nothing approach. But his timing was sometimes awry and there were occasions when he was too brave for his own good, which accounted for some of the war wounds.

Despite the tough image, Kevin possessed not a vestige of malice and it is a cruel shame that he should have earned immortal notoriety as the first man to be sent off in an FA Cup Final, against Everton in 1985.

TV cameras revealed clearly that he went for the ball and not Peter Reid in the offending tackle, and later he was presented with the winner's medal which was at first withheld. Any other outcome would have unjustly besmirched the honour of an honest and accomplished professional.

On leaving Old Trafford as a 32-year-old in the summer of 1988, it seemed likely that the intelligent Dubliner would wind down to retirement from the game and then pick up the reins of a new career. But not a bit of it. After a season in the Spanish sun Kevin resurfaced at Blackburn, harder to beat than ever, to play a major part in Rovers' rousing resurgence.

KEVIN MORAN

1978/79–1987/88

 287 24
GAMES GOALS

BORN ● Dublin, 29.4.56.
HONOURS ● FA Cup 82/3, 84/5. 71 Republic of Ireland caps (80–94).
OTHER CLUBS ● Sporting Gijon, Spain, 88/9; Blackburn Rovers 89/90–93/4 (147, 10).

One of his greatest assets was the ability to capitalise on unexpected opportunities.

1981/82–1988/89

272	67
GAMES	GOALS

BORN Belfast, 7.5.65.
HONOURS FA Cup 82/3, 84/5. 38
Northern Ireland caps (82–89).
OTHER CLUBS Everton 89/90–90/1 (29, 9).

For four fantastic years, Norman Whiteside was Roy of the Rovers incarnate. Until 1986/87, when the script began to show signs of going wrong, the mountainously built Irish boy-man was the plaything of the headline-writers, serving up sensations seemingly to order.

Norman Whiteside

He scored on his full debut for United, just a couple of months before becoming, at 17, the youngest player to appear in the World Cup Finals. Less than a year later, Norman was the youngest scorer in a Wembley final, contributing a deft strike on the turn against Liverpool in the Milk Cup. Two months on, he inscribed his name on another page of Wembley history as the youngest scorer in an FA Cup Final, thanks to a header against Brighton.

Admittedly there followed the occasional stutter as he fought for a place with the likes of Stapleton, Brazil and Hughes but, at the next whiff of glory, Norman proved there was no one like him for the big occasion. This time it was scoring the goal, a dream of a curler, which deprived Everton of the FA Cup in 1985.

By then the young striker had moved to midfield where his lack of out-and-out pace was less of a handicap and where his ball skills and strength were gainfully employed. One of his greatest assets was the ability to capitalise on unexpected opportunities, perhaps by switching play with an impromptu pass, or by shaping for a piledriver before delivering the most delicate of chips – the audacious duping of Ipswich 'keeper Paul Cooper at Old Trafford in the autumn of '82 comes to mind.

Sadly, there was a less savoury side to his progress. There were incidents, far too many of them, where his natural aggression escalated into raw violence. At times, perhaps, he lost his temper; at others he appeared to be chillingly cynical. Ultimately, as he must realise, such aberrations only punished himself and his team. Running a constant risk of suspension was hardly a help to a side chasing honours.

Such strife somehow seemed linked to a downturn in his playing fortunes. In November 1986 he suffered a

knee injury which cost him four matches. In his absence Alex Ferguson replaced Ron Atkinson and the young Ulsterman didn't appear the same player on his return, apparently giving undue weight to the physical side of his game. Thereafter his contribution was never as satisfying and he became disillusioned, eventually asking for a transfer. His request was granted but, after a run of poor form and being priced at £1 million, there were no takers. Norman was still unsettled, his career in the doldrums, when achilles and knee damage sidelined him for most of 1988/89. There were problems off the pitch, clashes with the manager took place and in July 1989 it was decided that a clean break would benefit both club and player. Accordingly – and sadly to fans who had retained faith that, somehow, there would be a miraculous reprieve for the fallen prodigy – he was sold to Everton for £600,000 down, another £150,000 payable later.

For a while at Goodison Park there were hopeful signs, but the knee trouble refused to go away and after two stop-start seasons, he was forced to retire at 25, an age when most players haven't even reached their peak. In truth, Norman had been descending from his zenith for some time, in a manner of which Roy of the Rovers would not have approved. Commendably, though, he did not wallow in self-pity, setting out instead to become a specialist in foot disorders in a manner that had nothing to do with comic-strip fantasy, a lot to do with real life.

GORDON STRACHAN

1984/85–1988/89

201 | **38**
GAMES | GOALS

BORN	Edinburgh, 9.2.57.
HONOURS	FA Cup 84/5. 50 Scotland caps (80–92).
OTHER CLUBS	Dundee 74/5–76/7 (60, 13); Aberdeen 77/8–83/4 (191, 54);
	Leeds United 88/9–94/5 (196, 37); Coventry City 94/5–96/7 (26, 0).
	MANAGER: Coventry City (96–).

Take a tiny, twisting jack-in-the-box, add a shock of red hair and an impish grin, and top it all with one of the canniest of soccer brains – and you've got Gordon Strachan. When Ron Atkinson paid Aberdeen boss Alex Ferguson £600,000 for his much-in-demand midfielder cum winger – after a tiresome transfer saga involving FC Cologne, who claimed Gordon had signed for them – there were those who reckoned the Scottish international sprite was too small for the English game. 'He'd need to play in a team of giants to survive' was the view of one respected judge.

In his first season Gordon did rather more than survive. He positively thrived, missing only one League game and scoring 15 goals, not to mention the addition of an FA Cup winner's medal to a trophy cabinet bulging with Scottish silverware. He had mixed fortunes with penalties though; at first he couldn't miss them, then he couldn't score them.

United fans took to him for his flair, industry and perky demeanour. They gloried in his ability to pick his way daintily through seemingly inpenetrable tangles of bodies and loved his line in defence-splitting passes.

In March 1989, to the surprise of many at a time when he was enjoying one of his most effective spells, he was allowed to join Leeds for £300,000. Ferguson reckoned that, at 32, Gordon had run out of steam in Manchester and needed a new challenge.

But no one could have imagined just how well he would do at Elland Road, where he went on to give six years of fabulous service, including an inspirational 1991/92 campaign in which his new club pipped his old one for the title. For that achievement, no words can convey sufficient credit.

The verdict on his days at Old Trafford? Well, at his best he was a match-winner who hinted at greatness, contributing width and variety to the Reds' attack. But, though he trotted out some memorable displays, he did not always live up to the promise of that first term.

If that sounds curmudgeonly, it is not intended to. Gordon was one of the few talents in British soccer who could transform a game with a moment of artistry. And he didn't need giants to help him do it.

In the words of one of Manchester soccer's sagest observers, the English game didn't teach much to Jesper Olsen. No one would dispute the diminutive Dane's rich talent but, equally, few could realistically describe his stay at Old Trafford as anything but frustrating.

Blind alleys seemed to hold a particular fascination for the £350,000 winger who arrived from Ajax of Amsterdam in July 1984 with a world-class reputation. This had been fuelled by the spectacular goal he scored for Denmark against England in the European Championship in 1982. Reds fans, as ever yearning for a new idol, expected so much and, to be fair, Jesper's first season did not wholly dash their hopes.

On his day he looked as though he had the ability to prise open the most clam-like of defences. Feinting, sprinting, shooting, he carried about him the aura of an exciting player and he completed a promising first campaign by helping United win the FA Cup. But thereafter he was frequently disappointing, drifting in and out of the action, rarely leaving a memorable mark. He seemed to run in the wrong directions, possessing the close control and speed to reach the byline yet choosing instead to make wayward darts across the pitch.

Though he was brave enough, Jesper exerted a markedly lightweight physical presence during the Atkinson regime. He became a more tenacious all-round performer under Alex Ferguson but he suffered injuries and it grew steadily more obvious that his style was not suited to the perpetual motion of English soccer.

It was no surprise when he returned to the Continent in November 1988, a £400,000 fee taking him to Bordeaux, where many believed he would rise to heights never scaled in this country. In fact, it never happened; his most effective days had proved to be earlier in his career. How sad that Manchester United never saw the best of Jesper Olsen.

JESPER OLSEN

1984/85–1988/89

175 24

GAMES GOALS

BORN Fakse, Denmark, 20.3.61.
HONOURS FA Cup 84/5. 45 Denmark caps.
OTHER CLUBS Naestved, Denmark; Ajax, Amsterdam; Bordeaux, France; Caen, France.

United knew that a willing and able Paul McGrath was an asset of rare quality.

1982/83–1988/89

198 GAMES **16** GOALS

BORN	Ealing, London, 4.12.59.
HONOURS	FA Cup 84/5. 83 Republic of Ireland caps (85–97).
OTHER CLUBS	Aston Villa 89/90–95/6 (253, 9); Derby County 96/7 (24, 0); Sheffield United 97/8 (12, 0).

In a perfect world, Paul McGrath would be recognised as one of the most accomplished British defenders in living memory. This Utopia would have no room for injuries or personal problems; a player would be free to express his talents untrammelled by life's frustrating realities. But there lies the rub in the case of the London-born Republic of Ireland centre-half.

Paul McGrath

There had never been any doubting the ability of Paul McGrath. It had been blindingly apparent to Ron Atkinson in April 1982 when he paid Dublin club St Patrick's Athletic £30,000 for the unknown youngster. The United manager was not exactly short of central defenders at the time with the likes of Gordon McQueen, Kevin Moran and Martin Buchan on his books but he predicted that his strapping acquisition could outdo them all.

Paul was strong, fast, good in the air and skilful with both feet. It seemed that all he lacked was experience. Accordingly, he made his debut the following season and impressed both at the back, where he showed every sign of developing into a dominant force, and in midfield, where his rather ungainly gait tended to conceal his all-round competence.

For the next two years Paul's appearance record, not helped by injuries, was intermittent and it was not until the second half of 1984/85 – culminating in a classy FA Cup Final performance against Everton – that he really came into his own. His confidence grew and, despite an occasional penchant for ball-watching, Paul matured into one of the outstanding centre-halves in the First Division.

In 1987 he played for the Football League in its centenary showpiece against the Rest of the World and many observers made him man of the match. It was only a friendly but such was his poise and power when confronted by Diego Maradona and company that soon his name was being linked with some of the top clubs in Europe.

But instead of being a platform for glory with the Red

Devils, the occasion proved something of a watershed in his fortunes. Knee problems plagued the Irishman with increasing regularity and off-the-pitch difficulties contributed to his woe, leading to lurid newspaper headlines and an acrimonious transfer request.

This was granted but any immediate move was scuppered by a series of cartilage operations and Paul was given the chance to rebuild his Old Trafford career. For three months in the spring of 1989 he appeared to be making the most of the opportunity, and all who marched beneath the United banner were hoping against hope that he would succeed. They knew, and no one was more aware of it than Alex Ferguson, that a willing and able Paul McGrath was an asset of rare quality.

But then the Irishman was involved in another spectacular incident, which proved one too many for the patience of the Old Trafford boss, and that summer Paul was transferred to Aston Villa for a cut-price £450,000. It was a last chance and, to his eternal credit, he grasped it avidly. Often the pain in those long-suffering knees precluded training, but invariably match days found him performing at his best.

In 1992/93, when Villa pushed United so hard for the League title, Paul was voted the players' player of the year; and though there were tales, still, of the occasional scrape, he had salvaged plenty from a career that had been heading, rapidly and unnecessarily, off the rails.

How deeply ironic, too, that as United hunted desperately for an experienced central defender during an injury crisis nearly four seasons later, the 37-year-old McGrath, who had moved on to Derby County, continued to turn in outstanding Premiership performances. If only . . .

JOHNNY SIVEBAEK ▼

1985/86–1986/87

34 GAMES **1** GOALS

BORN Vejle, Denmark, 25.10.61.
HONOURS Denmark caps.
OTHER CLUBS Vejle, Denmark; St Etienne, France.

Danish international Johnny Sivebaek's move to Old Trafford was ill-starred from the start. When United had agreed a £200,000 fee with his hometown club, Vejle, the skilful utility man failed the medical. Then, several weeks later in February 1986, the doctors had second thoughts and the deal went through.

Johnny was largely an unknown quantity but the fans' appetites had been whetted by his stunning goal, shown widely on television, for his country against the Republic of Ireland in a World Cup qualifier. His United debut was at Anfield where, playing in midfield, he showed neat touches but seemed disorientated and the game passed him by. He hardly played again for the rest of 1985/86, but was first choice at right-back for most of the next campaign.

Going forward, Johnny displayed running, crossing and shooting ability but there was doubt about his defensive work, and in August 1987 he joined St Etienne for £250,000, having never adjusted fully to the hectic British game.

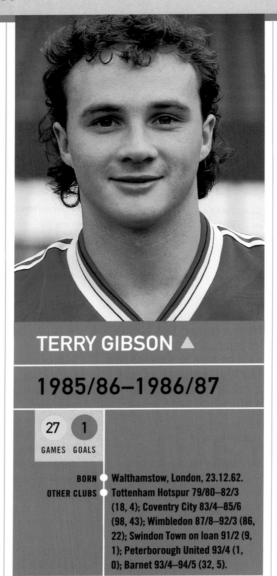

TERRY GIBSON ▲

1985/86–1986/87

27 GAMES **1** GOALS

BORN Walthamstow, London, 23.12.62.
OTHER CLUBS Tottenham Hotspur 79/80–82/3 (18, 4); Coventry City 83/4–85/6 (98, 43); Wimbledon 87/8–92/3 (86, 22); Swindon Town on loan 91/2 (9, 1); Peterborough United 93/4 (1, 0); Barnet 93/4–94/5 (32, 5).

There is a theory that if Terry Gibson was not good enough for Spurs, he could hardly have been up to playing for United. Although that ignores an admirable interim spell with Coventry – in which he proved that he could score goals in the top flight and without the benefit of star colleagues – there may be some truth in it. But here are some facts, not to prove a point, merely for reflection.

In the first ten League games he started for the Reds, they were undefeated. Ron Atkinson, in the 13 League matches which led to his sacking, picked Terry just once despite the team's goal drought and only three victories. When the terrier-like striker was finally given a run by Alex Ferguson, he was axed after the first defeat in eight games.

All this is not to say that Terry was the answer to United's problems but it does seem an odd way to treat a man who had cost around £400,000. Clearly he never had a chance. How he deserved the change of luck that brought him FA Cup glory so soon after moving to Wimbledon.

BILLY GARTON ▼

1984/85–1988/89

51 GAMES **0** GOALS

BORN Salford, Lancashire, 15.3.65.
OTHER CLUBS Birmingham City on loan 85/6 (5, 0).

Billy Garton was a useful utility defender who never quite convinced, never quite demonstrated the necessary blend of ability and confidence for the top level, though illness and injury made it difficult to gauge his true prowess. Eventually, indeed, poor Billy was forced out of the game by a debilitating condition which, no doubt, had restricted his level of performance.

He was a local youngster who came up through the Reds' youth sides and in 1984/85 progressed into the first-team reckoning, an increasingly rare phenomenon at Old Trafford at that time.

Though a versatile performer, Billy was at his best in the centre, sometimes looking ponderous at full-back. A good tackler and user of the ball, his longest and best unbroken run in the senior side was one of eight games in the middle of 1986/87 when Paul McGrath was absent. He let no one down but lacked a degree of dominance, and it was no shock when he was placed on offer at the end of the next campaign.

Then a projected move to Manchester City fell through and he resumed his role as perpetual stand-in until the poignant final verdict on his health was made in May 1990.

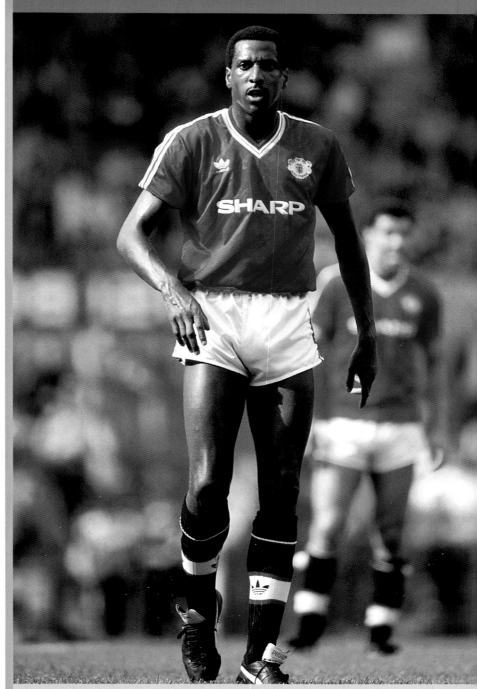

After Manchester United's 2–0 defeat of Arsenal on a murky afternoon in January 1987, Alex Ferguson left Old Trafford a deeply impressed man. It was not so much the performance of his team that moved the Reds' new boss – though that had been encouraging enough – but the spirited showing of the visitors' right-back Viv Anderson.

That day the England defender gave a display of such frenetic commitment and obvious hatred of losing that Ferguson recognised a kindred spirit. And he decided that here was a battle-hardened campaigner whom he would rather fight alongside than against. Accordingly, the following summer, Viv signed for United amid much acrimony over the fee – echoing previous ill-feeling with Arsenal over the purchase of Frank Stapleton – which a tribunal set at £250,000.

Though 31, the former Nottingham Forest stalwart seemed to be a bargain. He was tall and strong, fast and skilful, with long, spidery legs which seemed to pluck the ball away from opponents. And he was a top-class athlete, fitter than many players his junior.

Yet Viv's move to Old Trafford was to bring little joy. In his first season he was competent but not outstanding, perhaps being hampered by niggling injuries which cost him ten League appearances. Then heel and back problems sidelined him for most of 1988/89, which saw the emergence of the promising Lee Martin to increase competition for full-back places. Thereafter, for the next season and a half, the livewire Midlander strove to overcome his fitness problems, showing splendid good cheer and fortitude in the face of adversity.

In January 1991, by then 34, Viv moved to Sheffield Wednesday on a free transfer and, ironically, soon he was enjoying the sort of injury-free sequence that had characterised his days at Highbury. He became player-boss of Barnsley in 1993, then switched to Middlesbrough as Bryan Robson's assistant a year later. It will be surprising if such a determined individual, blessed with enthusiasm to burn, is not a long-term success in management.

VIV ANDERSON

1987/88–1990/91

69 GAMES   4 GOALS

BORN   Nottingham, 29.8.56.
HONOURS   30 England caps (78–88).
OTHER CLUBS   Nottingham Forest 74/5–83/4 (328, 15); Arsenal 84/5–86/7 (120, 9); Sheffield Wednesday 90/1–92/3 (70, 8); Barnsley 93/4 (20, 3); Middlesbrough 94/5 (2, 0). MANAGER: Barnsley (93–94).

PETER DAVENPORT ▼

1985/86–1988/89

106 GAMES **26** GOALS

BORN : Birkenhead, Cheshire, 24.3.61.
HONOURS : 1 England cap (85).
OTHER CLUBS : Nottingham Forest 81/2–85/6 (118, 54); Middlesbrough 88/9–89/90 (59, 7); Sunderland 90/1–92/3 (99, 15); Airdrieonians 93/4 (38, 8); St Johnstone 94/5 (22, 4); Stockport County 94/5 (6, 1); Macclesfield Town 97/8–98/9 (5, 1). MANAGER: Macclesfield Town (2000–).

Peter Davenport could be forgiven for seeing himself as a pawn in some celestial game in which Mark Hughes was very much the king. When the Welshman headed for Barcelona in 1986, United paid £570,000 for the spindly Nottingham Forest and England striker as his replacement. And when Alex Ferguson gleefully brought home the hero of the Stretford End two years later it was, ultimately, Peter who had to make way.

At first, Old Trafford must have seemed like rainbow's end to a man who had been a United supporter as a lad. But when he managed only one goal in his first dozen games, disturbing parallels were quickly drawn with the failure of another former Forest front-man, Garry Birtles. It was a difficult time for Peter to establish himself, a period of transition which saw the sacking of Ron Atkinson and the arrival of Ferguson, who made no secret of his yen for Hughes.

Peter battled manfully for his future and there were games when his deft control, body swerve and slick turning technique were out of the top drawer, even after he was pushed on to the wing. But 'Sparky's' shadow was ominously substantial and, when it became clear that Peter's role was merely that of a classy reserve, he took himself to Middlesbrough, then Sunderland, in search of the right stage on which to excel.

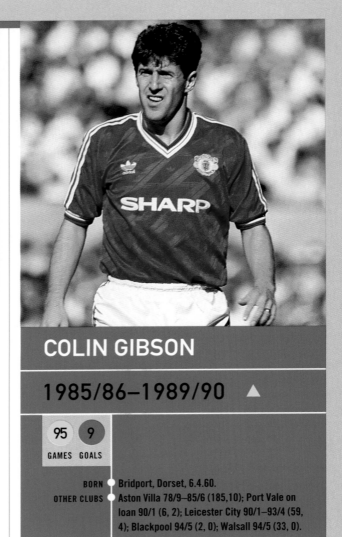

COLIN GIBSON

1985/86–1989/90 ▲

95 GAMES **9** GOALS

BORN : Bridport, Dorset, 6.4.60.
OTHER CLUBS : Aston Villa 78/9–85/6 (185,10); Port Vale on loan 90/1 (6, 2); Leicester City 90/1–93/4 (59, 4); Blackpool 94/5 (2, 0); Walsall 94/5 (33, 0).

Even before Colin Gibson's United career was plagued by mishaps to knee and hamstring he had become a victim of his own versatility. When he moved to Old Trafford at a cost of £350,000 from Villa Park in November 1985, he seemed earmarked as an alternative for the left-back berth occupied by the excellent, underrated Arthur Albiston. But any struggle between the two for that slot was quickly shelved as an injury crisis pitchforked Colin into midfield duty.

He did a spirited, if unspectacular job, foraging tirelessly and plugging gaps wherever he was needed, but in doing so his hopes of staking a strong claim to his specialist position suffered. Such frustration was not new to Colin. At Villa he had won League Championship honours at left-back and been mentioned as an England prospect in that role, only to become an emergency utility player.

On arrival at Old Trafford his task was made harder by terrace disappointment over the disappearance of a ten-point Championship lead and, not being a 'star', he became something of a target for an unenlightened but highly vocal fringe. Colin overcame that and, without becoming fully established, he chalked up workmanlike spells at the back and in midfield before injury relegated him to the sidelines once more. In December 1990, a £100,000 deal enabled him to make a fresh start at Leicester.

CHRIS TURNER ▲

1985/86–1987/88

79	0
GAMES	GOALS

BORN Sheffield, 15.9.38.
OTHER CLUBS Sheffield Wednesday 76/7–78/9 (91, 0); Lincoln City on loan 78/9 (5, 0); Sunderland 79/80–84/5 (195, 0); Sheffield Wednesday 88/9–90/1 (75, 0); Leeds United on loan 89/90 (2, 0); Leyton Orient 91/2–94/5 (58, 0).
MANAGER Leyton Orient (94–95); Hartlepool United (99-)

Chris Turner was a shot-stopper extraordinaire, a man who could perform wonders between the posts. But a 'keeper's jurisdiction extends beyond his white line. He must dominate his goal area, especially in the air, and, quite simply, Chris did not do so for Manchester United. When he left that line for high crosses, often he looked out of his element.

Alex Ferguson made no secret of the fact that he wanted a taller custodian, even though at 6ft Chris was the equal in stature of Peter Shilton and only an inch shorter than his medium-term successor, Jim Leighton.

Ron Atkinson had paid Sunderland £250,000 for Chris in the summer of 1985 to provide competition for Gary Bailey, whose form had been variable. It seemed the newcomer had made the right move when Gary suffered serious injury. Chris did well and was even mooted for the England squad, but then came the change of management and the blooding of young Gary Walsh.

Chris asked for a transfer and, after the arrival of Leighton in the 1988 close season, his wish was granted in the form of a second spell at Hillsborough.

GARY WALSH ▼

1986/87–1994/95

63	0
GAMES	GOALS

BORN Wigan, Lancashire, 21.3.68.
HONOURS European Cup Winners' Cup 90/1 (non-playing sub). FA Cup 93/4 (non-playing sub).
OTHER CLUBS Airdrieonians on loan 88/9 (3, 0), Oldham Athletic on loan 93/4 (6, 0); Middlesbrough 95/6–96/7 (44, 0); Bradford City 97/8–(92, 0).

A succession of serious injuries called an alarming halt to the impressive progress of Gary Walsh, reckoned by some seasoned professionals to be potentially the finest 'keeper Old Trafford has known since the war, despite suffering six seasons in the wilderness.

The tall, blond Lancastrian displaced Chris Turner towards the end of 1986/87 and kept the job as the next campaign began. His confidence was building steadily when he was concussed at Hillsborough, but he recovered to resume first-team duty, only to take another fearful blow to his head in a friendly in Barbados. His lengthy enforced absence allowed the selflessly supportive Turner to reclaim his place, then Gary's prospects took a further dive when the Reds bought Jim Leighton in May 1988. Ill fortune continued to dog the youngster as he returned from a loan spell at Airdrie with an ankle injury which, for a time, threatened his career. Thereafter Les Sealey was signed and, more crushingly still, Peter Schmeichel arrived in 1991.

But the England under-21 international soldiered on and, after excelling as a stand-in during spring 1994, he signed a new contract. But Alex Ferguson allowed that such a brave, agile and still-youthful performer deserved better than reserve status and in August 1995 the United boss accepted a £250,000 bid from Bryan Robson to take Gary to Middlesbrough. Later he helped Bradford City reach the top flight.

LIAM O'BRIEN ▼

1986/87–1988/89

36 GAMES **2** GOALS

BORN • Dublin, 5.9.64.
HONOURS • 16 Republic of Ireland caps (87–96).
OTHER CLUBS • Shamrock Rovers, Republic of Ireland;
Newcastle United 88/9–93/4 (151, 19);
Tranmere Rovers 93/4–98/9 (181, 11).

Liam O'Brien never looked short of skill during his short sojourn at Old Trafford. Sadly, he appeared rather less well endowed with confidence. The Eire international midfielder might have benefited from a settled run in the side but, unless outstanding performances are instantly forthcoming, that is an almost extinct luxury for rookies in top-level football.

So Liam never started more than three consecutive games and left for Newcastle, price £275,000, in November 1988. How big a potential asset was allowed to slip away? Well, the tall Irishman has been described as the right-footed Muhren; rather flattering, undoubtedly, but there were games when his passes conjured up visions of the creative Dutchman.

Liam was a composed footballer who was blessed with explosive, if under-used, shooting power, but one who appeared occasionally to lack urgency. He was criticised for being one-paced but could produce a turn of speed, as he showed in one of his latter appearances for United when he came on as substitute against Everton and almost turned the game. Come the middle and late 1990s, he was shining with Tranmere Rovers, proving that he could hold his own away from the intense pressures of the big time. Talent was never the problem for Liam, only self-belief.

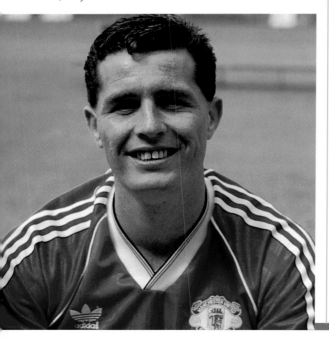

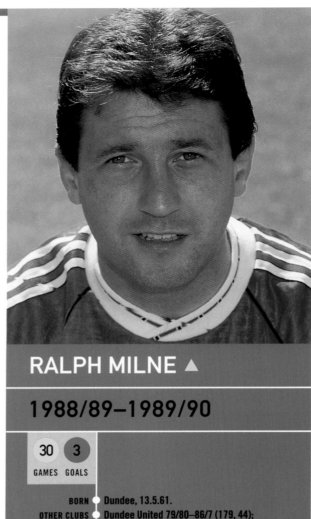

RALPH MILNE ▲

1988/89–1989/90

30 GAMES **3** GOALS

BORN • Dundee, 13.5.61.
OTHER CLUBS • Dundee United 79/80–86/7 (179, 44);
Charlton Athletic 86/7–87/8 (22, 0);
Bristol City 87/8–88/9 (30, 6).

Ralph Milne could hardly have made a more striking contrast with the man he replaced on Manchester United's left wing. Where Jesper Olsen cut a dashing figure, Ralph was an inelegant, rather hunched mover, with a suggestion of flat feet; where the Dane possessed extravagant talent which he often failed to harness, his Scottish successor was more modestly gifted yet, arguably, a better team man; where Jesper was tricky and unpredictable, Ralph was orthodox and direct; even in appearance the blond, tousle-haired one-time Ajax star and the neat, dark former under-21 international were worlds apart.

Was Ralph a surprise buy? Certainly he was to most United supporters, weaned on a diet of expensive stars. For a start, and most refreshingly, he arrived without the now customary transfer saga, his £170,000 move from Bristol City in November 1988 being presented to fans as a fait accompli.

Ralph was pitched straight into the team and mixed encouraging displays, notably against Oxford in the FA Cup, with nondescript ones. Occasionally he was incisive, more often he lurked on the edges of the action. Added consistency was vital to his Old Trafford future, but he never found it and was freed in June 1991.

Jim Leighton could be excused for cursing the day he joined Manchester United. He arrived with a reputation as one of the world's leading goal-keepers after a decade of success under Alex Ferguson at Aberdeen, and was seen as a key figure in the rebirth of the Red Devils as a major power; he left consumed with bitterness, his football world in tatters, after undergoing a public humiliation of excruciating proportions.

The sensitive Scot's ordeal unfolded during and after United's 3–3 FA Cup Final draw with Crystal Palace in May 1990, though the nightmare scenario had been building steadily for months. Jim had appeared to lose his confidence, together with several teeth, at Wimbledon in December and since then had performed so far below his best that some United fans were turning on him.

The manager deliberated long and hard before picking him for Wembley, only to suffer the mortification of watching the grey-faced custodian sink to his lowest ebb. Jim was blamed, to a lesser or greater degree, for all three Palace goals, as he failed to deal with two high balls and was beaten surprisingly by a low shot.

Ferguson was left with an agonising selection problem for the replay, a dilemma made all the harder by the two men's close previous relationship at Pittodrie. In the end, Alex made the right decision for United: poor Jim was axed in favour of Les Sealey and the Cup went to Old Trafford.

Inevitably in such traumatic circumstances, the rangy Leighton was finished as a Red. After loan spells understudying David Seaman at Arsenal and a more active stint at Reading, he joined Dundee for £150,000 in February 1992.

Ironically, the man who had cost five times that figure in May 1988 was, and remained into the next century, a good goalkeeper. Indeed, he had started splendidly at United, impressing hugely as a shot-stopper before aerial fallibility found him out.

Some swear to this day that he was merely the victim of a temporary loss of self-belief, a theory borne out by his international recall in 1994 at the age of 36. Others, it must be said, still shake their heads. But either way, after all he had endured, unlucky Jim deserved to bask in a little belated glory.

JIM LEIGHTON

1988/89–1990/91

94 GAMES   **0** GOALS

BORN ● Paisley, Renfrewshire, 24.7.58.
HONOURS ● 91 Scotland caps (82–98).
OTHER CLUBS ● Aberdeen 78/9–87/8 (300, 0); Reading on loan 91/2 (8, 0); Dundee 91/2–92/3 (21, 0); Hibernian 93/4–96/7 (151, 0); Aberdeen 97/8–(82, 0).

DANNY WALLACE

1989/90–1992/93

70 GAMES   **11** GOALS

BORN   London, 21.1.64.
HONOURS   FA Cup 89/90. European Cup Winners' Cup (non-playing sub) 90/1. 1 England cap (86).
OTHER CLUBS   Southampton 80/1–89/90 (255, 64); Millwall on loan 92/3 (3, 0); Birmingham City 93/4–94/5 (16, 2);Wycombe Wanderers 94/5 (1, 0).

When Danny Wallace faced Manchester United in a Southampton shirt, invariably he was a study in effervescence, all livewire enterprise and lethal intent, the sort of performer coveted by managers and fans alike. But transposed from Saint to Red Devil, all too often the chunky flankman appeared to be consumed by inhibitions, a sad little rubber ball that had lost its bounce.

So what went wrong for the cheerful Londoner after Alex Ferguson parted with £1.1 million to sign him in September 1989? One theory is that the high-pressure Old Trafford scene was too much for him, that he was better off as a major fish in a comparatively minor pond; another is that he was undermined by a series of niggling injuries.

But the most compelling explanation, perhaps, is that Danny was simply unsuited to the role demanded of him by United's style. At the Dell he had made his impact, even won an England cap, more as a left-sided striker than as an out-and-out winger. At Old Trafford, he was usually employed to bring width to the attack by hugging the touchline, a tough task for a raider whose natural game was to cut inside at every opportunity. Occasionally Danny was used as a central striker but that proved too much to ask of such a tiny man – as Tommy Docherty had it, he had to jump for low balls! – and his contribution was minimal.

In fact, the Wallace sojourn had begun promisingly enough, with a League Cup goal at Portsmouth on his debut, and in the spring of 1990 there were isolated moments of electric excitement, notably a brilliant FA Cup goal at Newcastle when he sidestepped his marker sublimely before crashing the ball home from a narrow angle.

He helped to lift the Cup that term before his 1990/91 campaign was ruined by fitness problems, though he did return from one lay-off looking sleeker and sharper than ever, and shone in the 6–2 League Cup humbling of Arsenal at Highbury.

In general, though, he seemed devoid of confidence, especially when delivering crosses, and gradually he was overhauled by the young brigade of Giggs and company. In October 1993, Danny joined Birmingham City for £250,000, leaving a tale of sad under-achievement behind him.

Clayton Blackmore was both a survivor and something of a curiosity during an enigmatic Old Trafford career. Without ever being a long-term regular – only in 1990/91 could he count on his place – the personable Welshman enjoyed nearly 250 outings and watched a procession of more illustrious names come and go during a ten-year span in the top-level reckoning.

Some said his ability to switch between midfield and full-back prevented him from settling in either role and therefore limited his appearances, while others saw that very versatility as the principal key to his long service.

There was a time, during United's disappointing 1988/89 campaign, when it seemed possible that Clayton might develop into the play-maker the side was so manifestly lacking. At his best – there was one masterful display against Sheffield Wednesday at Hillsborough – he showed poise and precision, spraying passes with confidence and vision.

But the feeling persisted that, while his distribution could be immaculate, he needed a tad too much time on the ball to make it tell consistently.

Clayton's in-and-out existence continued until August 1990, when squad circumstances afforded a new opportunity at left-back. Though right-footed, he took it magnificently, proving safe in defence and exhilaratingly effective as a launcher of attacks, crossing the ball with an accuracy unmatched by many a winger.

More compelling still was the Blackmore expertise from dead-ball situations, his explosive shooting bringing eight goals in his 56 matches, none more vital than the 30-yarder that squirmed through the Montpellier 'keeper's hands to set the Reds on their way to a place in the Cup Winners' Cup semi-final. His most crucial contribution to the European triumph, though, came near the end of the final when, as Barcelona pressed for an equaliser, he cleared Michael Laudrup's goal-bound shot off the line.

Thereafter, the Welshman's fortunes faltered. Paul Parker arrived, Denis Irwin switched to the left and Clayton was back in the shadows, squeezing out just enough appearances for a title statuette in 1992/93. A succession of injuries laid him low throughout 1993/94, after which he was freed to accept a much-needed new challenge under old chum Bryan Robson at Middlesbrough.

CLAYTON BLACKMORE

1983/84–1992/93

243 **25**
GAMES GOALS

BORN Neath, Glamorgan, 23.9.64.
HONOURS European Cup Winners' Cup 90/1. League Championship 92/3. FA Cup 89/90. 39 Wales caps (85–).
OTHER CLUBS Middlesbrough 94/5–97/8 (53,4); Bristol City on loan 96/7 (5,1); Barnsley 98/9 (7,0); Notts County 99/00– (21, 2).

GIULIANO MAIORANA ▼

1988/89–1989/90

8	0
GAMES	GOALS

BORN ● Cambridge, 18.4.69.

The football world of Giuliano Maiorana turned upside down in 1988/89, and in doing so fuelled the dreams of enthusiastic amateurs everywhere. The tall left-winger started the campaign working in his family's clothes shop and enjoying his game with Cambridgeshire part-timers Histon United; he finished it in the first-team squad at Old Trafford, with every chance of building on his fairytale foundation. There followed a season in the reserves, learning his trade, but then the script went agonisingly awry as, for no less than four years, Jools was afflicted by serious knee problems.

Events had moved swiftly after United had plucked the dashing teenager from under the noses of other interested clubs. After two brief senior appearances as substitute, he made his full debut against League leaders Arsenal and caused highly-rated full-back Lee Dixon enough problems to suggest that a top-flight future was not out of the question. Maiorana liked to run at defenders, and though he was fearfully raw, there was something in his style that encouraged the club to bear with him. However, with the wealth of brilliant flankmen at Old Trafford in 1994, United allowed Jools to leave on a free transfer. Thus a £30,000 flutter on an unknown flyer had proved unproductive, but it had been worth a try.

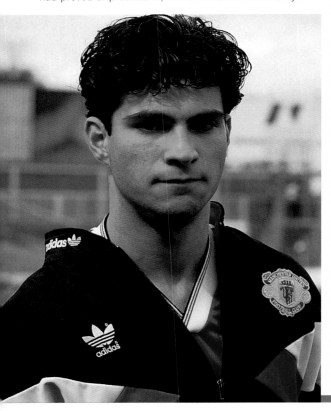

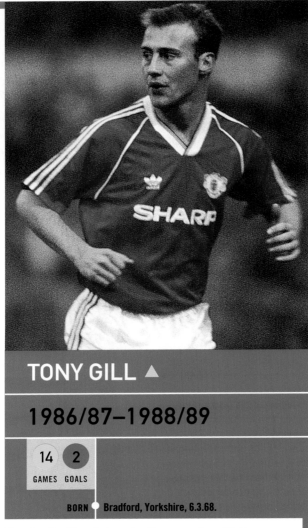

TONY GILL ▲

1986/87–1988/89

14	2
GAMES	GOALS

BORN ● Bradford, Yorkshire, 6.3.68.

The footballing fates dealt savagely with Tony Gill, an exuberantly confident utility player who had every chance of fashioning a long-term future at Old Trafford until his career was sabotaged by injuries.

He made his senior debut as an 18-year-old stand-in for Bryan Robson at Southampton in January 1987 and then suffered his first reverse. Achilles tendon trouble was diagnosed and it took two operations, and nearly two years, before he returned to contention. Indeed, some observers thought that, in the way of so many promising youngsters, Tony's flame had flickered briefly before being extinguished. But then, with United gripped by an injury crisis in November 1988, he returned to fill in at full-back and in midfield, making an excellent impression.

His second arrival saw him labelled as one of Fergie's Fledglings, a ludicrous and inappropriate reference to the Busby Babes. But, unmoved by the hype, Tony established himself in the squad and made some sterling contributions, including a sweet, half-volleyed equaliser in an FA Cup replay against QPR. Then came disaster: the young Yorkshireman broke an ankle that spring and never played again at senior level.

Typically, though, he didn't despair and made a fresh start as youth coach with Bristol Rovers.

Russell Beardsmore took the surest path into the hearts of Manchester United supporters – he put one over on Liverpool. Well, three actually.

He could hardly have chosen more glorious circumstances in which to prove his mettle: United had just gone a goal down to the old enemy in front of nearly 50,000 fans and a TV audience of millions. It was time for the crewcut kid with the scrawny frame of a pipecleaner and the air of a chirpy waif to take centre stage.

First he charmed his way past three men to make a spectacular equaliser for Brian McClair, next he helped set up a goal for Mark Hughes and then, joy of joys, he volleyed the third with all the panache Old Trafford demands of its heroes.

Did this heady extravaganza on New Year's Day 1989 herald the birth of a star? Poignantly, the answer is no. Russell, a stand-in full-back before moving to a wide midfield position in an injury crisis, had abundant skill, engaging eagerness and an instinct for taking up dangerous positions. And, more than any young Red for decades, he had the crowd on his side. Perhaps satiated with costly imports, the fans warmed to the 5ft 6in local lad; indeed, when he wasn't playing, they chanted for the England under-21 international's introduction.

But in the seasons that followed, Russell failed to impose himself with any degree of consistency. The ability was always evident, but his frail body was in chronic need of more beef; quite simply, he never seemed strong enough for the physical demands of top-flight football.

The arrival of costly new players and the rapid development of other youngsters brought more competition than he could handle, and he had faded to the periphery of the squad by the time a loan stint with Blackburn offered a fresh opportunity in December 1991.

Nothing came of that, though, and Russell was freed to join Bournemouth in the summer of 1993. For half a decade and more, he thrived at Dean Court, but when chronic back trouble ended the Beardsmore career in 1999, that glorious New Year's Day seemed a long, long time ago.

RUSSELL BEARDSMORE

1988/89–1991/92

 73 **4**

GAMES GOALS

BORN ● Wigan, Lancashire, 28.9.68.
OTHER CLUBS ● Blackburn Rovers on loan 91/2 (2, 0); Bournemouth 93/4–97/8 (178, 4).

LEE MARTIN

1987/88–1993/94

108 **2**
GAMES GOALS

BORN	Hyde, Cheshire, 5.2.68.
HONOURS	FA Cup 89/90.
OTHER CLUBS	Celtic 93/4–94/5 (19, 0); Bristol Rovers 96/7–97/8 (25, 0); Huddersfield Town on loan 97/8 (3, 0).

Plenty of shrewd judges reckoned Lee Martin was United's player of the year in 1989/90, and not just because the rookie full-back scored the goal that took the FA Cup to Old Trafford. He seemed to have arrived as a long-term fixture in the team and his subsequent reversal of fortune, culminating in departure to Celtic, represented a sorry anti-climax.

Locally-born Lee had broken into the senior reckoning during trying times for a United side toiling through a period of transition. Watching him perform with maturity and composure at home to Queen's Park Rangers in August 1988, it was hard to believe he was making his full debut. Clearly, here was a beacon of hope for the future.

That autumn Lee suffered an injury setback, but he was on hand to play a prominent role in revitalising the Reds' flagging fortunes at the turn of the year. The continued absence of Viv Anderson gave him the chance of a lengthy run in the team and he responded with a string of resourceful displays. By May 1990, the Martin outlook was bright indeed; England under-21 honours had been won and Ferguson was not alone in believing the youngster had prospects at full international level.

That golden moment in the Wembley replay against Crystal Palace, when Lee galloped forward to meet Neil Webb's beautiful pass and lash the ball high into Nigel Martyn's net, should have provided inspiring extra impetus. But just as he was set to consolidate, Lee suffered a back injury and managed only a few appearances during 1990/91. When he regained fitness, even his ability to play on either defensive flank was not enough to regain lost ground, with newly arrived Denis Irwin bedding in on the right and Clayton Blackmore in prime form at number three.

Suddenly, Lee was on the margins, no fitting place for a natural full-back whose all-round efficiency needed, perhaps, only a smidgin more aggression to propel him towards the highest class. It was scant consolation that he became skipper of the reserves, in which he remained until Lou Macari paid £250,000 to rescue him in January 1994. Sadly, he was no luckier at Parkhead than he was at Old Trafford, breaking his leg in a freak accident against Falkirk. On recovery, he headed west to seek better fortune with Bristol Rovers, only for back problems to end his League career.

Alex Ferguson dubbed Mark Robins the best finisher at Old Trafford – and then he sold him. Here was an apparent contradiction between word and deed, yet both the manager's initial statement and his subsequent course of action made sense.

Certainly, when confronted with a clear goal-scoring opportunity, the predatory little Lancastrian was likely to make the most of it with a straightforward economy missing in the work of, say, Mark Hughes. Not for Robins the dramatic flourish, the breathtaking athleticism; instead, a simple, brisk efficiency that was considerably more reliable.

Yet, the act of scoring aside, there was simply no comparison between the overall contribution of the two Marks. While the younger man was skilful enough, he offered little outside the box; in contrast, the Welshman exerted huge presence in all attacking areas, being especially adept at holding the ball, a knack crucial to United's style.

Not that Alex had wanted to get rid of the popular 'Mark II'. Even after the prolific 22-year-old had made it plain he was not happy to operate as a perpetual substitute – though that was his most effective niche – his boss asked him to change his mind. But, wisely perhaps, the player decided that he was likely to remain dispensable as a Red and accepted an £800,000 move to Norwich City in August 1992.

Mark had tasted senior action for the first time in 1988/89, but was goalless until the following term. Then, though granted only 13 full outings, he scored ten times, including a precisely nodded winner at Nottingham Forest in the FA Cup, a strike which, rightly or wrongly, has entered Old Trafford folklore as the goal that saved the hard-pressed Ferguson's job. Mark went on to net the semi-final replay winner against Oldham, a deliciously cool piece of work that summed up his value.

Come the autumn he ousted Hughes on merit and did well, but at the first lapse in form he was out, destined never to be first choice again. There might have been a chance in 1992, when a goal drought cost United the title, but he was unfit and the moment was gone. So when the Canaries came calling, Mark Robins flew the United coop, making a fine start at Carrow Road before more injuries interrupted his progress. A subsequent move to Leicester brought further frustration, tempered by a League Cup winner's medal in 1997.

MARK ROBINS
1988/89–1991/92

 69 **17**
GAMES GOALS

BORN Ashton-under-Lyne, Lancashire, 22.12.69.
HONOURS European Cup Winners' Cup 90/1 (non-playing sub). FA Cup 89/90.
OTHER CLUBS Norwich City 92/3–94/5 (67, 20); Leicester City 94/5–96/7 (56, 12); FC Copenhagen, Denmark, on loan 96/7; Reading on loan 97/8 (4, 0); Orense, Spain, 97/8; Panionios, Greece, 98/9; Manchester City on loan 98/9 (2, 0); Walsall 99/00– (38, 6).

DEREK BRAZIL
1988/89–1989/90

DEFENDER

2 GAMES   **0** GOALS

BORN:
Dublin, 14.12.68.

OTHER CLUBS:
Oldham Athletic on loan 90/1 (1, 0); Swansea City on loan 91/2 (12, 1); Cardiff City 92/3–95/6 (115, 1).

GARTH CROOKS
1983/84

On loan from Tottenham Hotspur

FORWARD

7 GAMES   **2** GOALS

BORN:
Stoke, Staffordshire, 10.3.58.

OTHER CLUBS:
Stoke City 75/6–79/80 (147, 48); Tottenham Hotspur 80/1–84/5 (125, 48); West Bromwich Albion 85/6–86/7 (40, 16); Charlton Athletic 86/7–90/1(56, 15).

LAURIE CUNNINGHAM
1982/83

WINGER

5 GAMES   **1** GOALS

BORN:
Holloway, London, 8.3.56.

HONOURS:
6 England caps (79–80).

OTHER CLUBS:
Orient 74/5–76/7 (75, 15); West Bromwich Albion 76/7–78/9 (86, 21); Real Madrid, Spain; Marseille, France; Leicester City 85/6 (15, 0); Charleroi, Belgium;Wimbledon 87/8 (6, 2).

DIED: 15.7.89.

MARK DEMPSEY
1983/84–1985/86

MIDFIELDER

2 GAMES   **0** GOALS

BORN:
Manchester, 14.1.64.

OTHER CLUBS:
Swindon Town on loan 84/5 (5, 0); Sheffield United 86/7–87/8 (63, 8); Chesterfield on loan 88/9 (3, 0); Rotherham United 88/9–90/1 (75, 7).

DEINIOL GRAHAM
1987/88–1988/99

FORWARD

3 GAMES   **1** GOALS

BORN:
Cannock, Staffordshire, 4.10.69.

OTHER CLUBS:
Barnsley 91/2–93/4 (38, 2); Preston North End on loan 92/3 (8, 0); Carlisle United on loan 93/4 (2, 1); Stockport County 94/5 (11, 2); Scunthorpe United 95/6 (3, 1).

MARK HIGGINS
1985/86

CENTRE - HALF

8 GAMES   **0** GOALS

BORN:
Buxton, Derbyshire, 29.9.58.

OTHER CLUBS:
Everton 76/7–83/4 (152, 6); Bury 86/7–87/8 (68, 0); Stoke City 88/9–89/90 (39,1).

STEVE PEARS

1984/85

GOALKEEPER

 5 **0**
GAMES GOALS

BORN:
Brandon, County Durham,
22.1.62.

OTHER CLUBS:
Middlesbrough on loan 83/4 (12, 0); Middlesbrough
85/6–94/5 (327, 0); Hartlepool United 96/97 (16, 0).

JEFF WEALANDS

1982/83–1983/84

GOALKEEPER

8 **0**
GAMES GOALS

BORN:
Darlington, County Durham
26.8.51.

OTHER CLUBS:
Darlington 71/2 (28, 0); Hull City 71/2–78/9 (240, 0);
Birmingham City 79/80–81/2 (102, 0); Oldham Athletic on
loan 84/5 (10, 0); Preston North End on loan 84/5 (4, 0).

NEIL WHITWORTH

1990/91

DEFENDER

1 **0**
GAMES GOALS

BORN:
Stoke, Staffordshire,
10.3.58.

OTHER CLUBS:
Wigan Athletic 89/90 (2, 0); Preston North End on loan
91/2 (6, 0); Barnsley on loan 91/2 (11, 0); Rotherham
United on loan 93/4 (8, 1); Blackpool on loan 93/4 (3, 0);
Kilmarnock 94/5 -97/8 (76, 3); Wigan Athletic 97/8 (4, 0);
Hull City 98/9–99/00 (19, 2).

IAN WILKINSON

1991/92

GOALKEEPER

1 **0**
GAMES GOALS

BORN:
Warrington, Lancashire, 2.7.73.

OTHER CLUBS:
Crewe Alexandra 93/4 (3, 0).

DAVID WILSON

1988/89

MIDFIELDER

6 **0**
GAMES GOALS

BORN:
Burnley, Lancashire, 20.3.69.

OTHER CLUBS:
Lincoln City on loan 90/1 (3, 0); Charlton Athletic on loan
90/1 (7, 2); Bristol Rovers 91/2–92/3 (11, 0).

NICKY WOOD

1987/88–1988/99

FORWARD

4 **0**
GAMES GOALS

BORN:
Oldham, Lancashire, 6.1.66

PAUL WRATTEN

1990/91

MIDFIELDER

2 **0**
GAMES GOALS

BORN:
Middlesbrough,Yorkshire, 29.11.70.

OTHER CLUBS:
Hartlepool United 92/3–93/4 (57, 1).

MAL DONAGHY

1988/89–1991/92

118	0
GAMES	GOALS

BORN — Belfast, 13.9.57.
HONOURS — 89 Northern Ireland caps (80–94).
OTHER CLUBS — Luton Town 78/9–88/9 (410, 16); Luton Town on loan 89/90 (5, 0); Chelsea 92/3–93/4 (68, 3).

Some players catch the eye, their every move on – and sometimes off – the pitch provoking reaction from supporters and media alike. Others can spend a match, a season or even a career, playing a vital role unobtrusively yet with consummate efficiency. Mal Donaghy is a perfect example of the latter category.

He joined United, the team he idolised as a boy, after ten years at Luton during which he barely missed a match. His consistency, usually at full-back or in the centre of defence but occasionally in midfield, was a byword and, with every respect to Luton, it's a wonder that a big club had not lured him away from Kenilworth Road much earlier.

When Alex Ferguson, beset by injuries, needed an all-purpose defender of proven ability, Mal was the natural choice. The manager was criticised in some quarters for shelling out £650,000 for a 31-year-old but he knew that the Northern Ireland international was fitter than many a younger man and could point to a remarkably injury-free decade.

So, in the autumn of 1988, Mal realised his childhood ambition to become a Red Devil. He lined up alongside Steve Bruce and became an unflappable bastion of the side for the remainder of that campaign, showing subtle positional sense and a sure touch on the ball. His presence helped to stabilise a season that was going downhill fast and to create a platform for the youth-inspired New Year revival.

Hamstring injuries plagued Mal for much of the following term, and when he was loaned back to Luton in midwinter it seemed that his taste of the high life was to be brief. But Ferguson knew what a gem of a standby the quiet Ulsterman was, and in 1990/91 Mal excelled when Bruce was sidelined. His calm reliability alongside Gary Pallister was particularly evident at home to Montpellier in the Cup Winners' Cup and in the second leg of the League Cup semi-final at Leeds.

In August 1992, a month before his 35th birthday, he joined Chelsea for £150,000, having given invaluable service to the club closest to his heart. When Mal Donaghy was in the team he played well, when he was out he didn't complain; no manager could have asked for more.

There was no trace of stardust about Mike Phelan. No hush of expectation descended on Old Trafford when he received the ball, eager interviewers didn't hang on his every word, the United souvenir shop was not festooned with posters of the down-to-earth Lancastrian. But every top club needs men like him, and if that sounds like a patronising reference to a performer who tends to be placed all too glibly in the 'bits-and-pieces' category, then this writer apologises unreservedly.

True, he was adaptable and fulfilled the popular image of the honest journeyman, labouring ceaselessly but unspectacularly, filling in ably wherever he was needed in midfield or defence. But it should not be forgotten that after his £750,000 transfer from Norwich in July 1989 – the first of Alex Ferguson's five major deals that summer and autumn – Mike completed a full set of domestic medals, adding a European Cup Winners' Cup gong for good measure. No mean achievement, no mean player.

Indeed, during his first season at Old Trafford he was United's only ever-present in the League, then missed a mere handful of outings the next term before injury curtailed his contribution in 1991/92. After that the competition for places hotted up, but still he made enough appearances to deserve his title statuette come the spring of 1993.

At first, the presence of Bryan Robson and the rest had forced the right-sided Mike into a role on the left flank of midfield in which he looked out of place, and it was only later, when injuries to others allowed him to move into the centre, that his all-round competence was seen to full advantage.

At various junctures the former Canaries captain – he succeeded Steve Bruce in that job – also excelled at right-back and alongside the centre-half, a position which some authorities reckoned to be his best. He was an expert man-marker, too, as he proved to Roy Keane's chagrin in the 1992 League Cup Final triumph over Nottingham Forest.

Though Mike was approaching 33 by the summer of 1994, most clubs might have found continued use for his fitness, experience and general nous, but such was the pressure from a new generation of young Red Devils that he was granted a free transfer.

Thereafter he served West Bromwich Albion before an interlude as Stockport's assistant manager was followed by a welcome return to Old Trafford as a coach.

MIKE PHELAN

1989/90–1993/94

145 **3**

GAMES GOALS

BORN ● Nelson, Lancashire 24.9.62.
HONOURS ● European Cup Winners' Cup 90/1. League Championship 92/3. FA Cup 89/90. League Cup 91/2. 1 England cap (89).
OTHER CLUBS ● Burnley 80/1–84/5 (168, 9); Norwich City 85/6–88/9 (156, 9); West Bromwich Albion 94/5–95/6 (21, 0).

A dynamo in defence, attack and all points between, he became a motivator supreme.

1981/82–1993/94

459 GAMES **97** GOALS

BORN ● Chester-le-Street, County Durham, 11.1.57.
HONOURS ● European Cup Winners' Cup 90/1. League
Championship 92/3, 93/4. FA Cup 82/3, 84/5,
89/90. 90 England caps (80–91).
OTHER CLUBS ● West Bromwich Albion 74/5–81/2 (198, 39);
Middlesbrough 94/5–96/7 (25, 1).
MANAGER: Middlesbrough (94–).

When Steve Bruce placed the crown-shaped lid of the Premiership trophy on the head of Bryan Robson at the climax of one of Old Trafford's most unforgettable nights, nothing could have been more appropriate. It was May 1993, the long League wait was over and the player who had striven most ceaselessly to end it was honoured in a manner befitting his regal contribution. That term his outings had been strictly rationed, but his great fighting heart was as inspirational as ever in lifting his team with counsel both sage and stirring. And when he did take the field, there was not the slightest doubt that, even though mobility had declined in his 37th year, the appetite for the fray was as sharp as ever. Once or twice, it's true, the frustration at enforced inactivity boiled over into excessive vigour, but there was no condemnation from the game at large. In the context of such magnificent defiance in the face of anno domini, it seemed that the odd aberration from a favourite son could be excused.

Bryan Robson

'Robbo' had always been a lion-like competitor, as evidenced by the countless minutely documented incidents which bejewelled his glorious career. Yet 20 seconds of hectic action in a long-forgotten 1982 encounter with Notts County summed up his qualities as forcefully as any of them. The Reds' skipper scrapped for possession on the edge of his own box, won it, bamboozled two opponents with an immaculate turn and gave the ball to Moses. Then he sprinted for County's goal as the move continued through Duxbury and Muhren and arrived in time to nod the Dutchman's cross inside the far post from eight yards. It was a typically dashing contribution by 'Captain Marvel', who had arrived at Old Trafford for a record £1.5 million fee in October 1981.

Though Bryan, already an England midfielder, was clearly an outstanding player, there were rumbles at the time that the price was exorbitant and Ron Atkinson's judgement in handing so much cash to his former club was called into question. But Ron, who had been advised by Bill Shankly, no less, to pay whatever it took to get Robson, had no doubts. As he said at the time: 'Now we have someone who can take a game by the scruff of the neck and make things happen.'

And so he did. After a solid, unflashy start, Bryan Robson became an ever more dominant force. Soon he took over the captaincy, both of club and country, from Ray Wilkins and proceeded to lead by example. A dynamo in defence, attack and all points between, he became a motivator supreme. At its peak, Bryan's game had no discernible weakness. His tackling, passing, shooting and heading were all exemplary; power and pace he possessed in abundance; and his reading of the game was mature, even looking back to his early days at the Hawthorns.

But Bryan was cursed with one bane – injury. With West Brom he broke a leg three times in 12 months; after moving north he missed scores of games, often at crucial times for United and England. Some blamed him for being too brave – it's a testimony to his stature that critics turned what would have been a virtue in anyone else into a supposed blemish in Bryan's case – but this was patently absurd. To have asked him to hold back, even slightly, would have been to deny his nature and therefore nullify what was special about him.

After playing a comparatively minor, but still telling, part in winning a second successive Championship, Bryan left to manage Middlesbrough. Now United faced a playing future without a man in whose absence they had shrivelled so often, a man who hefted the FA Cup a record three times, a man apart. Meanwhile 'Boro looked to 'Robbo' to prove once again that he is, as Ron Atkinson put it more than once, pure gold.

Webb ruptured an achilles tendon while playing for England. He was never the same again.

1989/90–1992/93

109 **11**
GAMES GOALS

BORN ● Reading, Berkshire, 30.7.63.
HONOURS ● European Cup Winners' Cup 90/1 (non-playing sub). FA Cup 89/90. League Cup 91/2 (non-playing sub). 26 England caps (87–90).
OTHER CLUBS ● Reading 79/80–81/2 (72, 22); Portsmouth 82/3–84/5 (123, 34); Nottingham Forest 85/6–88/9 (146, 47) and 92/3–93/4 (30, 3); Swindon Town on loan 94/5 (6, 0); Grimsby Town 96/7 (4, 0).

It was a day of bravado at Old Trafford, a day of flattering to deceive. First Michael Knighton, who purported to be on the verge of buying the club, did party tricks with a football in front of the Stretford End; then Neil Webb, the new midfield general, played beautifully and scored a spectacular goal in an uplifting 4–1 victory over reigning Champions Arsenal. It was the perfect start to the 1989/90 campaign; the sun shone on a shirtsleeved crowd and everyone went home happy, fantasising about the Reds' latest new dawn, indulging in careless talk about the title.

Neil Webb

The idyll didn't last: Knighton withdrew his offer, the team slumped towards the wrong end of the table and, after only four League outings, poor Neil Webb ruptured an achilles tendon while playing for England. He was never the same again.

The mild-mannered schemer had arrived from Nottingham Forest in the close season, two years after United's initial bid had been rejected by Brian Clough. Now the player was out of contract and the £1.5 million fee was determined by a transfer tribunal.

Neil's attraction was as a creator who could also score goals. Alex Ferguson wanted his vision and range of passing, his composure and control, and never mind an awkward, rather languid style that gave rise to accusations of lack of urgency. With Bryan Robson and the soon-to-be-signed Paul Ince supplying the physical edge, the manager felt the balance would be right. The humbling of Arsenal boded well, but then came a chronic blow to Ferguson's plans, the accident in Sweden that sidelined the right-sided play-maker for seven months.

On his return in March, Neil was bulkier and slower than before but able still to exert a telling influence on a lacklustre side. He helped them stave off relegation and made a compelling contribution to their FA Cup triumph, most memorably in the final replay against Crystal Palace when his raking 50-yard crossfield pass set up Lee Martin's winner.

Yet over the next two seasons, Neil was an enigma. Sometimes he sprayed the ball around delightfully, but too often his presence was anonymous, as though he were consumed with self-doubt, his distribution lacking the degree of penetration his natural ability promised.

In 1990/91 he struggled manfully to improve his all-round fitness and was devastated when omitted from the Cup Winners' Cup Final starting line-up. The autumn of 1991 saw him apparently brighter and hungrier than ever before, and he did so well as United led the title race that he was recalled to the international scene, captaining England 'B' in December.

But then it all went wrong. In March he was involved in a spat with Ferguson over his non-release for an England friendly, and he was dropped; indeed, some even blamed the Reds' subsequent failure to win the League on that decision. Whatever, from that point Neil's days at Old Trafford were numbered and in November 1992 he returned to Forest for £800,000. Whether he had been 'too nice' to meet United's exacting expectations, or had been treated unsympathetically, or been plain unlucky, was all a matter for conjecture.

In hindsight, Celtic's original evaluation of McClair no longer seemed quite so extraordinary.

1987/88–1997/98

468 GAMES **126** GOALS

BORN	Airdrie, Lanarkshire, 8.12.63.
HONOURS	European Cup Winners' Cup 90/1.
	League Championship 92/3, 93/4, 95/6, 96/7.
	FA Cup 89/90, 93/4. League Cup 91/2.
	30 Scotland caps (86–93).
OTHER CLUBS	Motherwell 81/2–82/3 (39, 15); Celtic 83/4–86/7
	(145, 99); Motherwell 98/9 (11,0)

From the Red Devils' most prolific goal-scoring hero in 20 years, to selfless midfield workhorse, to faithful retainer on the fringe of the first team and the reserves' eminence grise: Brian McClair ran a gamut of decreasingly glamorous roles during the Alex Ferguson years. Yet there was never a murmur of public discontent from the versatile, ever-willing Scottish international, whose influential role in the renaissance of Manchester United should never be underrated.

Brian McClair

When Brian walked into the strikers' graveyard of Old Trafford, it became clear immediately that he was not destined to be the latest in a long line of expensive stiffs. Early goals, combined with a fatalistic attitude to missed chances, furnished clues to the calibre of the man for whom Celtic had demanded £2 million before settling for £850,000 after arbitration in July 1987.

Yet on the face of it the ordeal facing the stocky marksman, who had netted 41 times and been voted Scotland's player of the year in his final campaign north of the border, was more daunting than for most United newcomers. Firstly, he had to acclimatise himself to the more rigorous demands of the English game; secondly, he was saddled with the unwelcome burden of possibly becoming the first Red since George Best in the 1960s to score 20 League goals in a season. The pressure from media and fans was intense, and Alex Ferguson added his two penn'orth by declaring that Brian was just the man to lay the ghost. The intelligent, level-headed 'Choccy' didn't flinch: he merely got on with the job and duly notched his 20 goals. Well, 24 in fact, not to mention another seven in the major cup competitions.

The following term he started slowly as he strove to build a partnership with returned favourite Mark Hughes. Gradually, as an understanding showed signs of blossoming, Brian began to find the net with some regularity again, never more rousingly than with a slickly executed scissor-kick at home to Liverpool on New Year's Day. Then came a late-season lull, during which his talents were deployed occasionally in midfield, thus signalling a new phase in his career. The next three campaigns saw him giving his all, sometimes up front, at others lying deep, before settling in the engine room during 1992/93.

Brian began that term motoring up and down the right flank, later occupying a central berth as the arrival of Eric Cantona prompted a reshuffle. Some reckoned he possessed insufficient weight of tackle for his new position, but none questioned his stamina or commitment, and his nine goals were of huge significance in the final Championship analysis.

He had been Ferguson's first major signing, so it was fitting that the man whose 100th senior goal for the club settled the 1992 League Cup Final against Nottingham Forest should be instrumental in the overdue title triumph. But a cruel setback awaited: Roy Keane arrived that summer and the 29-year-old Scot found himself reduced to stand-in status.

However, the manager predicted Robsonesque longevity for his ultra-fit countryman and demonstrated good faith by offering a new contract. 'Choccy' accepted and buckled down to continue his trusty part in United's never-ending trophy quest. He was still trucking in 1997/98, after which he was freed to complete his playing days at Motherwell before moving to Blackburn to assist his chum, Brian Kidd. With the benefit of hindsight, Celtic's original valuation of Brian McClair no longer seemed quite so extraordinary.

The most important of Steve Bruce's footballing attributes was the unquenchable spirit of the man.

1987/88–1995/96

410 **51**
GAMES GOALS

BORN — Hexham, Northumberland, 31.12.60.
HONOURS — European Cup Winners' Cup 90/1. League Championship 92/3, 93/4, 95/6. FA Cup 89/90, 93/4. League Cup 91/2.
OTHER CLUBS — Gillingham 79/80–83/4 (205, 29); Norwich City 84/5–87/8 (141, 14); Birmingham City 96/7–97/8 (72, 2); Sheffield United 98/9 (10, 0). MANAGER: Sheffield United (98-99); Huddersfield Town (99–).

You're in the trenches, up to your neck in muck and bullets and the enemy is closing in. Hope is waning fast, though maybe one final, gargantuan effort might yet turn the tide. But who will lead you over the top? In the footballing equivalent of such desperate straits, there was never any doubt that Manchester United would rally behind Steve Bruce, the sort of man any soldier would be glad to call his comrade.

Steve Bruce

They did so most famously one sunlit spring afternoon at Old Trafford, at a crucial stage of the 1992/93 campaign, when he transformed imminent defeat by Sheffield Wednesday into joyously improbable victory. After 86 minutes, United were a goal down and seemingly doomed to lose vital ground in the title race, when up charged Steve to equalise with a majestic header. Now the Reds were rampant and, some seven heart-stopping minutes into injury time, the skipper lunged forward once more to nod a priceless winner. In that wildly exhilarating moment, as the battered Bruce features dissolved into glee, many believed for the first time that United were destined, at last, to don that elusive crown.

Of course, though Steve's attacking exploits were of inestimable value – notably his 19 strikes (including 11 penalties) in 1990/91 – it was as a courageous central defender that he earned his corn. In fact, when he arrived from Norwich in December 1987, eyebrows were raised at the manager's choice of a solid alternative to the infinitely more gifted but less reliable Paul McGrath. Certainly it was acknowledged that the enthusiastic stopper would battle to the last drop of his blood but where, in heaven's name, was the class expected of a United player?

Yet gradually this roughest of soccer diamonds, while he remained unlikely to graduate from the Alan Hansen Academy of Smooth Operators, emerged as the classic case of an honest trier who made the absolute most of limited natural ability, getting better and better as an all-round footballer along the way. Poise and grace would never be Steve's hallmarks, but his ball control, distribution and general composure improved out of all recognition, and while he could be discomfited by cleverly deployed pace, his experience ensured that he was rarely exposed. Add, for good measure, a fierce tackle and aerial strength, and the picture of a truly formidable centre-half was almost complete.

In fact, the final ingredient was the most important of all – the unquenchable spirit of the man. It sustained him when he was rejected by three top clubs as a boy; it ensured that, once given his chance at Old Trafford, he didn't waste it; it drove him to play on with injuries that would have brought lesser men to their knees; and it supplied the motivational powers needed to succeed Bryan Robson as captain of the Reds.

By common consent, he should have won full caps; indeed, Bobby Robson has admitted his mistake in never calling Steve to his country's colours, and Jack Charlton would have picked him for Eire had he not been disqualified by an England youth appearance.

That must be an eternal frustration for the affable north-easterner himself, but United fans could live with it. They were content to reflect that, of the many millions Alex Ferguson lavished on building his new team, no slice was better spent than the relatively modest £800,000 which secured the signature of Steve Bruce.

However, though his appetite for the Premiership fray remained undiminished, by the spring of 1996 the 35-year-old warhorse could no longer resist the challenge of the improving David May and, rather than hang around on the Old Trafford periphery hoping for an occasional outing, he accepted a summer move to Birmingham City. His footballing expertise, United would be able to replace. But that heroic heart? It wouldn't be easy.

There followed a spell as player-boss of Sheffield United, with whom he learned plenty, before Steve made a hugely promising start in the management chair of Huddersfield Town.

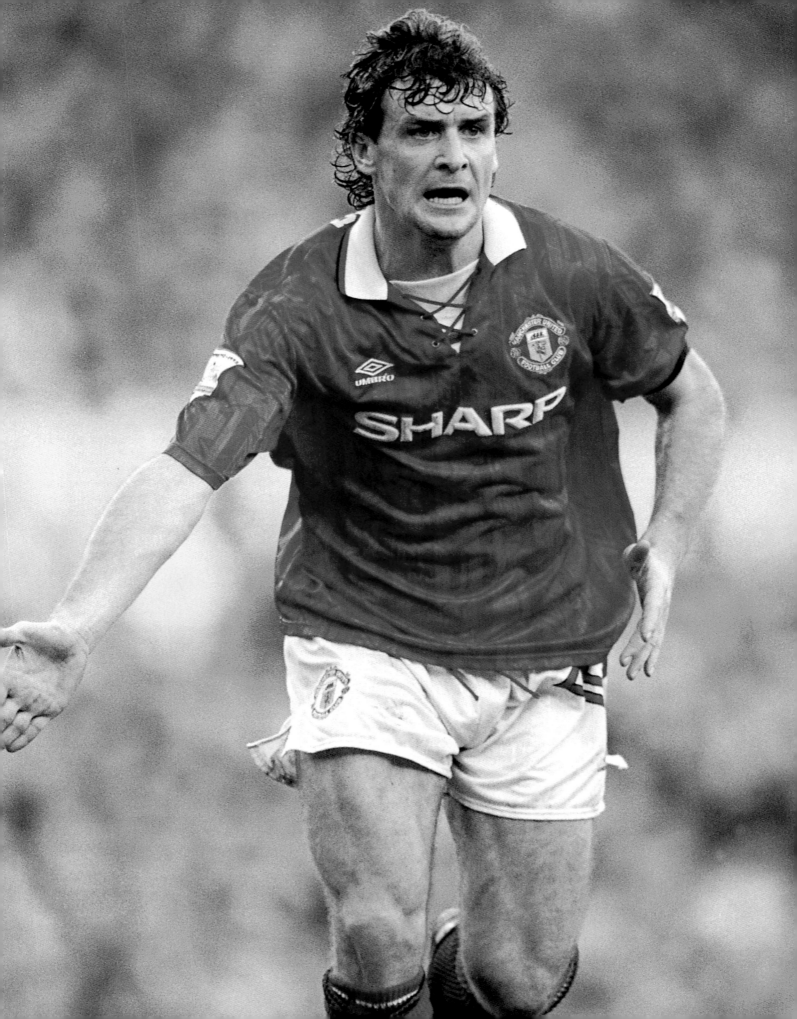

Few Red Devils have left behind them a deeper fund of pulsating memories than 'Sparky'.

1983/84–85/86 & 1988/89–94/95

462 GAMES   **162** GOALS

BORN — Wrexham, Denbighshire, 1.11.63.
HONOURS — European Cup Winners' Cup 90/1. League Championship 92/3, 93/4. FA Cup 84/5, 89/90, 93/4. League Cup 91/2. 72 Wales caps (84–99).
OTHER CLUBS — Barcelona 86/7 (28, 4); Bayern Munich on loan 87/8 (18, 6); Chelsea 95/6– 97/8 (95, 25); Southampton 98/9– 99/00 (51, 2); Everton 99/00– (9, 1). MANAGER: Wales (99–).

In his Red Devil days, a compelling aura of impending drama surrounded Mark Hughes. Every time he walked on to a football field, he carried with him the promise of tumultuous action. Frequently it took the form of a goal, invariably of the spellbinding variety, the type that emblazoned itself on the memory of all those privileged to witness it; occasionally his darker side was evident, when thunderclouds gathered on his brow and that celtic fire blazed. Even on less eventful days there was a stirring trial of strength with defenders, an exhibition of centre-forward play that blended power with subtlety in a manner unique in the contemporary game. Like him or not – and he did have his critics – there was no denying the star quality of 'Sparky'.

Mark Hughes

When the Welshman emerged as the cream of United's surfeit of strikers in 1984/85 – claiming his place at the expense of Brazil and Whiteside, and scoring 25 goals in senior competitions – a glow of collective contentment radiated from the Stretford End. Premature, perhaps, but the Red legions, sorely debilitated by the deeds of Dalglish, Rush and company, sensed that here they had a hero to slay the Anfield dragons.

The first months of the following campaign did nothing to disillusion them. Mark, a product of the club's youth sides, signed a five-year contract and plundered ten goals in 13 matches as United galloped to a ten-point lead in the title race. But the idyll was annihilated as results fell away and it was announced that Hughes was to join Barcelona for around £2 million. Outraged fans accused the Old Trafford board of betrayal and there were some unsavoury exchanges, illustrating vividly the esteem in which the young marksman was held. In similar vein, when he returned for £1.6 million two years later, he was embraced once more as a favourite son. Mark was the signing the supporters wanted above all others and when

they got him, by and large, he didn't disappoint them.

'Sparky' combined charisma with a rare range of talents of which arguably the most important – eclipsing even the most fearsome shot in British football – was the adhesive control and bull-like muscle which allowed him to retain possession against all-comers. This made him the physical focus of the Reds' fast-flowing attack, enabling team-mates to play the ball to him in the knowledge that he could keep it safe while they hared into new positions. He could pass with precision over long distances, too, if irking some observers with the occasional sloppy short-range lay-off.

Various detractors claimed that he was difficult to play alongside because he held the ball too long, that he spent too much time with his back to goal, that he squandered simple chances, that he was old enough to keep his temper; but all that withered before a veritable mountain of acclaim. His peers queued up to sing his praises – he was players' player of the year in both 1989 and 1991 – and the fans positively drooled over those wondrous goals. They are too numerous to list, but this writer's favourites include the savage narrow-angled drive in the Cup Winners' Cup Final against Barcelona, the looping 25-yarder lashed home against Manchester City as if in answer to speculation about his place following the arrival of Eric Cantona in late 1992, and the last-gasp firecracker of a volley to equalise against Oldham in the 1994 FA Cup semi-final. During that campaign, in his 31st year, Mark Hughes reached new heights of all-round excellence alongside the Frenchman and was more critical than ever to United's quick-breaking style.

It couldn't go on indefinitely, of course, and in the summer of 1995 he was allowed to depart – prematurely according to some observers who doubted the suitability of Andy Cole as his replacement – to Chelsea in a £1.5 million deal. All who wished him well were delighted by his success at Stamford Bridge and, later, his appointment to manage Wales. Meanwhile back at Old Trafford, though the last thunderbolt has exploded and the final tackle has been ridden, 'Sparky' is lionised still. Few Reds have left behind them a deeper fund of pulsating memories.

He was a perceptive reader of the game whose positional sense rarely let him down.

1991/92–1995/96

145 **2**
GAMES GOALS

BORN ● West Ham, London, 4.4.64.
HONOURS ● League Championship 92/3, 93/4. FA Cup 93/4.
League Cup 91/2.
19 England caps (89–94).
OTHER CLUBS ● Fulham 80/1–86/7 (153, 2); Queen's Park
Rangers 87/8–90/1 (125, 1); Derby County 96/7
(4, 0); Sheffield United 96/7 (10, 0); Fulham 96/7
(3, 0); Chelsea 96/7 (3, 0).

Old met new in Paul Parker. The nimble little Londoner was a master of the crisp-tackling and tight-marking techniques which occupied pride of place in any self-respecting full-back's armoury before modern trends turned flank defenders into quasi-wingers, often at the expense of their traditional duties. But whereas the majority of his old-fashioned counterparts tended to rely more on power than pace, United's tenacious England international could match most Premiership speed merchants stride for stride. Quicksilver on the turn, he recovered instantly if an opponent did slip past him and usually could be relied upon to bite back with a second challenge before too much damage had been done.

Paul Parker

But Paul was no mere greyhound. Although close (some might say pernickety) observers detected the occasional lapse in concentration, he was a perceptive reader of the game whose positional sense rarely let him down. Thus a Parker interception marked the demise of many an opposition raid, and he offered an invaluable line in cavalry-style rescues, invariably being on hand to cover if the twin centre-halves were hard-pressed.

In fact, Paul expressed a preference for operating permanently in the middle and was used there in an experimental sweeper system during part of 1991/92, his first term as a Red Devil following his close-season £1.7 million transfer from Queen's Park Rangers. On occasion, too, the dapper right-back deputised competently for Gary Pallister, and the way he shackled former team-mate Les Ferdinand at Old Trafford in October 1993 offered impressive proof of his man-marking capabilities. But despite being a prodigious jumper, at only 5ft 7in he couldn't achieve the consistent aerial dominance demanded by a central role, and he continued to look most comfortable in the number-two shirt.

One weakness to which Paul's critics never tired of referring was his distribution and, fair enough, it was not on a par with that of his smooth-passing colleagues. However, he strove to improve his delivery, with some success, and it should be stressed that any periodic inaccuracy hardly would have attracted comment were he playing for a team containing fewer gifted individuals than United.

A less-than-serious shortfall in the Parker game was goals, Paul netting only twice in senior competition for the Reds and inevitably being ribbed by his team-mates as the lowest-scoring outfielder. His first strike was rather special, though, a perfectly angled cross-shot from close range that climaxed a sweetly executed one-two passing interchange with Brian McClair at home to Spurs in January 1993; on the other hand his second, a spectacular effort from near the right touchline during an FA Cup tie at Reading in 1996, might have owed more to a bobble on the Elm Park pitch than precision delivery!

However, to dwell on the Parker strike rate is like concentrating on Cantona's goal-line clearances, merely an aside. Overall, and despite revealing the occasional need to boost Paul's confidence, Alex Ferguson was delighted with the versatile defender who, at the time of his arrival, had just returned to action following knee problems which had threatened his career. There were to be protracted fitness worries in Manchester, too, a strained hamstring costing him much of 1991/92, then further injury sidelining him for the first three months of the subsequent title-winning campaign.

Sadly, there was worse to come. After moving into his thirties in April 1994, Paul was unavailable for long stretches of two more seasons, during which he was overhauled in the pecking order by the Neville brothers. Consequently it was no surprise when he was freed in the summer of 1996 to join Derby County, though it was a pity. A fully-fit Paul Parker would have offered ideal cover when United's back-four was devastated by injuries early in 1997.

LES SEALEY

1989/90–1990/91 & 1993/94

55	0
GAMES	GOALS

BORN	Bethnal Green, London, 29.9.57.
HONOURS	European Cup Winners' Cup 90/1; FA Cup 89/90.
OTHER CLUBS	Coventry City 76/7–82/3 (158, 0); Luton Town 83/4–88/9 (207, 0); Plymouth Argyle on loan 84/5 (6, 0); Aston Villa 91/2 (18, 0); Coventry City on loan 91/2 (2, 0); Birmingham City on loan 92/3 (12, 0); Blackpool 94/5 (7, 0), West Ham United 95/6 (2, 0); Leyton Orient 96/7 (12, 0); West Ham United 96/7– 97/8 (2, 0).

Sometimes he was United's 'Mr Angry', a ranting extrovert between the posts; mostly he was a gleeful eccentric whose madcap antics delighted the many while alienating the few. But the bottom line was that Les Sealey served the Reds royally in no fewer than four cup finals during two spells at the club – and without costing a penny in transfer fees.

Londoner Les arrived on loan from Luton Town in December 1989 after injury to Gary Walsh left United without cover for Jim Leighton. Seasoned and reliable, he was not seen as a world-beater, but Alex Ferguson had no hesitation in pitching him into the FA Cup Final replay against Crystal Palace after the Scot's traumatic experiences in the first match.

Les responded superbly, refusing to be intimidated either by the occasion or the physical force exerted by Mark Bright and company. As he picked himself up after one early, over-robust challenge, the light of battle was in his eye and soon he had shown his prowess with a crucial, if somewhat lucky save with his legs from Andy Gray's 20-yard free-kick. This was typical of a brave, unorthodox performer who was technically flawed – witness his occasionally erratic positioning – but adept at protecting his net with any part of his anatomy.

He was rewarded for his part in the victory by a one-year contract, becoming first-choice custodian for 1990/91 and keeping in two finals. First came the League Cup defeat by Sheffield Wednesday, made memorable by his, er, forthright refusal to be substituted after his knee was cut to the bone. A few hours after the game he fainted, and might have lost his leg, yet three weeks on he was between the posts to help beat Barcelona in the Cup Winners' Cup.

Now Les wanted a two-year contract, but left to join Aston Villa after being offered only 12 months' security of tenure. But in January 1993 he was back at Old Trafford as deputy to Peter Schmeichel and was called to arms when the Dane was suspended for the '94 League Cup Final.

United lost to Villa but the 36-year-old standby was blameless, and he was disappointed to be given a free transfer at the end of the season. Since then Les has banished dullness from the dressing rooms of Blackpool, West Ham and Leyton Orient.

But for the identity of his father, there is a good chance that Darren Ferguson would be enjoying a lengthy career with Manchester United. The Scotland under-21 midfielder did enough during his brief spell in the Old Trafford spotlight, especially throughout an uninterrupted sequence of 15 League games at the outset of 1992/93, to establish credentials of undeniable quality. However, being the manager's son was sure to place the youngster under intolerable pressure at some stage and, reluctantly but wisely, the Fergusons decided on a parting of their professional ways.

Darren, the subject of an inquiry from Nottingham Forest during his progress through the Red Devils' junior ranks, made his senior debut at Bramall Lane in February 1991, coming on as substitute for Neil Webb and impressing with his efficient distribution in the face of vigorous challenges. Bright pre-season form won him a place on the left of midfield that August, but then knee problems which demanded three operations put him temporarily out of contention.

Fit again a year later, Darren began another new term in the first team and now revealed his true potential. Though he wasn't quick, he was a lovely passer, especially with his left foot and rarely did he squander possession. He was adept at shielding the ball, too, and while not a ball-winner in the accepted sense, he tackled forcefully enough, occasionally showing flashes of the family spirit! One criticism was that he rarely got forward and that when he did his finishing was poor, but he was giving enough in other areas for that to be overlooked.

Without making extravagant claims for the promising 20-year-old, pundits began to praise his unobtrusive but consistent contribution to United's recovery from a slow start. But after he was sidelined by a hamstring strain in November, the side began to take off in his absence and he never regained his place, though the Championship statuette he received at season's end was rich consolation.

That autumn the Fergusons spoke of Darren's need to look elsewhere and when Wolves bid £500,000 in January 1994 he headed for Molineux. Mystifyingly, his progess in the Black Country proved disappointingly fitful and he hoped to make the most of a fresh start at Wrexham.

DARREN FERGUSON

1990/91–1993/94

30 GAMES **0** GOALS

BORN ● Glasgow 9.2.72.
HONOURS ● League Championship 92/3.
OTHER CLUBS ● Wolverhampton Wanderers 93/4–98/9 (117, 4); Cosenza, Italy, and Sparta Rotterdam, Holland, both on loan 98/9; Wrexham 99/00- (35, 4).

DION DUBLIN ▼

1992/93–1993/94

17	3
GAMES	GOALS

BORN • Leicester, 22.4.69.
HONOURS • League Championship 92/3. 4 England caps (98-).
OTHER CLUBS • Cambridge United 88/9–91/2 (156, 53);
Coventry City 94/5–98/9 (146, 60); Aston Villa
98/9– (50, 23).

After a desperate shortage of goals in the second half of 1991/92 cost United the League Championship, Alex Ferguson acted decisively.
First he tried to sign Alan Shearer from Southampton, but lost out to Blackburn; then he switched his attention to Dion Dublin, the shaven-headed six-footer who had been at the sharp end of Cambridge United's long-ball success story. The Abbeymen had conducted the sale of their leading scorer by video, circulating a tape of his goals to all top clubs. Alex had been impressed by the variety of the 23-year-old Midlander's strikes and came up with the requisite £1.1 million.

Clearly Dion was not a typical Old Trafford signing, lacking the finesse of most expensive acquisitions, but his size and physical presence offered a different attacking option. He responded by scoring a late winner at Southampton in his first full game, only to fall victim to cruel fortune in his third. A tackle from Crystal Palace's Eric Young, later exonerated from blame by all concerned, left him with a fractured leg and horribly damaged ligaments. Less resilient characters might never have played again, but he fought back in time to take a seat on the substitutes' bench that spring. However, subsequent opportunities proved few and in September 1994 he joined Coventry for £2 million, a deal which satisfied all the participants. Dion left Old Trafford with his all-round game improved immeasurably, the Sky Blues had obtained an effective spearhead and United had doubled their money. His subsequent rise to England status was a resounding triumph for brave perseverance.

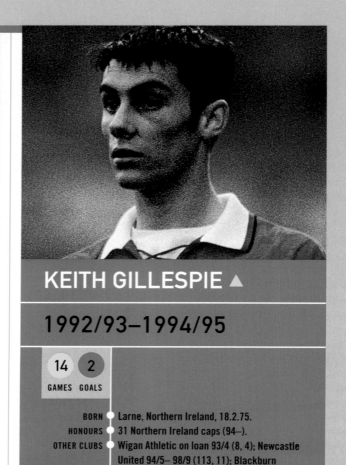

KEITH GILLESPIE ▲

1992/93–1994/95

14	2
GAMES	GOALS

BORN • Larne, Northern Ireland, 18.2.75.
HONOURS • 31 Northern Ireland caps (94-).
OTHER CLUBS • Wigan Athletic on loan 93/4 (8, 4); Newcastle
United 94/5– 98/9 (113, 11); Blackburn
Rovers 98/9– (38, 3).

When Keith Gillespie ghosted unstoppably past two Newcastle defenders before netting thrillingly from 16 yards at Old Trafford in October 1994, he made an indelible impression on visiting manager Kevin Keegan. So much so that come January, when Alex Ferguson enquired about the availability of Andy Cole, Kevin agreed to sell – providing Keith joined the Geordies as a £1 million component in the £7 million deal. Alex was reluctant to part with his richly promising rookie but so keen was he on Cole, and with Andrei Kanchelskis then blocking the 19-year-old flankman's path to the senior side, he accepted Newcastle's terms.

Had Ferguson known of the Ukrainian's growing determination to depart, maybe his decision would have been different. Whatever, that is history and while the Reds' new striker blew hot and cold, Keith's breathtaking skills established him quickly as a favourite on the Tyne.

Glancing back at his early development, that was hardly surprising. Wingers have an extra cross to bear at Old Trafford, especially if, like Keith, they are slim and dark and hail from Ulster. But his head was not for turning, either by meaningless comparisons or the natural ebullience of youth. Quick and confident enough to take players on at need, he knew when a safe pass was the more sensible option, and the accuracy of his centres was improving at the time of his transfer. Despite fitness problems and relegation after a later move to Blackburn, Keith still has plenty of Premiership potential. Good luck to him and, it must be said, well done to Kevin Keegan.

MICHAEL APPLETON

1996/97

MIDFIELDER

2 GAMES **0** GOALS

BORN:
Salford, Manchester, 4.12.75.

OTHER CLUBS:
Lincoln City on loan 95/6 (4, 0); Grimsby Town on loan 96/7 (10, 3); Preston North End 97/8– (89, 7).

PAT McGIBBON

1995/96

CENTRAL DEFENDER

1 GAMES **0** GOALS

BORN:
Lurgan, Northern Ireland, 6.9.73.

HONOURS:
6 Northern Ireland caps (95–).

OTHER CLUBS: Portadown, Northern Ireland; Swansea City on loan 96/7 (1, 0); Wigan Athletic 96/7– (113, 8).

COLIN McKEE

1993/94

FORWARD

1 GAMES **0** GOALS
BORN:
Glasgow 22.8.73.

OTHER CLUBS:
Bury on loan 92/3 (2, 0); Kilmarnock 94/5–98/8 (76, 11); Falkirk 98/9 (4, 0)

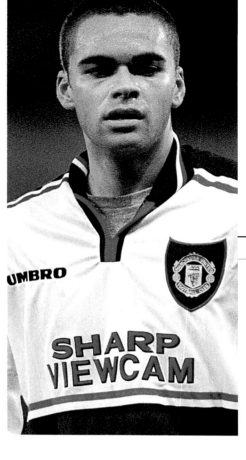

JOHN O'KANE

1994/95–1996/97

FULL-BACK

7 GAMES **0** GOALS

BORN:
Nottingham, 15.11.74. OTHER CLUBS: Bury on loan 96/7 (13, 3) ; Bradford City on loan 97/8 (7, 0); Everton 97/8–98/9 (14, 0); Burnley on loan 98/9 (7, 0); Bolton Wanderers 99/00– (11, 1).

WILLIAM PRUNIER

1995/96

CENTRAL DEFENDER

2 GAMES **0** GOALS

BORN:
Montreuil, France, 14.8.67

HONOURS:
France caps.

OTHER CLUBS:
Auxerre 84/5–92/3 (221, 20); Marseille 93/4 (35, 4); Bordeaux 94/5 (20, 0).

GRAEME TOMLINSON

1994/95

FORWARD

2 GAMES **0** GOALS

BORN:
Watford, Hertfordshire, 10.12.75.

OTHER CLUBS:
Bradford City 93/4 (17, 6); Luton Town on loan 95/6 (7, 0); Bournemouth on loan 97/8 (8, 1); Millwall on loan 97/8 (3, 1); Macclesfield Town 98/9– (46, 5).

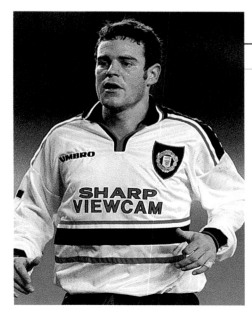

Exuding energy and enterprise, Ince was not far from being the complete modern midfielder.

1989/90–1994/95

GAMES 277 **GOALS** 28

BORN Ilford, Essex, 21.10.67.
HONOURS European Cup Winners' Cup 90/1. League Championship 92/3, 93/4. FA Cup 89/90, 93/4. League Cup 91/2. 48 England caps (92–).
OTHER CLUBS West Ham United 86/7–89/90 (72, 7); Inter Milan 95/6–96/7; Liverpool 97/8–98/9 (65, 14); Middlesbrough 99/00– (32, 3).

The void was gaping, the situation potentially desperate. Manchester United had suffered debilitating disappointment on the last lap of the 1991/92 title race and as they regrouped for what many saw as a make-or-break new campaign for Alex Ferguson's expensively assembled team, one question gave rise to grave concern. The years were finally catching up with Bryan Robson, no longer the unquenchably dynamic force of seasons past, so to whom would the Red Devils turn for midfield motivation? Who would drive them, lift them, inspire them by mammoth personal example? Cometh the hour, cometh Paul Ince.

Paul Ince

He was, of course, the obvious candidate, having improved steadily over his three seasons at the club, but now came a crossroads. Some reckoned he would remain in that heavily populated category of value-for-money competitors destined to fall marginally short of the top class. Others had faith that he could step up to join the select band who can seize a game and mould it, make the difference between winning and losing by sustained excellence and application – and they were right.

Throughout 1992/93 Paul asserted himself majestically to become the new hub of the side, compiling a sequence of colossal performances as United won the League at last. Shuttling ceaselessly between penalty areas, he exuded energy and enterprise, sometimes scything into tackles like a runaway motor-mower, though more often winning possession crisply and neatly. He carried the ball with skill and purpose, too, and his right-footed distribution was invariably sensible, occasionally incisive.

As a bonus, he obliged with a few goals, hitherto a shortfall in his game, including an emphatic low 25-yarder with his weaker left foot in the Manchester derby at Old Trafford and an overhead kick at Loftus Road that would not have shamed Denis Law. Most welcome of all, though, and one which summed up Paul's surging, irrepressible

presence, was the late clincher at Crystal Palace as the Reds closed in on the title. Bursting unstoppably on to a pass from Eric Cantona, he hustled past a defender, bore down on the 'keeper and netted with a fierce cross-shot.

That summer Paul was elevated, albeit temporarily, to the exalted rank of England captain, underlining the wisdom of Ferguson's gamble in taking the immature and rebellious but immensely promising 21-year-old from West Ham in September 1989. It had been a messy transfer, with the player posing for the press in a red shirt long before the deal was completed, and one complicated by a mystery pelvic injury which resulted in a pay-as-he-played agreement up to the reported fee of £1.7 million.

At the time, Paul seemed to be nursing a grievance against the world, a legacy of an unsettled childhood, and United set to work on his attitude as well as his football. During a first season in which he demonstrated his all-round ability by filling in as an emergency full-back, he proved his basic pedigree; thereafter, gradually, he enhanced every aspect of his play as he helped to compile a glittering collection of trophies. A combination of marriage, fatherhood and sound advice speeded up the maturing process; moaning at referees decreased, snarls became less frequent than smiles and, while an underlying narkiness would always remain, the temper was on a tighter rein.

Throughout the double-winning term of 1993/94 and much of the ultimately disappointing 1994/95 campaign Paul continued to exert a towering influence, though following his part in the Cantona affair at Selhurst Park in January '95 his effectiveness decreased. Thereafter certain tensions surfaced within the club and that summer, to the dismay of many but not all United-lovers, the self-styled 'Guv'nor' was sold to Inter Milan for a reported £7 million.

Though his play lacked the perception of Roy Keane's, Paul was not far from being the complete modern midfielder, and there was understandable anxiety about how he would be missed. Ferguson's answer was to pair Keane with Nicky Butt and to win everything, while there were no medals for the 'Guv', either in Milan, or later at Liverpool and Middlesbrough. So the final verdict on Paul Ince? A magnificent player, yes. Indispensable, by no means.

1990/91–1994/95

158	36
GAMES	GOALS

BORN ● Kirovograd, Ukraine, 23.1.69.
HONOURS ● League Championship 92/3, 93/4. FA Cup 93/4. League Cup 91/2.
USSR and CIS caps (89–).
OTHER CLUBS ● Dynamo Kiev 88–89 (22, 1), Shakhtyor Donetsk 90–91 (21, 3), both USSR; Everton 95/6–96/7 (52, 20); Fiorentina, Italy 96/7– 97/8; Glasgow Rangers 98/9– (58, 10).

There was no more potent weapon in the Premiership for transforming defence into penetrating attack.

Andrei Kanchelskis

Of the three heroes whose departures ruffled the summertime calm of Old Trafford in 1995, the one most sorely missed, and by a considerable distance, was Andrei Kanchelskis. The gaps left by Messrs Ince and Hughes were filled with relative ease, the first directly, the second by a tactical variation. But while David Beckham offered his own special delights in Andrei's right-flank slot, and even though the 'double double' was secured, United were immeasurably the poorer for losing the options afforded by the flying Ukrainian's extreme pace.

Kanchelskis was a refreshing footballer. Ironically for a fellow who failed ultimately to find happiness at a succession of clubs, he played the game with a smile never far from his face and, when the ball was at his feet, it was a fair bet that the fans were enjoying themselves, too. Whether devastating defenders with searing straight-line speed or beguiling them on jinking, shoulder-shrugging runs, he was an entertainer and a match-winner. During 1993/94 there was no more potent weapon in the Premiership for transforming defence, suddenly and explosively, into penetrating attack. In that most riveting of campaigns, United were blessed with a trio of brilliant but contrasting flankmen, each of whom captivated crowds in their turn. So what a telling tribute it was to Andrei that, with due respect to Ryan Giggs and Lee Sharpe, he was the most consistently productive of the three.

When the 22-year-old outside-right arrived as a £1 million signing from Donetsk in May 1991, it was a clear case of 'Andrei Who?' Though he was a Soviet international, he was little known outside his native land, but before long the Old Trafford regulars had taken him to their hearts. When he was on form, they thrilled to his free-running style, his close skills and his rasping shot, while applauding his willingness to forage. Equally important to a young man making his way in an alien environment while worrying about events in his strife-torn homeland, they warmed to him as a personality, appreciating the boyishly wholesome air and the perky optimism which suffused his play. Nevertheless, Andrei was not the finished article as a

player, either in 1991/92, when he missed only a few senior games, or in the subsequent title-winning term, when his outings were limited by Sharpe's return from injury and illness. Though his potential was never in doubt, he lacked awareness of passing options, too often pounding forward naively as though fitted with blinkers, and his crossing quality was variable.

However, he became frustrated when left out of the side and there was speculation that he would move in June 1993. The manager, though, was loth to lose such a gem and persuaded Andrei that, with patience, there was a bountiful future for him at Old Trafford. Sure enough, the next term another enforced absence for the unlucky Sharpe presented Kanchelskis with an extended opportunity and he shone as never before. Now his game had matured, he slotted smoothly into the team pattern and United never looked more incisive than when he was in full cry.

Examples of Andrei's verve clamour for description, none more so than an incandescent piece of individualism in the FA Cup semi-final replay against Oldham, when he cut inside from the right, danced across the face of the Latics' defence, then swivelled to dispatch the sweetest of 20-yard curlers just inside the far post with his unfavoured left foot. More typical were any number of grass-singeing dashes from deep inside his own half which climaxed invariably with low, crisply struck shots.

Yet the Reds' squad was extensive and, still haunted by doubts and with top Continental clubs dangling untold riches before him, the popular winger spoke once more of departing in 1994. The threat evaporated for a time but a season later – one in which he had contributed 15 goals, including a rampaging hat-trick against Manchester City – he declared that his differences with Ferguson were irreconcilable. He was upset over tactical omissions from the side and dogged by nagging fitness problems, but the suspicion lingered that money came into it somewhere.

Whatever the whole truth, there was no way any club could hang on to such an unhappy player and he was sold, oh so reluctantly, to Everton for £5.5 million. Even that acrimonious exit could not mar the memory of his achievements as a Red, but how frustrating it remained for United fans that Kanchelskis' prime years were being spent elsewhere. As it turned out, though, Andrei's exploits on Merseyside, in Italy and in Scotland were to prove less than wholly satisfying.

One shrewd observer reckoned that Lee could have become the finest left-winger the club had ever had.

1988/89–1995/96

262 GAMES **36** GOALS

BORN ● Halesowen, Birmingham, 27.5.71.
HONOURS ● European Cup Winners' Cup 90/1. League Championship 92/3, 93/4, 95/6. FA Cup 93/4. League Cup 91/2. 8 England caps (91–).
OTHER CLUBS ● Torquay United 87/8 (14, 3); Leeds United 96/7–98/9 (30, 5); Sampdoria loan 98/9; Bradford City 98/9– (27, 2).

The relative decline of Lee Sharpe and his departure from an Old Trafford stage which he had illuminated with a rare talent for more than half a decade was frustratingly premature. By the time he joined Leeds for £4.5 million in August 1996 he seemed little more than a squad player, a shadow of his former vibrant self and no longer a likely match-winner, despite his involvement in all but eight matches of the 1995/96 double-winning campaign.

Lee Sharpe

Yet still he was only 25, quick and skilful, bright and brave. He worked hard during games and was unselfish to a fault; his temperament was even and he was vastly experienced for such a young man. A fair combination. In fact, one veteran monitor of the Old Trafford scene, a perceptive and frequently astringent observer not given to fulsome praise, reckoned that Lee possessed the raw materials to become the finest left-winger the club had ever had. Alex Ferguson, too, had waxed lyrical, especially about the Sharpe contribution to the 1992/93 Championship triumph, pointing out that, while Lee netted only once, he supplied no fewer than 18 'assists' between his November return from a career-threatening bout of meningitis and season's end.

Indeed, it was the rare quality of the England international's final ball that marked him out as special, particularly when he was forced to deliver under pressure. Lee demonstrated a priceless knack of bending his crosses with perfect weight, teasing defenders to distraction, delighting his own front-men with his accuracy. Glorious examples on the road to that first title included the raking dispatch that set up Andrei Kanchelskis to score at Loftus Road in January, the exquisite centre that met Eric Cantona's forehead for an equaliser at Maine Road two months later, three Boxing Day presents to his strikers at Hillsborough . . . the point is made. On his day Lee could produce a devastating finish, too. Consider his Highbury hat-trick in November 1990, comprising a 25-

yard scorcher, a neat glancing header and a precisely angled shot; or, more spectacular still, the long-range volley out of the blue that stunned Everton at Goodison in October 1993.

However, life was not all hip-wiggling goal celebrations after Lee's £200,000 purchase from Torquay, a deal struck at Plainmoor one night in May 1988 after Alex Ferguson, fearful of being spotted by rival scouts, had disguised himself in a balaclava to watch his quarry in action. Apart from facing the sternest imaginable competition for a place from Giggs, Kanchelskis and then a new wave of brilliant youngsters, Lee was plagued by injury and illness. There was a hernia operation, protracted groin problems and, most serious of all, that horrifying 1992 encounter with meningitis. His resilience in recovering from each setback seemed remarkable but, in the long term, maybe they left their mark.

Also, if we are searching for reasons for Lee's loss of impetus, he might not have been helped by occasional role switches made by his manager in the team's broader interests. Admittedly he had looked typically unflustered at left-back – notably when an injury crisis pitched him into top-flight action shortly after his arrival from Torquay – but, emphatically, he is not a natural defender. More simply, Lee is a refreshingly easy-going fellow who enjoyed the privileged life of a handsome young star to the full. Whether he retained the necessary raw hunger for success in such tempting circumstances, or whether a modicum of complacency crept in, can only be the subject of conjecture.

Back in 1991, still only 19, he was voted young player of the year and won his first full cap, and as the century ended he ought to have been enjoying his prime. But at Elland Road he found a club in a difficult stage of transition and his early form, while not disastrous, was hardly convincing either. Thereafter he lost the whole of 1997/98 to injury, then slipped out of the first-team picture. A new start beckoned with ambitious Bradford City, but if Lee Sharpe is going to meet the expectations created during the vivid highlights of his Old Trafford sojourn, the next couple of seasons are crucial.

Pally proved to be less white elephant than a mammoth asset.

1989/90–1997/98

431 **15**
GAMES GOALS

BORN ● Ramsgate, Kent, 30.6.65.
HONOURS ● European Cup Winners' Cup 90/1. League Championship 92/3, 93/4, 95/6, 96/7. FA Cup 89/90, 93/4, 95/6. League Cup 91/2. 22 England caps (88–).
OTHER CLUBS ● Middlesbrough 85/6–89/90 (156, 5); Darlington on loan 85/6 (7, 0); Middlesbrough 98/9– (46, 1).

'Bargain' was not the word which sprang to mind in the weeks immediately following Manchester United's £2.3 million purchase of 24-year-old Gary Pallister from Middlesbrough in August 1989. The coltish 6ft 4in centre-half oozed anxiety, shouldered the blame for several goals and left many Old Trafford loyalists fearing that Alex Ferguson had made a towering blunder. However, the manager was to claim handsome vindication for a bold piece of business carried out under mounting pressure to improve his team. Indeed, five years on Gary was at least the equal of any British stopper – many within the game put him in a class of his own – and in terms of the fees mooted in the 1990s to secure players in key positions, yes, most certainly he could be considered a bargain.

Gary Pallister

In fact, Reds fans needed only moderate patience to discover that Pally was less white elephant than mammoth asset. That same term he steadied himself to play an increasingly commanding role as United won the FA Cup, and was made supporters' player of the year for his pains. Two years later he received even more meaningful approbation, that of his peers, in the shape of the PFA players' player award; and come 1993 he laid persuasive claim to a regular England place while being spoken of as a possible future United skipper. At that point it was pleasing to reflect that the club had turned to Gary only when Liverpool pipped them for the signature of Glenn Hysen. With every respect to the imposing Swede, that was one race which, in retrospect, the Mancunians were delighted to lose.

Indeed, Pally became a truly majestic, all-round central defender; and he was still near the height of his powers in 1997/98, when it appeared possible that he might serve United – sore back permitting – until the turn of the century. In the air he was well-nigh impregnable, his massive presence subduing attackers psychologically as well as physically; on the ground he controlled the ball

deftly with either foot, passed it accurately and intelligently, and was capable of carrying it past opponents in the imperious manner of a latter-day Alan Hansen. Crucially, too, he was blessed with a startling turn of speed for such a big fellow, leaving only an occasional tendency to lose concentration as an area for concern. He worked hard to eradicate that flaw though, and instances of 'dozing off' on the field became rare, an advance due partly, no doubt, to some well-judged metaphorical boots up the behind from manager and team-mates. True, there remained anxious moments of apparent casualness, but such was Gary's assurance that the fans' palpitations were seldom justified.

Clearly, Pally's progress owed most to his own natural ability, but the club deserved credit for ensuring that he made the most of it. On arrival he was altogether too slender, unable to 'punch his weight' and lacking in stamina, but specialist training wrought a gradual transformation into a bull-necked colossus who remained as strong at the final whistle as at the first. Gary's outlook, too, needed toughening, but there can be few men more adept at inbuing single-mindedness and 'devil' than the Reds' boss. The result was self-evident, as Wimbledon's renowned warrior John Fashanu found out in an FA Cup clash at Selhurst Park in February 1994. 'Fash' ran out breathing fire, an intimidating prospect before which many a so-called hard-man has faltered. But Pally met the challenge implacably, refused to be unsettled and reduced the Dons' destroyer to helpless anonymity.

Despite the efficiency of Messrs Johnsen and Berg during 1997/98, United's rearguard never seemed quite right when Gary was sidelined for a worrying spell by a recurrence of the back injury which cost him his England place for Euro '96. He was the only player to have shared in all nine of the major triumphs during the Ferguson reign to date, and it did not seem fanciful to suggest that still he had not finished. But the signing of Jaap Stam alerted Bryan Robson to a possible scoop and Pally completed a £2 million return to Middlesbrough in the summer of 1998. The Dutchman's excellence dispelled fears that United had dropped a costly clanger and one of the most accomplished defenders in Old Trafford history went on to play an influential, if injury-plagued part in consolidating 'Boro's Premiership future.

Peter's near-omnipotence confirmed him as an all-time goal-keeping great.

1991/92–1998/99

392 GAMES **1** GOALS

BORN Gladsaxe, Denmark, 18.11.63.
HONOURS European Cup 98/9. League Championship 92/3, 93/4, 95/6, 96/7, 98/9. FA Cup 93/4, 95/6, 98/9. League Cup 91/2. Denmark caps (87–).
OTHER CLUBS Gladsaxe-Hero, Hvidovre, Brondby, all Denmark; Sporting Lisbon, Portugal, 99–00.

As the living embodiment of United's superiority – and widely perceived arrogance – for the better part of a decade, Peter Schmeichel was never the most popular person in English football.

Peter Schmeichel

His combination of excellence and self-assurance, coupled with his ranting at anyone within earshot at moments of stress, made him despised by fans all over the country and even alienated many of his fellow professionals. That is the inescapable conclusion from the players' decision to vote for David James as the best 'keeper in the Premiership during 1995/96, then David Seaman in 1996/97 and Nigel Martyn in both 1997/98 and 1998/99. Quite simply, with the giant Dane's monumental input to United's modern success outstripping that of any single colleague, and with every respect to the aforementioned trio, there must have been an element of 'I'm not supporting that bad-tempered so-and-so' when the votes were cast. In reality, surely, Schmeichel's frequent near-omnipotence was more than enough to confirm his stature as one of the all-time goalkeeping greats, let alone merely the pick of one English season.

Consider: in spring '96 as United clawed themselves back into a title race which had seemed dead, the lion's share of the bouquets went to Eric Cantona, yet Peter's saves earned at least as many points as the Frenchman's goals. His contribution was encapsulated in microcosm at St James' Park in March when once, twice, three times he denied Les Ferdinand when it seemed the England striker was certain to score. Without those priceless interventions, Eric's dramatic volley would have been no more than a consolation, rather than the dagger to Newcastle's heart it turned out to be. Not that Peter had it all his own way as a Red Devil following his £750,000 transfer from Brondby in August 1991. He had to survive an uncertain start while he adjusted to the greater incidence of crosses in British football and, like any net-minder, he knew his share of palsied moments and feeble fumbles.

But, in general, Peter flourished on the grand scale. Some individual saves will never be forgotten – for instance, the Banks-like plunging scoop to keep out Rene Wagner's downward header in Vienna in December 1996 – but it was to be his astonishing expertise in one-on-one confrontations

which was to become his trademark. As a lone attacker bears down on any goalkeeper, there is an analogy to be drawn with a predator approaching its prey. But somehow; when the 'keeper was Schmeichel, it was the forward who took on the role of likely victim. Quick off his line for such a big fellow, the Dane offered precious little goal to aim at and frequently saved the apparently unsaveable with a spreadeagled parry. In addition, Peter was a formidable launchpad for attacks, hurling the ball instantly and accurately to beyond half-way. Occasionally, too, if the Reds were trailing late on, he would charge upfield in search of a goal, his only success being the header against Rotor Volgograd in September 1995 which preserved, albeit temporarily, the club's unbeaten home record in Europe.

Clearly, such an accomplished performer with more than a century of international caps to his credit might be expected to rejoice in widespread affection as does, say, David Seaman. But in Peter's case, a few little, er, eccentricities, got in the way. Though his seemingly hysterical bombast at the first hint of a problem – nothing was ever his fault – did little for his public image, he declared there was no malice involved, that it was merely his method of self-motivation. This explanation was accepted readily by his oft-abused team-mates, who were inspired by his reassuring presence and welcomed his elevation to the captaincy for most of 1997/98 following Roy Keane's injury. However, nothing could gainsay the fact that his tantrums could strike an offensive note, appearing especially inappropriate when they coincided with a run of indifferent personal displays, for example towards the end of 1993/94.

After that, though, Peter regained his pedestal, his customary authority dented only marginally by fleeting aberrations of form, most notably in the middle of 1998/99. It was during this clanger-strewn lean spell, when he was troubled by back problems, that he announced his intention to quit United at season's end, explaining that he no longer felt able to cope with the intense demands of the English game. Ironically, after a mid-term holiday, he returned to his best, but would not change his mind about leaving. In Keane's absence, Peter led United to European Cup glory, even contributing to the equaliser against Bayern with his late sortie into attack, and there could be no more fitting climax to his imperious reign. Has there been a better goalkeeper in the world than big Schmeichel during the modern era? In the view of this humble layman, the answer is an emphatic 'no'.

BEN THORNLEY ▼

1993/94–1997/98

14	0
GAMES	GOALS

BORN ● Bury Lancashire, 21.4.75.
OTHER CLUBS ● Stockport County (10,1) and Huddersfield Town (12, 2) on loan 95/6; Huddersfield Town 98/9– (63, 5).

It is right to remember Ben Thornley amidst the euphoria that has engulfed Manchester United during the honour-strewn 1990s. A thrustful young winger with tantalising skills and a startling change of pace who had helped to lift the FA Youth Cup in 1991/92, he made his senior debut as a substitute at West Ham in February 1994. Thereafter he hit top form on the reserves' left flank and six weeks on, as his 19th birthday approached, a major breakthrough seemed possible.

With Ryan Giggs out of sorts and Lee Sharpe injured, Ben came under serious consideration for United's FA Cup semi-final against Oldham. But four days before that Wembley date, his world caved in. A tackle by Blackburn's Nicky Marker in a reserve game left Ben with a chronic knee injury and his footballing future in jeopardy. He spent much of 1994/95 in an excruciating limbo of mental and physical anguish, eventually returning to action and gaining experience in loan spells the following term.

By 1996/97 he was back in senior contention, displaying commendable craft and crossing ability during sporadic outings as Giggs' deputy, but lacking the pace to be truly penetrative. Several hefty bids for his services were rejected but in the summer of 1998 he moved to Huddersfield. Good luck to Ben Thornley at the McAlpine Stadium; he deserves massive credit for courage in the face of adversity.

KEVIN PILKINGTON ▲

1994/95–1997/98

8	0
GAMES	GOALS

BORN ● Hitchin, Hertfordshire, 8.3.74.
OTHER CLUBS ● Rochdale on loan 95/6 (6, 0);
Rotherham United on loan 96/7 (17, 0);
Port Vale 98/9– (23, 0).

Kevin Pilkington is a competent young goalkeeper for whom it is difficult not to feel a smidgin of sympathy. Following his installation as understudy to Peter Schmeichel during 1994/95, the plucky youngster attempted to grow up – in a footballing sense – in the mighty one's all-encompassing shadow, and it was not easy.

After excelling on his senior debut as the Dane's substitute in a home victory over Crystal Palace in November 1994, Kevin knew some trying moments between the Manchester United posts. For instance, he was on duty for the 3–0 League Cup humiliation by York City in September 1995 and although he did not deserve particular blame, he was targeted by whingers who sighed: 'If only Peter'd been here … '

In fact, Kevin was a promising all-rounder but he failed to do himself justice in most of his senior appearances. Accordingly United sought more experienced men, first Tony Coton and then Raimond van der Gouw, to serve as second string while the blond rookie was loaned to other clubs.

He did well in spells with Rochdale and Rotherham and extended his horizons further at Celtic in the spring of 1998. However, on his return it was decided that Kevin was not good enough to become Schmeichel's long-term successor and he was given a free transfer.

SIMON DAVIES ▼

1994/95–1996/97

20 GAMES **1** GOALS

BORN	Middlewich, Cheshire, 23.4.74.
HONOURS	1 Wales cap (96–).
OTHER CLUBS	Exeter City on loan 93/4 (6, 1); Huddersfield Town on loan 96/7 (3, 0); Luton Town 97/8–98/9 (22, 1); Macclesfield Town 98/9– (48, 3).

English-born Welsh international flankman Simon Davies was more of a jinker than a flier.

On his day he could produce a beguiling stepover and purvey a dummy with bewildering persuasion, yet his pace was unremarkable and he did little to suggest that he would make the leap from Central League stalwart to Premiership regular with Manchester United.

As a lanky left-sided teenager, Simon displayed much skilful promise during the successful FA Youth Cup campaign of 1991/92, then consolidated in the reserves. The next step came with League Cup and European outings during 1994/95, the highlight being his goal against Galatasaray at Old Trafford. Showing commendable composure, Simon chested down a cross from Gary Neville before unleashing an emphatic ten-yard cross-shot to start the Reds on their way to a 4–0 victory.

Though that senior opportunity had been due largely to the rules then restricting the number of foreigners to be used in European competition, Simon had done enough to earn several appearances at League level.

Understandably in view of the murderous competition for wing and midfield berths at Old Trafford, he could not cement a place and became unsettled. A transfer request was granted but a move never materialised and he signed a new contract in 1996.

However, in summer '97 United accepted a £150,000 offer and Simon joined Luton, then Macclesfield.

CHRIS CASPER ▲

1994/95–1996/97

7 GAMES **0** GOALS

BORN	Burnley Lancashire, 28.4.75.
OTHER CLUBS	Bournemouth on loan 95/6 (16, 1); Swindon Town on loan 97/8 (9, 1); Reading 98/9– (47, 0).

When Chris Casper was locking up the centre of defence for United's 1992 FA Youth Cup winners, he was rated as likely to succeed as most of his talented team-mates. But given Alex Ferguson's understandable caution over that key position, the tall, dark Lancastrian found progress frustratingly slow.

At first his road was blocked by Steve Bruce and Gary Pallister, a formidable barrier indeed, yet even after Steve's departure, Chris found himself in a queue behind the likes of David May, Ronny Johnsen and Henning Berg. Beyond that, his confidence could hardly have been boosted by the arrival of Dutch star Jaap Stam and the encouraging start made at Premiership level by young Wesley Brown.

Admittedly there were a handful of senior opportunities during a 1996/97 injury crisis and the England youth international, the son of former Burnley hero Frank Casper, stepped into the breach calmly and efficiently enough.

However, though there were no particular howlers and Chris maintained his reputation as a stylish, footballing centre-half, there remained question-marks over his authority and ruthlessness. Season 1997/98 brought a successful loan spell with Swindon and a new two-year contract, but with the certainty of ferocious ongoing competition for places with United, he opted for a £300,000 switch to Reading.

Grins replaced glowers, as if some obscure chip was being shed from the Cole shoulder.

1994/95–

225 GAMES **103** GOALS

BORN	Nottingham, 15.10.71.
HONOURS	European Cup 98/9. League Championship 95/6, 96/7, 98/9, 99/00. FA Cup 95/6, 98/9. 7 England caps (95–).
OTHER CLUBS	Arsenal 90/1 (1, 0); Fulham on loan 91/2 (13, 3); Bristol City 91/2–92/3 (41, 20); Newcastle United 92/3–94/5 (70, 55).

The advent of Dwight Yorke in August 1998 might have shattered the aspirations of Andy Cole, whose remarkable strike rate of approximately a goal every two starts in his three and a half seasons as a Red Devil had failed to earn the acceptance, much less the affection, which he might have considered his due. But instead of shrinking at the prospect of further high-class competition – remember he had Messrs Solskjaer and Sheringham to contend with already – the much-maligned Midlander struck up a joyful professional and personal empathy with the irrepressible Tobagan. The result was a deluge of goals for both men and the transformation of a widely held, if rather unkind, image of Andy.

Andy Cole

Now the so-called morose misfit was perceived anew as a gleeful executioner, a top performer at peace with himself and his world. Grins became more commonplace than glowers, as if some obscure chip was being shed from the Cole shoulder, and the swashbuckling pair cut swathes through bewildered defences with their lightning interplay and untrackable dummies as they spearheaded United's progress towards an unprecedented treble.

Come 1999/2000, his technique ever more refined, Andy contributed a new series of nerveless masterpieces, notably the bicycle kick at home to Leicester, the scintillating swivel, sprint and dink that sunk Leeds at Elland Road, and the quicksilver turn and half-volley as Fiorentina were outgunned at Old Trafford.

In truth, Andy had done more than enough back in pre-Yorke 1997/98 to repudiate his doubters. He netted 25 times, he was runner-up to Dennis Bergkamp as the players' player of the year and he gave the lie to accusations that he couldn't produce in crucial matches, witness fabulous examples of individual opportunism at Liverpool, Chelsea and Blackburn. Finally he demoralised Everton at Old Trafford with a chip so sublime that, had it emanated from the hallowed boot of Eric Cantona, it would have been hailed as a stroke of genius.

Yet while statistics proved that Andy was no flop, one fact which no amount of number-crunching could disguise was

that, at times, he had made supporters weep with his profligacy, cutting a poignantly abject figure as chance after chance had gone begging. That image was most vivid at West Ham in the final League game of 1994/95, when United lost the title for the want of one goal and Andy squandered a succession of late openings. Unjust or not, it seemed that some supporters would never forgive him for that. His apologists could assert, with justification, that until 1997/98 he had never enjoyed a lengthy settled sequence without injuries or illness. Fully fit at last, they could add, he proved himself comprehensively.

And indeed, whereas earlier it had been reasonable to ask whether Andy lacked the skill and composure to capitalise on an acceptable percentage of the openings which his own searing pace and predatory instinct helped to fashion, the question has become no longer valid. Unquestionably, he can do it.

Following his shock arrival in January 1995 in exchange for £6 million and Keith Gillespie, he became something of an aunt sally, the chemistry between crowd and footballer somehow lacking something even in times of triumph, yet he has matured gradually into a splendid all-round forward, even apart from his goals. The speed and variety of his movement off the ball creates confusion which can be exploited by colleagues, and he has become as much a maker as a taker of chances. All along he has worked assiduously, never hiding from responsibility even at his lowest ebb as a whipping boy. For that, and for a performance graph that has soared during the past three campaigns, he deserves enormous respect.

Clearly his link with Yorke is important, but it can be overstressed to Cole's detriment. There was a feeling that Andy was overawed by Cantona and there is no doubt that Dwight is his most suitable partner since Peter Beardsley at Newcastle. But it would be monstrously unfair to give the newcomer all the credit for their joint prosperity. Often the glory in which Yorke has bathed has been made possible only by the selflessness of his fellow striker, a largely untrumpeted circumstance.

And so, at last, it is time for United fans everywhere to cherish Andy Cole. In 1998 this writer paid tribute to him, but pondered: 'When will he be loved?' After his fabulously adroit title-clincher against Spurs in May '99 had laid the ghost of Upton Park, and another term of shining achievement had followed, there was only one conceivable answer: 'Now!'

The Red Devils required a genius – and they found him in Eric Cantona.

1992/93–1996/97

182 **80**
GAMES GOALS

BORN • Caillols, near Marseille, 24.5.66.
HONOURS • League Championship 92/3, 93/4, 95/6, 96/7. FA Cup 93/4, 95/6. 45 France caps (87–).
OTHER CLUBS • Auxerre 83/4–85/6 (13, 2); Martigues 85/6 (0, 0); Auxerre 86/7–87/8 (68, 21); Marseille 88/9 (22, 5); Bordeaux on loan 88/9 (11, 6); Montpellier 89/90 (33, 10); Marseille 90/1 (18, 8); Nimes 91/2 (17, 2), all France; Leeds United 91/2–92/3 (28, 9).

Manchester United had been waiting a long time for such a man; since the early 1970s, in fact, when a certain Irishman's progress down a sad and slippery slope became, in sporting terms, distressingly irreversible.

Eric Cantona

Back then, a little boy was playing in the hills of his native Provence, unaware of the aching need that was to grow steadily at Old Trafford, not knowing that to him would fall the glorious destiny of meeting that need.

The Red Devils required a genius, no less, one who could supply the final frisson of inspiration and style that would transform a collection of fine players into champions. In November 1992, United found their messiah in Eric Cantona.

As Alex Ferguson has admitted, his purchase of the tempestuous but supremely brilliant Frenchman owed plenty to sheer good luck. The unexpected deal, which had most Leeds fans groping for the sackcloth and ashes, sprang from no more than a casual inquiry by the Reds' boss. Old Trafford's latest title challenge had been endangered by a goal drought and reinforcements were being sought when – pouf! – the Gallic charmer, whose late contribution had helped Leeds land the 1991/92 Championship at United's expense, simply fell into Fergie's lap.

The reason for the Yorkshiremen's readiness to sell – and for a mere £1.2 million – has never been explained satisfactorily, but really it doesn't matter. The fact was that the Reds had signed one of the world's most gifted footballers. Now, could they use him to best advantage? Many critics dismissed him as an unwarranted luxury whose flicks and tricks were an attractive but impractical adornment; others reckoned his propensity for falling foul of authority would see him sink without trace. All of them were wrong.

Eric strutted proudly on to the Old Trafford stage, and before long his flair and imagination had given United an extra dimension, a decisive edge which resulted in an exhilarating title triumph in 1992/93 followed by the hallowed League and FA Cup double a year later.

There might even have been a third successive title, but for Cantona's eight-month ban after attacking a lout who had goaded him at Selhurst Park in January 1995. After that, as personal oblivion beckoned, he confounded his detractors to emerge impressively rehabilitated from a period of self-examination. The upshot was yet another Championship, with Eric's goals winning match after match as Newcastle's vast lead was steadily overhauled. All that remains to mention of 1995/96 is that United appointed their Frenchman as captain and they won the FA Cup, courtesy of a late and lordly winner from . . . Eric Cantona.

Notwithstanding his darker side, which has tainted his talent and resulted in disruptive suspensions, his football was unique. Often he seemed to saunter disdainfully while others strained every muscle, but suddenly he would find space where there was none. Then Eric the innovator would reveal the perfection of his touch with passes of the sweetest subtlety, orchestrating incisive attacks with a distinctive swagger. Yet despite such delicacy, the Cantona cocktail contained strength and athleticism, too, frequently enabling him to brush defenders aside with an imperious shrug.

For all that, it was Eric's goals which provoked the purest wonder. Whether he wielded the rapier (his chips were particularly exquisite) or the bludgeon (long-range bombshells a speciality), the result was the same – utter beauty. Naturally he was feted with awards, notably by fellow players in 1994 and, more controversially, by football writers two years later when his rebirth as well as his ability was being honoured.

After that, after everything, what was left for United's turbulent talisman, who had entered his 31st year just two weeks on from the double double? The early months of 1996/97 saw his form falter for the first time, but a melancholy autumn gave way to a more fruitful spring as a renewed quest for glory gathered momentum. However, his wan contribution to the European Cup semi-final prompted suggestions that the end of a magnificent reign was nigh, and so it proved. Just a week after leading the Reds to a fourth Premiership crown in half a decade, he announced his retirement. Not for him a slow descent into mediocrity; he left as he had arrived, dramatically and on his own terms. Given the nature of the man, the decision to depart at the top was a correct one. The multitudes who lionised him, and his young colleagues in whose development he played such a mammoth part, were left to bid a graceful farewell and cherish the profusion of deathless memories this unique player left behind him.

Back in 1992, Eric Cantona was described as an uncontrollable free spirit, a capricious bird of passage who would never linger. In the four and a half years that followed he became the single most influential footballer in the English game. Touché!

On occasion, in appreciation of Giggs' unique talent, even the fans of his victims have been moved to applaud.

1990/91–

394 GAMES 83 GOALS

BORN ● Cardiff, 29.11.73.
HONOURS ● European Cup 98/9. League Championship 92/3, 93/4, 95/6, 96/7, 98/9, 99/00. FA Cup 93/4, 95/6, 98/9. League Cup 91/2. 26 Wales caps (91–).

The eyes are cold, the expression deadpan. The slim body hovers over the ball, swaying mesmerically. One enchanting step-over follows another and he is gone, more elusive than a mayfly, as uncatchable as a shadow.

Ryan Giggs

Yet again, Ryan Giggs is running free, flowing through a defence as smoothly, as cleanly, as water ripples over the stones on a river bed. In a flash, the sheer beauty of the moment is overtaken by high drama as he changes direction, wriggles like some frenzied eel past several unavailing challenges and draws back his left boot. The ball is struck, the net is found; the stadium erupts and the day is made for all who prize the extraordinary in sport. The Welsh prodigy plays for Manchester United but he belongs to the world and on occasion, in rapt appreciation of his unique talent, even the fans of his victims have been moved to applaud.

After being snatched from Manchester City – he had been enrolled in the Blues' School of Excellence, only to sign schoolboy forms with United on his 14th birthday – Ryan made meteoric progress at Old Trafford. Soon he was the coruscating focal point of an outstanding youth team, then tasted senior action as a 17-year-old in the spring of 1991, before emerging as the footballing phenomenon of the subsequent season. Extravagant claims for boy wonders are rarely warranted, but in this case there was simply no room for doubt, not enough superlatives to do justice to the Giggs ability.

The combination of qualities which sets Ryan apart from his fellows reads uncommonly like a blueprint for soccer perfection. The total mastery over the ball and the startling acceleration, the exquisite balance and the deceptive strength, they meld together to irresistible effect. There is courage and industry, too, and crucially, his head is not for turning by any amount of adulation. The native nervelessness which enhances his efforts on the pitch is mirrored by a level demeanour off it; indeed, had he been any other way, then Alex Ferguson's strenuous efforts to protect him from media predators must have proved fruitless.

Yet for all that gilded glory, is Ryan capable of assuming the mantle of true, lasting greatness? Without tempting fate, it began to seem possible in the spring of 2000 when, per-

haps, a lengthy purple patch – highlighted by the torture of Fiorentina at Old Trafford – announced the onset of his prime. Certainly the 26-year-old's running with and without the ball was more destructive than ever, he appeared increasingly aware of the passing options available in United's fluid system, and his crossing was more frequently devastating than dreadful.

The improvement came as a relief to supporters perturbed by earlier fluctuations of confidence, noticeable even as he contributed thrillingly to United's first double in 1993/94. There followed a year during which the Giggs input became ominously fitful as he attempted to play on despite debilitating injury problems and he began to look distressingly like a victim of his own fame. The question was unavoidable: was he being sucked in by outside interests to the detriment of his football?

Ever alert to danger signs, Alex Ferguson reacted with firm understanding, offering periodic rests, extra coaching and sound advice. The results were plain to see in 1995/96 when a re-galvanised, fully fit Ryan, often roaming from midfield, played the best all-round football of his life to that date. The impetus was maintained over the next four terms as he married that familiar explosive brilliance ever more surely to gratifying consistency, especially in a succession of fabulous displays in the Champions League, during which he terrorised some of the world's most accomplished defenders.

Ryan is best deployed on his natural left flank, offering balance to the team as he torments victims on the touchline while adding periodic spice by cutting inside like some high-velocity sidewinder, although he can be deadly, too, in central midfield. Meanwhile, the unforgettable memories pile up: the sublime run and goal at Loftus Road in early '94 that was Giggs in microcosm; the near-post howitzer that jolted Juventus at Old Trafford in October '97; a far-post header of which Tommy Taylor would have been proud at home to Barcelona a season later; and, most compelling of all given its context of unhinging the tightest defence of modern times, the bewitching dribble and thunderous drive which evicted Arsenal from the 1999 FA Cup near the end of a spellbindingly dramatic semi-final replay.

His value is incalculable and during his distressingly frequent absences through hamstring injuries, United tend to be less penetrative, sometimes looking half the side without him. Awesome talent, an endless appetite for work, a lovely temperament and still getting better after nine years at the top – is Ryan Giggs for real?

Gary radiates mature efficiency, an astute, well-organised defender who remains eager to learn.

1992/93–

245 GAMES **2** GOALS

BORN ● Bury Lancashire, 18.2.75.
HONOURS ● European Cup 98/9. League Championship 95/6, 96/7, 98/9, 99/00. FA Cup 95/6, 98/9. 34 England caps (95–).

Subject to unavoidable multi-coloured exceptions, Gary Neville's working togs are the red shirt and white shorts of Manchester United. Yet somehow it requires no quantum leap of the imagination to picture the cool, sensible Lancastrian bedecked immaculately in pinstripe suit, complete with briefcase and brolly, striding briskly in the direction of Civil Service desk or accountant's ledger.

Gary Neville

Truly Gary is a manager's dream. On the field he radiates mature efficiency, an astute, well-organised defender who, despite winning more than 30 England caps by the age of 25, remains engagingly eager to learn. Off the park, too, he seems almost too good to be true, his professionalism equalled only by his commitment to the Old Trafford cause. That last-mentioned quality was illustrated with vivid clarity in September 1996 when, after appending his name to a five-year contract, he declared: 'I'd be happy to sign for ten years if they asked me!'

The rise and rise of Gary Neville began as a 16-year-old trainee Red in July 1991, gathering pace rapidly as he forged a promising central defensive partnership with Chris Casper at junior level and captained United's victorious FA Youth Cup side in spring '92. That September marked his senior debut, then came a lull, but a major breakthrough was imminent.

Injuries to Paul Parker and David May in autumn '94 offered an opening at right-back which Gary seized, impressing with his composure, intelligent reading of the game and unfussy tackling. He excelled at smuggling the ball away from danger, unobtrusively but effectively, and he was above average in the air for a full-back. He showed commendable initiative as a speedy overlapper, too, and there was the attacking bonus of his long throw.

That term the slim rookie enjoyed two settled first-team spells, one in midwinter, the other in the closing weeks of what proved to be a numbingly disappointing campaign for United. For Gary, though, the learning curve had been not so much steep as well-nigh vertical and his aptitude was underlined dramatically in the summer when he was elevated to the England team, having made just 17 Premiership starts. Predictably enough, this extraordinarily calm youngster was not fazed by finding himself so unexpectedly on the international stage. Whether operating at full-back or on the right of a back three, he did well enough to nudge towards the status of England regular. But then, perhaps inevitably there occurred a momentary blip in Gary's runaway success story.

During periods of 1995/96 his customary consistency was less pronounced and there were moments when his habitually fierce concentration appeared to slip. In striving to remedy the situation, perhaps he tried too hard, and the point came when the manager decided that Gary needed a rest. Ironically, the man to benefit was his younger brother Phil, who denied Neville Snr a start in the FA Cup Final against Liverpool. That said, Gary missed only seven League appearances during United's second double-winning campaign and returned resiliently to feature in Euro '96.

Over subsequent seasons he played the best football of his life on the right flank of the Reds' rearguard – his well-oiled link with his chum, David Beckham, proving particularly effective – though it is much to his boss's chagrin that Gary lacks the physical stature (at 5ft 10ins) to operate dominantly in the middle. In all other respects, particularly his ability to order a back four and to cover for team-mates under pressure, he is a natural for the job. No doubt he will continue to deputise there, as he did so superbly at home to Liverpool in September 1998, when his speed and anticipation reduced the brilliant Michael Owen to impotence.

But for the moment, after recovering from a long-standing groin injury, and despite a few uncharacteristic lapses which might be ascribed legitimately to battle fatigue – notably two frightful errors against Vasco de Gama in Rio which effectively ended the Reds' World Club Championship chances – he remains a right-back of formidable quality. No recognition of that worth could be more emphatic than his selection by his peers for the PFA Premiership teams of '96, '97, '98 and '99, a phenomenal achievement for one so young.

For the future, bolstered by a burgeoning authority and with his loyalty, dedication and all-round proficiency beyond question, Gary Neville seems destined to become an outstanding captain of Manchester United. Already he has donned the armband in emergencies; one day, surely, it will be his by right.

For all his admirable solidity, though, Ronny is no slouch with the ball at his feet.

1996/97–

112 **6**
GAMES GOALS

BORN ● Sandefjord, Norway 10.6.69.
HONOURS ● European Cup 98/9. League Championship 96/7, 98/9.
FA Cup 98/9. Norway caps.
OTHER CLUBS ● Tonsberg 91–92; Lyn Oslo 92–93 (31, 7); Lillestrom
94–95 (23, 4), all Norway; Besiktas, Turkey 95/6 (22, 1).

Ronny Johnsen is virtually a one-man football team, and though no media fanfares accompanied his £1.5 million arrival from the Turkish club Besiktas in the summer of 1996, the versatile Norwegian represents one of Alex Ferguson's canniest excursions into the transfer market. An admirable first season at Old Trafford, at the end of which he pocketed a Championship medal, was followed by even more influential second and third terms in which he emerged as one of United's most reliable players. Indeed, although a recognised 'first eleven' has become unfashionable in these days of ceaseless squad rotation, Ronny would be a prime candidate for any notional selection along those lines, based on his sheer consistency. That in itself is an enormous achievement, as it would leave such estimable performers as Henning Berg, David May, Wes Brown and probably even new signing Mickael Silvestre on the sidelines.

Ronny Johnsen

Primarily a central defender, Ronny can also operate to the Red Devils' lofty standards in midfield, and has filled in at full-back, too. And there is yet another dimension to the slim six-footer's commendable adaptability. As recently as 1994 he was employed regularly as a striker, the position in which he began his soccer career, in Norway's first division. Indeed, it's a fair bet that such a splendid natural athlete would acquit himself soundly even if pressed into emergency duty between the posts. Ronny is the ideal squad player, then, but that does not imply a lack of specialist expertise in any given role. As a centre-half for instance, he is sure-footed, sharp-eyed and intelligent, challenging decisively both in the air and on the ground. He is extremely quick, too, a priceless asset, though he must guard against an admittedly infrequent tendency to ball-watch, a flaw which can be punished ruthlessly at the top level.

Johnsen was seen at his best at Stamford Bridge in February 1997, coping more coolly than most Premiership defenders when confronted with Chelsea's Gianfranco Zola. After scoring an early goal, the brilliant Italian threatened to run amok against the startled Reds during a one-sided first half. But Ronny tracked his elusive quarry faithfully, eventually wearing down Zola's effectiveness and United duly regained a foothold in the game. Another emphatic example of the Johnsen class came in the home victory over Aston Villa the following December, when he earned man-of-the-match accolades for his composed dominance of Stan Collymore and Savo Milosovic.

However, it is as an energetic midfielder that Ronny has delivered some of his most telling performances. In Turkey in October 1996 he completed a sternly efficient marking job on Fenerbahce's key man, the Nigerian Okocha, then excelled as a rock-steady holding player at home to Porto, allowing Giggs, Cantona and company the freedom to inspire one of United's most rousing European victories. Similarly he was outstanding when Juventus were overcome at Old Trafford.

For all his admirable solidity, Ronny is no slouch with the ball at his feet, either. Though not especially creative, his distribution is invariably sensible, his control is assured and he has been seen to leave an opponent for dead through sheer sleight of foot. Scoring goals is not his prime concern, but after failing to hit the target during his first campaign, he became more of a threat during 1997/98. Indeed, Ronny did much to prolong United's faltering Championship challenge with timely springtime efforts at home to Wimbledon and Liverpool.

Unfortunately, after contributing royally to the treble triumph of 1998/99, he succumbed to knee problems which put him out of contention for virtually the whole of the subsequent campaign. Having regained fitness, though, he can expect to play an integral part in the Red Devils' plans for several more years. The experienced Norwegian was by no means an obvious transfer target and stands as a telling tribute to United's continental scouts. For recommending Ronny Johnsen, congratulations are in order.

DAVID MAY

1994/95–

106	8
GAMES	GOALS

BORN	Oldham, Lancashire, 26.6.70.
HONOURS	League Championship 95/6, 96/7. FA Cup 95/6, 98/9.
OTHER CLUBS	Blackburn Rovers 88/9–93/4 (123, 3).

The broadest grin at the Riverside on May 5, 1996, belonged to David May, and no one had more heart-felt reason for celebration than the affable blond centre-half. It was the day Manchester United clinched their third Championship in four years and David had headed the opening goal in a 3–0 victory over Middlesbrough, then gone on to play a blinder as Bryan Robson's men had briefly threatened to stage a party-pooping revival.

Beyond that, the man signed as a possible long-term successor to Steve Bruce could feel that he had finally arrived as a Red Devil, having survived some torrid times since his £1.2 million acquisition from Blackburn in the summer of 1994. When the deal was announced, his capture from United's local rivals was hailed as a coup by the fans. Not only had Rovers been outstripped in the recent title race, but now one of their most promising youngsters had been lured to Old Trafford.

Soon, however, that sunny scenario was to take on a gloomy aspect. David took time to adapt to the Reds' slick passing style and cruel jibes began emanating from the direction of Ewood Park. Then, when the squarely-built six-footer proved woefully sluggish during a run in his unfavoured role of right-back – notably in the European Cup debacle in Gothenburg, where he was substituted after being tormented by Jesper Blomqvist – he became the butt of many so-called United supporters, too.

Sadly, just when he needed to play to restore his confidence, David was sidelined by a hernia, not returning until the spring of 1995, ironically about the time his former club was relieving his new employers of their Premiership crown. It was a situation demanding enormous courage and determination, and the former Rover displayed both in abundance. Overcoming further fitness problems in the course of 1995/96, he offered competent cover when Gary Pallister suffered a midwinter injury and attained new heights when called up again in March. Indeed, so dominant was David during the run-in to the League and FA Cup double that Steve Bruce, no less, could not gain a Wembley place.

Infectiously enthusiastic, a doughty aerial battler and a first-rate tackler whose shrewd reading of the game compensates for a lack of outright pace, he had learned to cope with every United game being a high-pressure affair and there could be no doubting his worthiness to wear the red shirt.

Thereafter David excelled as the title was retained in 1996/97, but a combination of further debilitating injuries and heightened competition from Messrs Johnsen, Berg, Stam and Brown raised uncertainty about his Old Trafford future. Even so, he performed nobly when called upon during the final month of the momentous treble-winning campaign, notably in the Wembley eclipse of Newcastle's Shearer and Ferguson. Come 1999/2000, Dame Fortune frowned once more. Just as mishaps to central defensive rivals caused vacancies, he suffered knee damage and was out for three months. On his return David was loaned to Huddersfield, only to be struck down yet again.

The lack of a work permit cost Manchester United a cool £5 million and the services of Henning Berg for a decade. During the late 1980s, the blond Norwegian defender arrived at Old Trafford for a trial and Alex Ferguson liked what he saw. But that crucial piece of paper was not forthcoming and the richly promising teenager departed to continue his fledgling career in his native land. Ten years on, the Red Devils' boss finally got his man, but not before Henning had been a key component in the Blackburn Rovers side which had denied United the Premiership title in 1994/95.

In fact, Alex had made further protracted attempts to complete the signing during 1996/97, a deal reportedly falling through because of strained relations between Ewood Park and Old Trafford. However, the player was desperate to join the club he had supported since boyhood and when he got his wish in August 1997 it signalled the temporary end of United's worldwide quest for a centre-half. Though Messrs Pallister, Johnsen and May were already in situ, the manager was determined that his plans would never again be undermined by an injury crisis in such a key area.

After a somewhat shaky start during which he appeared ill at ease with United's offside trap, Henning settled seamlessly into the side. Icily composed, immensely strong and an assured distributor, he read the play so shrewdly that he seemed to stroll through the most tumultuous sequences of action. At times he excelled, particularly under heavy fire away to Juventus and in the siege at Monaco, but at others he appeared ponderous when faced with pacy opponents and, handicapped by a niggling hernia problem, gradually he slipped down the pecking order.

Come 1998/99, Stam, Johnsen, Gary Neville, May and Brown comprised a daunting quintet of rivals and by autumn speculation about Berg's future was mounting. But when squad circumstances furnished an extended first-team run in the New Year, Henning responded magnificently and at the San Siro in March the Norwegian truly captured the hearts and minds of United fans with his coolly polished display against Ronaldo and company. A series of implacable tackles on some of the world's most talented forwards was a colossal factor in the Reds' triumph, while one acrobatic scooped clearance from the head of Zamorano offered vivid evidence of his athleticism and powers of improvisation.

That April Henning fell prey to further injury, but he was back in the side at the outset of 1999/2000, only to be ousted by newcomer Mickael Silvestre following a costly error against Fiorentina in Florence. At that point his prospects seemed bleak, but when the Frenchman lost form in the spring, back bounced Berg, as composed and competent as ever, to play an influential part in the climax to yet another momentous campaign.

HENNING BERG

1997/98–

 99 **3**

GAMES GOALS

BORN	Eidsvell, Norway, 1.9.69.
HONOURS	League Championship 98/9, 99/00. Norway caps.
OTHER CLUBS	KFUM Oslo, Valerengen, Lillestrom, all Norway; Blackburn Rovers 92/3–97/8 (159, 4).

1992/93–

240 GAMES **18 GOALS**

BORN ● Manchester, 21.1.75.
HONOURS ● European Cup 98/9. League Championship 95/6,
96/7, 98/9, 99/00. FA Cup 95/6. 8 England caps (97–).

> *Butt's self-belief appears to be total, he simply cannot be intimidated and his apparent disregard for reputations is remarkable.*

Nicky Butt has not been blessed with the breath-taking flair of a Beckham, the sweet skills of a Scholes or the coolness and poise of the brothers Neville. But while those fellow graduates from the Old Trafford academy of soccer excellence have attracted a deafening chorus of approval from some of the game's shrewdest judges, United's red-haired midfield buzz-bomb is not exactly lacking in eminent admirers himself.

Nicky Butt

When Bryan Robson departed for Middlesbrough in 1994, he picked out Nicky as the rookie Red Devil most assuredly bound for the top, while Kevin Keegan, who had managed the combative Mancunian at England under-21 level, predicted the long-term international future which now is under way.

But Nicky's most enthusiastic advocate, and undoubtedly the most influential, is Alex Ferguson. Since the uncomplicated, hard-working youngster muscled his way to the fringe of the senior reckoning in 1992 – having assisted in the capture of the FA Youth Cup several months earlier – the United boss had appeared to feel a particular affinity with him, perhaps perceiving in the boy a mirror image of his own passionate desire to succeed.

In the summer of 1995, Alex was to demonstrate his faith in unequivocal manner, parting with Paul Ince and paying Nicky the mammoth compliment of not replacing the England star with an expensive new recruit. Indeed, he went further, declaring that he had pondered the wisdom of buying Paul Gascoigne but decided it would not be fair on Old Trafford's crop of youthful talent, particularly Butt, whom he asserted could be held back no longer.

Those who questioned the manager's judgement – and there was no shortage of sceptics during a controversial interlude which also saw the sale of Mark Hughes and Andrei Kanchelskis – needed only to re-examine one of United's darkest footballing hours for evidence to back Ferguson's viewpoint. Not many plus points emerged from the Reds' annihilation by Barcelona in November 1994, but certainly the performance of Nicky Butt was

one. On that sorry Nou Camp night, he was a study in unshakeable resolution and controlled fire, standing tall as the walls caved in around him and taking responsibility like a veteran.

Since then there has been ample opportunity to appreciate the midfielder's many admirable qualities. A hyper-active ground-coverer with a biting tackle and no mean ability in the air, he is unselfish, endlessly persistent and his sinewy strength makes him devilishly difficult to dispossess. His toughness, though not in doubt, tends to be of the calmly uncompromising rather than malicious variety and, unlike some dispensers of hard knocks, he can take them without complaint.

As a distributor, Nicky is at his most effective when he keeps it simple, which he does most of the time. In fact, he can dispatch the occasional delightfully cute delivery, but there have been moments when he has been a tad over-ambitious for his capabilities, especially during his early Premiership days. Perhaps he felt, having risen to the senior side, that he should be doing more than winning the ball and giving it sensibly, a misapprehension that seems to have vanished.

Nicky is not a prolific goal-scorer, though a couple of his strikes remain vivid in the memory, namely his flying header from David Beckham's exquisitely driven cross in the 1996 Charity Shield drubbing of Newcastle and his savage 20-yarder which won a tight encounter with Leeds at Old Trafford in November 1998.

Crucially in the mega-competitive environment of the modern game, his self-belief appears to be total, he simply cannot be intimidated and his apparent disregard for reputations has always been remarkable. Indeed, whether whipping the ball from the foot of an illustrious opponent or directing Monsieur Cantona where to pass (!) Nicky has given every appearance of being nerveless. He thrives on responsibility, too, as he has shown during lengthy absences of fellow enforcer Roy Keane.

Above all, and despite finding himself in occasional competition for a place with his chum, Paul Scholes, it is clear that Nicky Butt belongs in the top flight.

With his input ever more efficient and mature as the new millennium dawned, this phlegmatic yet spikily formidable 25-year-old remained an integral cog in the Manchester United trophy-winning machine.

> *There isn't a player in the country who spots a passing option more perceptively and he runs many a game.*

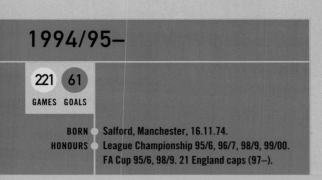

1994/95–

221 GAMES **61** GOALS

BORN Salford, Manchester, 16.11.74.
HONOURS League Championship 95/6, 96/7, 98/9, 99/00.
FA Cup 95/6, 98/9. 21 England caps (97–).

After years in the shadow of more flamboyant, though not necessarily more gifted performers, Paul Scholes has emerged as a star in his own right.

Paul Scholes

The articulate Emmanuel Petit, a fierce but respectful midfield rival at both club and international level, nominated the chunky redhead as the League's outstanding player of 1998/99, while after Paul's head-hand-and-foot hat-trick against Poland at Wembley, England boss Kevin Keegan quipped that 'the little fellow deserves a knighthood.'

Sir Paul Scholes? At first glance, he more closely resembles a refugee from the pages of Just William. With his scamp's face and stockily boyish build, he lacks only a scruffy school cap and a catapult protruding from a torn blazer pocket to complete an irresistible picture. But place a ball at his feet and a Manchester United shirt on his back, and our young scallywag is transformed into a soccer thoroughbred, one of the most subtle and perceptive talents of an Old Trafford generation.

Though the calmly undemonstrative, almost painfully modest Paul has tended, until recently, to be underrated in the media, there has never been the remotest doubt about his quality in the mind of the Red Devils' manager, who once affectionately dubbed him a 'bloody little nuisance' for putting so much pressure on the selection process by his sustained excellence.

Indeed, Sir Alex Ferguson has even likened Scholes to a callow Kenny Dalglish, paying tribute to a shrewd footballing brain which capitalises assuredly on delightful ball control, incisively imaginative distribution and a priceless instinct for scoring goals. Paul possesses an innate knack of drifting unnoticed into space, even when closely marked in the heart of enemy territory, a capacity which yielded particularly bountiful dividends during the 1995/96 League and FA Cup double-winning campaign. Despite making only 18 senior starts that term, he returned 14 goals to finish as the club's second-highest scorer, behind Eric Cantona.

Telling testimony to the pedigree of Scholes the marksman is offered by the sheer variety of his finishing repertoire. Both delicate, eye-of-the-needle placements and savage, long-range howitzers – mention must be made of that perfect vol-

ley from David Beckham's corner at Bradford in March 2000 – are upliftingly within his compass, although clinical clips and nondescript nudges tend to be equally productive. Paul's aerial work is outstanding, his timing and courage compensating amply for lack of inches, and he is strong enough to withstand challenges, too, while speed of thought makes up for absence of pace over distance.

However, for all that striking success, it has been Scholes the midfielder who has riveted the attention in recent campaigns. While continuing to notch important goals – notably a succession of European gems, including his icily composed Champions League quarter-final clincher at the San Siro in March '99 – he excelled in the deep-lying role, especially during Roy Keane's lengthy absence in 1997/98 when he was majestic both as play-maker and ball-winner, his creative vision matched only by his abrasive physical impact. There isn't a player in the country who spots a passing option more perceptively nor one who can deliver the ball more surely, and he runs many a game. The value of his aggression cannot be overstated, either, though he is not a tidy tackler and perhaps more care is needed. Certainly his build-up of indiscretions has led to costly suspensions, notably the one which caused him to miss the 1999 European Cup Final.

When Cantona reigned supreme, Paul had to be patient, often occupying the bench when his exceptional ability screamed out for inclusion. But that stage was over by the turn of the century, when he had emerged as a leading light for club and country, both teams lacking a certain imaginative dimension in his absence.

Where best to employ this three-in-one jewel, this deadly finisher, inspirational creator and quiet enforcer? At first it seemed that he should play at the front, but recent seasons have showcased his value as the chief orchestrator in central midfield, while some pundits reckon he is most productive in the 'hole' behind the strikers.

Of course, the greatest compliment to United's Salford-born nugget is that he is admirably equipped to shine in any of these roles. As for his fans, proud that sometimes it seems easier for him to make the England team than the Reds' but worried that repeated exclusions might drive him elsewhere, they can rest assured: wherever he plays, their hero's days on the Old Trafford periphery are over at last. In the years ahead, publicity-shy Paul Scholes is going to find it increasingly difficult to achieve the low public profile he craves.

JORDI CRUYFF

1996/97–1999/00

52 GAMES **8** GOALS

BORN Amsterdam, Holland, 9.2.74.
HONOURS League Championship 96/7. Holland caps.
OTHER CLUBS Barcelona 94/5–95/6 (41, 11); Celta Vigo on loan 98/9.

There is no dressing up the bald fact that Jordi Cruyff has not been a success with Manchester United. True, he has been unfortunate with injuries but, even when fully fit, the tall, slender Dutchman has failed to convince, partly because there is something about him which conveys a distinct, if misleading, impression of languor. Even in the tumult of Premiership combat, Jordi can exude an incongruous serenity, like some preoccupied young aristocrat heading for drinks on the terrace. In fact, under that blond thatch and graceful demeanour, there exists a footballer alive with immense possibilities. Fiery he is not, but he can play.

His blessings are many, but most important are the silky technique and sharp intelligence which befits the son of Johan Cruyff, Europe's premier soccer talent of the 1970s. Watch Jordi when he receives the ball in a wide position and ponders a cross into a crowded penalty box. Only seldom will he hit and hope; instead he will attempt to thread a pass to a specific colleague. Of course, he is risking tame anti-climax, for the odds are against him when confronted by a forest of opponents, yet it's a mark of his quality that he attempts the harder but potentially more rewarding option.

For lengthy spells Jordi can seem anonymous, appearing to drift on the action's outer edge, but then suddenly he will dispatch a lovely raking pass, unleash an unexpected shot or jink away from an unwary marker. He boasts deceptive pace without having to strain for it, can finish forcefully and his aerial prowess is not inconsiderable. An abrasively physical cutting edge is not on offer, and neither is heart-on-sleeve passion, but there is a measure of beauty in his football.

Jordi developed under his father's management at Barcelona, leaving the Nou Camp for Old Trafford in an £800,000 deal soon after the 22-year-old had performed promisingly for Holland during Euro '96. To Alex Ferguson he offered a classy option as central striker or wide midfielder and, due partly to United's injury situation, he started the League campaign.

To the surprise of some pundits, who had thought him lightweight, he fared pretty well and was in the team more often than not until the late autumn of 1996. Since then, though, the injuries have piled up and sometimes he has looked a Red without much devil. Still, he re-emerged as a useful squad member in October 1998, playing some of the most effective football of his Old Trafford tenure before being loaned to Celta Vigo in January 1999.

Later that year, after making his fourth consecutive Charity Shield appearance, he revealed new-found urgency and earned lavish praise from his manager after rising from the bench to equalise at home to Wimbledon. Understandingly, though, Jordi had become sick of life on the periphery and he seemed certain to leave in the summer of 2000.

One delicious moment of outrageous invention during Euro '96 saddled Karel Poborsky with a burden of expectation under which he laboured anxiously throughout a disappointing Old Trafford tenure. Indeed, that steeply flighted chip which settled the Czech Republic's quarter-final clash with Portugal took on a poignant once-in-a-lifetime aspect as its diminutive author struggled, manfully but sometimes painfully, to come to terms with Premiership life.

Karel was the fleet-footed right-flanker for whom Alex Ferguson had been scouring the world since Andrei Kanchelskis had decamped to Everton and his signing that summer, for £3.5 million from Slavia Prague, was seen as a coup. As a prime factor in both his country's progress to the European final and Slavia's to a UEFA Cup semi-final, the scampering Czech had been feted for his cocktail of industry, tenacity and sparkling skill, and had been courted by Liverpool as well as leading Continental clubs. With his distinctive gaunt features and flowing locks, Karel was portrayed as the latest addition to United's roster of high-profile characters. All that remained was for the newcomer to perform.

He started perkily enough and cut a dash in several early games, most upliftingly at Elland Road in September when he tortured his hosts mercilessly and received what is possibly a unique tribute for a Red Devil. After waltzing through the home defence to set up goals for Nicky Butt and Eric Cantona, and netting brilliantly himself, he was cheered from the pitch by Leeds supporters! After that, it seemed that Karel was on the right track, that his verve and imagination would be given full rein, but somehow the 'Czech Express' began to splutter. The potentially destructive distribution became depressingly errant, the darting incursions reduced to fitful wanderings and, despite plenty of encouragement from the stands, Karel's confidence evaporated almost visibly.

Some sympathy was in order. Not speaking English, it could hardly have been easy to adjust to everyday life in a strange land, let alone cope with the searching demands of the Premiership. To his credit, he continued to work hard and, in fairness, he managed some reasonable performances. Of course, a settled sequence in the side would have helped, though that was always an unlikely luxury given his form.

Karel's discomfort ended in December 1997 when he swapped a regular seat on the Reds' bench for a place in the Portuguese sun by joining Benfica for a reported £2 million. He had once said: 'I want United's fans to remember Poborsky.' So they will, but not in the manner he intended.

KAREL POBORSKY

1996/97–1997/98

47 GAMES **6** GOALS

BORN	Jindinchuv-Hradec, Czechoslovakia, 30.3.72.
HONOURS	League Championship 96/7. Czech Republic caps.
OTHER CLUBS	Ceske Budejovice 91/2–93/4 (82, 15); Viktoria Zizkov 94/5 (27, 10); Slavia Prague 95/6 (26, 11), all Czech Republic; Benfica, Portugal, 97/8-.

Time will tell, but Phil Neville just might be outstanding ... even by the standards of Manchester United.

1994/95–

185 **2**
GAMES GOALS

BORN ● Bury, Lancashire, 21.1.77.
HONOURS ● League Championship 95/6, 96/7, 98/9, 99/00.
● FA Cup 95/6, 98/9. 23 England caps (96–).

Phil Neville could be forgiven had he been flummoxed by two mighty jolts which disrupted the runaway success story that his early career had become – and the fact that he wasn't speaks volumes for his resolution. First, in 1996/97, he fell victim to glandular fever; then, perhaps still struggling to regain prime form in the wake of that severely debilitating illness, he was a last-minute omission from the England party for France '98.

Phil Neville

Thus a draining physical ailment was followed by a crushing psychological blow, and the leaps-and-bounds progress which had characterised Phil's rise was not maintained during the first half of 1998/99, when he did not seem his former confident self. What a tribute to the young man, then, that he bounced back to play an effective part in the club's massively ambitious spring programme, and continued to thrive after another indifferent start in 1999/2000.

At this point, a glance back at Phil's pedigree is in order. By the time the Reds took their burgeoning title challenge to Newcastle in early March 1996, he had already provided ample evidence to suggest that he was an exceptionally gifted defender. In addition to his impeccable all-round accomplishments, including the capacity to fill either full-back berth with equal dexterity, he exuded a colossal sang-froid, way beyond the norm for a boy of 19. Yet if there did exist any flaw in Phil's cool, surely it would be revealed by what was certain to be a remorselessly searching test on Tyneside. After all, it was the crossroads of United's season, demanding strength and maturity at the back, dash and invention going forward.

How calmly Neville the younger faced his black-and-white striped inquisitors. In the first half, as Newcastle went for a quick kill, he defended sensibly, occasionally brilliantly, against the likes of Asprilla and Beardsley at their most voracious. Then, shortly after the interval, he set up the only goal of the game. Sprinting down the left flank, Phil exchanged passes neatly with Andy Cole before dinking a tantalising cross for Eric Cantona to supply the coup de grace with a far-post volley.

A heady business, indeed, yet no one who had followed Phil's sporting development would have been surprised. Since childhood he had excelled at ball games, even having to decide whether his future lay with the Reds or as a batsman with Lancashire CCC. Having chosen to follow Gary – always as much a friend as a sibling – into football, he emulated his big brother's absolute dedication and rose smoothly through the junior ranks.

Come January 1995, aged 18, he was pitchforked into senior action against Wrexham in the FA Cup, coping coolly with the step-up in standard and underlining his potential two weeks later in the Manchester derby at Maine Road. Though that was his final senior start that term, the season ended upliftingly for Phil when he captained United to victory in the FA Youth Cup. Clearly there was only one outlet for such talent – the first team, which is where he found himself for most of the euphoric double-winning campaign which ensued. A natural right-footer who appeared even more comfortable on the left, where he enjoyed the majority of his outings, Phil combined pace with intelligence, easy ball control with deceptive strength, adding for good measure a finely honed attacking instinct.

Twelve days after the FA Cup Final defeat of Liverpool, Phil's career gathered further prodigious momentum when he was capped by England at the age of 19, but sooner or later there had to be a setback. Cue an ankle problem followed by glandular fever, from which he fought back to complete the 1996/97 title-winning campaign and hold his place throughout most of 1997/98, including an enterprising stint in midfield during an injury crisis. Sometimes, though, his customary verve seemed muted.

And so to 1998/99 when, with competition for places hotter than ever, he spent more time on the bench than he would have liked, yet remained an integral and increasingly versatile part of the squad, his man-to-man marking of Gianfranco Zola in the FA Cup victory at Stamford Bridge attracting particularly lavish plaudits.

Still in his early twenties, restored to England duty by Kevin Keegan and with bags of priceless experience behind him, Phil has every expectation of a glittering future. However, to underline his stature and ensure that his career does not stagnate, he needs to cement a position in United's perceived best eleven, which must exist in the manager's mind even in these days of frenetic player rotation. When Denis Irwin finally stands down, Phil Neville must ensure that it is he who steps into the breach.

TERRY COOKE ▼

1995/96–1996/97

8	1
GAMES	GOALS

BORN ● Marston Green, Warwickshire, 5.8.76.
OTHER CLUBS ● Sunderland on loan 95/6 (6, 0); Birmingham City on loan 96/7 (4, 0); Wrexham on loan 98/9 (10, 0); Manchester City 98/9- (34, 7); Wigan Athletic on loan 99/00 (10, 1).

Not many youngsters, no matter how talented, find themselves compared to Diego Maradona on their debut, but it happened to Terry Cooke. To be fair to the journalist with the ultra-fertile imagination, he was referring to just one fleeting moment of inspiration – and it was a bit special.

It happened like this at home to Bolton in September 1995: operating in his favoured attacking position near the right touchline, Terry delivered a sweet, first-time backheel to Paul Scholes, took the instant return in his stride and delivered a perfect cross for Ryan Giggs to score. Of course, it set an awesome standard for the pacy, industrious but rather lightweight little Midlander to maintain and further opportunities proved to be limited, even before a serious knee injury cost him most of the 1997/98 season. Thus in April 1999, after a perky loan stint, Terry was sold to Manchester City for £600,000 down with a possible £400,000 to follow, and he starred in the Blues' successful promotion campaign.

PHIL MULRYNE ▲

1997/98–1998/99

4	0
GAMES	GOALS

BORN ● Belfast, 1.1.78.
HONOURS ● 8 Northern Ireland caps (97–).
OTHER CLUBS ● Norwich City 98/9– (16, 2).

When Philip Mulryne scored a fine hat-trick against Birmingham City in one of United's friendly preambles to the 1998/99 campaign, it begged an obvious question.

Was the skilful, tenacious right-sided midfielder of sufficient quality to make the Old Trafford grade?

Particularly with widespread speculation at that time about the future of David Beckham in the light of his World Cup trauma, the matter had immediate relevance. However, the England star buckled down to work, Philip receded to the outer fringes of Alex Ferguson's sizeable squad and when Norwich City placed a £500,000 offer on the table in March, it was accepted.

There were those close to the club who regretted the departure of the Belfast-born 21-year-old, who had won full international honours before making his senior debut for United in a League Cup tie at Ipswich in October 1997.

They believed that, if he was given time to build up his stamina, Philip was capable of demonstrating his worth. Now he has the opportunity to prove them correct, or otherwise, at Carrow Road, where he made a commendably impressive start only to have his impetus halted by a broken leg early in 1999/2000.

MICHAEL CLEGG ▲

1996/97–

20	0
GAMES	GOALS

BORN Tameside, Manchester, 7.7.77.
OTHER CLUBS Ispwich Lown on loan 99/00 (3, 0); Wigan Athletic on loan 99/00 (6, 0).

The most meaningful compliment that can be played to Michael Clegg is that whenever the rookie right-back has been plunged into senior action he has not looked out of his depth.

Even in the frenzied atmosphere of an FA Cup encounter with Wimbledon at Old Trafford in January 1997, he was utterly self-possessed, turning in a cool, competent performance that would not have shamed a first-team veteran.

Michael passed sensibly, joined in attacks with enterprising overlaps and made crucial tackles, notably one athletic challenge on Marcus Gayle which prevented a probable goal. In addition, he faced up to the Dons' formidable aerial threat with courage and sound judgement and his positional play earned plaudits for its maturity.

He took the eye equally as forcibly in March 1998 when he rose from the bench to enter the European Cup quarter-final fray at home to Monaco. Quick and combative, he stormed forward convincingly and came close to scoring with one fierce drive.

However, having shown exceptional application to rise through United's junior ranks – in the process confounding observers who doubted that he would make it – the Mancunian faces an much tougher task, that of winning a regular place in the Premiership side.

Even for the determined and capable England under-21 international, that seemed an increasingly tall order during 1999/2000, the final months of which he spent on loan, first to Ipswich Town and then to Wigan Athletic.

JOHN CURTIS ▼

1997/98–

18	0
GAMES	GOALS

BORN Nuneaton, Warwickshire, 3.9.78.
OTHER CLUBS Barnsley on loan 99/00 (28, 2).

John Curtis faces an extra opponent every time he runs on to the pitch. Having been tipped constantly for stardom since he entered his teens and having captained England at a succession of junior levels, the athletic utility defender has been saddled with massive expectations beneath which many a lad would be crushed.

However, it would seem that John can handle it. An archetypal old head on young shoulders and a born leader, he radiates composure, determination and a certain brand of cool certainty that marks out winners from also-rans. Of course, he can play a bit, too. The Curtis method is to read the game intelligently, spot danger early and deal with it decisively, an approach buttressed by a splendid all-round technique.

In his mid teens John seemed a natural centre-half, but when he failed to grow beyond 5ft 9ins he switched to fullback, where he made an impressive impact in sporadic senior appearances during 1997/98. Something of a chasing by Arsenal's Marc Overmars at Old Trafford in March showed that there was still much to learn, but there was no disgrace in struggling against a world-class player at the top of his form and John gained from the experience.

Thereafter his United opportunities proved frustratingly few as competition for places stepped up, and in 1999/2000 the England 'B' and under-21 international was loaned to Barnsley, where he figured prominently in the Tykes' push for promotion to the Premiership.

In his first term as a Red, this modest fellow attained a chemistry with the fans which others must have envied.

1996/97–

155 / 60
GAMES GOALS

BORN ● Kristiansund, Norway 26.2.73.
HONOURS ● European Cup 98/9. League Championship 96/7, 98/9, 99/00. FA Cup 98/9. Norway caps.
OTHER CLUBS ● FK Clausenengen 89/90–94/5; Molde 95/6.

Ole Gunnar Solskjaer is a study in gleeful audacity, a quicksilver elf of a striker who made the transformation from virtual unknown to the apple of Old Trafford's eye in the space of one exhilarating campaign. Since then he has sparkled despite limited opportunity, his four goals in 11 minutes at Nottingham Forest in February 1999 and his European Cup Final winner against Bayern Munich both highlighting his brilliance and emphasising the dilemma facing the personable Norwegian.

Ole Gunnar Solskjaer

Should he settle for life as a perennial substitute, continuing to be the major long-term casualty of the Old Trafford rotation system, or should he leave to become the main man elsewhere? Thus far he has taken the former option, reasoning that his chances of glory are greater with United than anywhere else, and certainly his decision to spurn Tottenham's advances in August 1998 was to prove eminently sound by that season's climax.

Since then, his value has mushroomed due to further uninhibited opportunism in 1999/2000. For example, a rare start against Everton yielded another four-goal extravaganza, then a deft shuffle and slick finish secured a home draw with Liverpool. But it was Ole's majestic control of a plummeting ball followed by a typically ruthlessly conversion in Bordeaux which proclaimed his attributes most persuasively to would-be suitors around the globe.

Solskjaer's instant success after arriving in July 1996 was a revelation even to Alex Ferguson, who had viewed him as a £1.5 million investment for the future. However, that theory was shattered, comprehensively and joyously, when pre-season training got under way. One moment smiling cherubically on the touchline, the next Ole was fizzing between startled defenders like some demonic firecracker and embarrassing Peter Schmeichel with the power and accuracy of his shooting.

Duly Solskjaer was introduced to the Premiership fray as a substitute during the visit of Blackburn in August. Soon the bank holiday crowd was transfixed as the effervescent newcomer administered a much-needed dose of pure adrenaline to the hitherto sluggish home attack. A darting, twisting, high-velocity wraith, he nonplussed Rovers' defence with his constant movement, got in half a dozen attempts on goal and equalised from one of them. Ole had arrived, and he was to be involved in most of United's matches during the remainder of a hectic campaign.

The son of a champion wrestler, the wand-like Solskjaer bears scant resemblance to an archetypal grappler, though he has inherited his father's supple strength and natural balance. He has been blessed, too, with searing acceleration, a knack of turning and shooting in one blur of action, and an enviable range of ball skills. Ole is quick-witted, so that when the ball is played into a crowded box, he tends to be the first to react, whipping decisively away from his markers; and he will make run after run into unexpected areas.

All that, and ideal temperament to boot, make Solskjaer a rare bargain, though some observers fear that he may be too lightweight physically to hold his own throughout an English season. Fair point: while not lacking in pluck or determination, he is no Mark Hughes when it comes to retaining possession, and may be best suited to sudden, sharp bursts when defenders are tired.

Whatever, in his first term as a Red, this modest fellow attained a chemistry with the fans which others must have envied. His boyish looks and endearing enthusiasm had much to do with that, but his goals – 18 in only 33 starts – were the crucial factor. Indeed, how avidly his new admirers came to relish the trademark Solskjaer strike, the slide-rule effort dispatched unerringly with right foot or left, after he has glimpsed just a tiny area of unguarded net.

At season's end, the 24-year-old must have been barely able to credit his meteoric rise, and his second campaign, inevitably laden with higher expectations, proved more difficult. Fitness worries, the absence of Cantona, being used in an unfamiliar left-sided role on occasions, the fact that he was no longer an unknown quantity – all this militated against him. But then came two more years of deathless derring-do to establish Ole as the world's deadliest substitute. Clearly he deserved better than eternal bench occupancy, yet still he smiled and proclaimed his loyalty to the Reds' cause. Whether that would survive the purchase of another world-class striker, such as Ruud Van Nistelrooy if the Dutchman regained fitness, only time would tell.

The task facing the tall, inventive, but rather ponderous marksman at United was an unenviable one.

1997/98–

105 GAMES   **25** GOALS

BORN   Highams Park, London, 2.4.66.
HONOURS   European Cup 98/9. League Championship 98/9, 99/00. FA Cup 98/9. 38 England caps (93–).
OTHER CLUBS   Millwall 83/4–90/1 (220, 93); Aldershot on loan 84/5 (5, 0); Nottingham Forest 91/2–92/3 (42, 14); Tottenham Hotspur 92/3–96/7 (166, 76).

Technically accomplished, immensely experienced, an England regular, respected by his peers ... Teddy Sheringham was all these things when he joined Manchester United from Tottenham Hotspur in a surprise £3.5 million deal in the summer of 1997. Yet by the end of his first season as a Red Devil he had been dropped by club and country and could be fairly described as a considerable disappointment.

Teddy Sheringham

End of story? Not quite. After recovering from a knee operation in February 1999, Teddy shone on occasional outings, culminating in his man-of-the-match Wembley display against Newcastle, when he rose from the bench to score one goal and create another. Then, for a golden encore, he tucked away the life-giving European Cup Final equaliser against Bayern Munich. Despite being in his 34th year, he had emphasised spectacularly that his usefulness was not at an end. To paraphrase the words of his erstwhile mockers: 'Oh Teddy, Teddy. You went to Man United and you won the lot!'

In all fairness, the task facing the tall, inventive, but rather ponderous marksman at Old Trafford was a supremely unenviable one. No matter how strenuously he or Alex Ferguson chose to deflect attention from the circumstance, Teddy was bought to fill the vacuum left by the sudden retirement of Eric Cantona. Not surprisingly, it proved beyond him, as it would have proved beyond most men. He had his moments of achievement, indeed he gave a handful of splendid performances, but overall his influence in that first term was peripheral.

The Londoner kicked off with a stinker, performing anonymously against his former club at White Hart Lane. It was impossible not to feel sympathy for him as he faced a barrage of scorn from his former admirers, which intensified as he cracked a spot-kick against a post, the first of three successive misses which was to cost him the job of penalty-taker.

Thereafter, however, as he settled into the United system, more as a deep-lying linkman than a front-runner,

he began to show the attributes for which he was renowned. Terrific in the air, a beautiful controller and passer of the ball and a subtle prompter who brought colleagues into the game, Teddy began to have a positive influence on a winning team. On the debit side, he was never the sprightliest of movers, his finishing was horribly unreliable and his impact was inconsistent, but there were grounds for hope.

These redoubled when he gave two of his most productive displays: at home to Juventus in October he timed his run to perfection to equalise with a towering header from a Ryan Giggs cross, then returned the compliment by laying on United's third for the Welshman; at Arsenal in November he netted twice, with a firm header after slipping his marker and with a first-time left-footer on the turn from 20 yards.

But it was one exquisite moment against Feyenoord in Holland which, for this onlooker, gave rise to real hope that Teddy might prove an acceptable replacement for Cantona. Taking a short ball from Giggs on the edge of the centre-circle, he looked up and took out three defenders with a sumptuous dispatch to Denis Irwin, who was breaking down the left. Sheer wonder, but sadly it was not to prove typical over the difficult months that lay ahead.

While the Reds were purring in mid-term, the Sheringham input was fine, but when the team's fluency evaporated ominously after Christmas, and seasoned campaigners such as he might have been expected to lead by example, he became ever more lacklustre.

Come 1998/99 his prospects deteriorated as newcomer Dwight Yorke gelled spectacularly with Andy Cole, while Ole Solskjaer returned to form. To make matters worse Teddy fell victim to injury and was adopted as a scapegoat by many fans, who felt he was a liability. But an enterprising autumn display in Munich offered a telling reminder of his capabilities, then came that fairytale spring revival. After that the nature of the epitaph to Sheringham's Manchester sojourn, when it is eventually needed, will be radically warmer than the one envisaged merely a short time earlier.

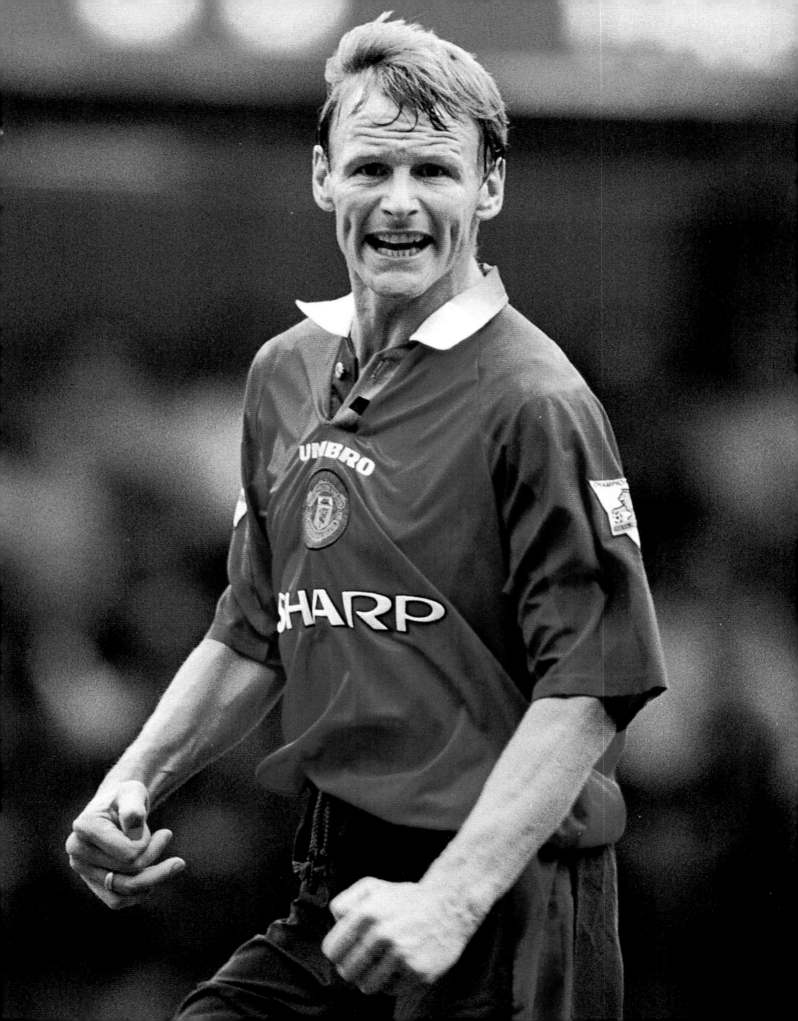

He will face an insistent challenge for both full-back slots but the quiet man from Cork is far from finished.

1990/91–

468 **31**
GAMES GOALS

BORN ● Cork, Republic of Ireland, 31.10.65.
HONOURS ● European Cup 98/9. European Cup Winners' Cup
90/1. League Championship 92/3, 93/4, 95/6,
96/7, 98/9, 99/00. FA Cup 93/4, 95/6. League
Cup 91/2. 56 Republic of Ireland caps (90–99).
OTHER CLUBS ● Leeds United 83/4–85/6 (72, 1);
Oldham Athletic 86/7–89/90 (167, 4).

The young bucks continue to clamour for his place, but Old Man Irwin, he just keeps rolling along. Indeed, such was the unobtrusive thirtysomething's consistency at the turn of the century, it is possible that the new contract which takes him to 2001 may not be the last he signs at Old Trafford.

Denis Irwin

Clearly, Arsenal do not have a monopoly on venerable defenders. When his Premiership peers voted Denis the League's best left-back in the spring of 1994 – an accolade they repeated in 1999 – they were merely confirming a belief that had been growing steadily in Manchester for several seasons. Indeed, after United had lifted the Championship in 1992/93, Alex Ferguson described Denis as one of the finest flank defenders in the world. No voice was raised in argument then – and the silence in the success-laden years since has been deafening. No player was more consistent as the Reds yomped to League and FA Cup doubles in 1993/94 and 1995/96 and the treble in 1998/99, and if the public plaudits have rained inevitably on the heads of Cantona et al, that hasn't bothered the unassuming Irishman, whose £650,000 capture from Oldham Athletic in June 1990 was to prove, in retrospect, an absolute steal.

By the time United faced the Latics in two FA Cup semi-final clashes that year, they had already been tracking the progress of the 24-year-old right-back who had revived his career at Boundary Park after being released, cheaply and surprisingly, by Leeds in 1986. His calm and class on both occasions made up Ferguson's mind, and Denis was wearing the Reds' number-two shirt as the new campaign got under way. In typically unspectacular fashion, he used that term to bed himself in, honing his talents as he tasted top-flight competition for the first time. At the back, he impressed with his pace, precise passing and resourceful reading of the game, while his ability to deliver wickedly curving crosses, low-trajectory missiles that bent around defenders and lured 'keepers from their lines, became a potent offensive weapon.

Then 1991/92 brought change and a challenge to which

the Eire international – he was capped for the first time shortly after joining the Reds – responded magnificently. The manager's decision to deploy new arrival Paul Parker at right-back saw Denis switch flanks, and initially he looked a little out of place. But though naturally right-sided, he is blessed with splendid touch in both feet and soon he settled seamlessly at number three. Thereafter, while remaining admirably solid in defence, he blossomed as an attacking force. His incisive overlaps became a joy to behold and, as his confidence mushroomed, his knack of hitting the ball cleanly brought rich rewards.

That season Denis netted four times and in the next he went one better, with no strike more welcome than his low 20-yarder which claimed the points in a tight April confrontation at Coventry. Come 1993/94 the all-round Irwin game reached new heights, his rearguard duties being discharged with the usual unshowy excellence, while two of his efforts at the other end would have done credit to any star in the Old Trafford constellation. At Anfield in January, Denis curled the sweetest free-kick imaginable past Liverpool's wall; then the following month, at Selhurst Park against Wimbledon in the FA Cup, he exchanged passes cleverly with Paul Ince before conjuring his way past two opponents with Giggs-like élan, then applying the most clinical of finishes.

If United's largely unsung hero has a weakness, it is in the air (he stands only 5ft 8in), though even when he cannot win the ball outright, usually he manages to distract the opposition with a well-timed leap. In any case, to dwell on such a marginal flaw is to be over-fussy. Though he was in his 35th year as season 1999/2000 drew to a close, an Irwin error remained a collector's item and Denis stood firm as a mature defensive anchor of enduring value. He will face an insistent challenge for both full-back slots from the Neville brothers, Wes Brown, John Curtis, Michael Clegg and others, but the quiet man from Cork is far from finished. Indeed, his enduring stature was underlined in autumn '97 when he replaced the unfortunate Teddy Sheringham as penalty-taker and in the following spring when he stood in for Peter Schmeichel as skipper. Long may Denis Irwin remain part of the Old Trafford furniture.

It was typical of 'Keano'. One moment scrapping like a yard-dog, the next passing like a master.

1993/94–

268 GAMES **37** GOALS

BORN ● Cork, Republic of Ireland, 10.8.71.
HONOURS ● League Championship 93/4, 95/6, 96/7, 98/9, 99/00. FA Cup 93/4, 95/6, 98/9. 46 Republic of Ireland caps (91–).
OTHER CLUBS ● Nottingham Forest 90/1–92/3 (114, 22).

He is booed like a pantomime villain on grounds up and down the land, yet without doubt Roy Keane is Manchester United's most influential on-field figure, bar none. Never was this more apparent than in Turin in April 1999, with the Reds two adrift after 11 minutes and facing Champions League oblivion. Then, when the need was most dire, the feisty Irishman transformed the contest as if by pure force of will.

Roy Keane

He headed an unstoppable goal which sent visible tremors through Juventus and, more crucially still, dictated midfield play with an implacable authority which rapidly established psychological supremacy.

It was typical of 'Keano'. One moment scrapping like a yard-dog, the next passing like a master, he was both a physical colossus who breathed confidence into team-mates, and a creative fixer with a hand in every phase of play. That night, as has become the norm since his recovery from a career-threatening knee injury which sidelined him for most of 1997/98, Roy was the heartbeat of Alex Ferguson's pulsating side. He has proved himself the natural choice to succeed Eric Cantona as skipper and, despite the bookings which cost him his place in the European final, has demonstrated that he can, for the most part, achieve the fine balancing act between vigour and excess.

After becoming a Red Devil for a British transfer record of £3.75 million in July 1993, the Eire midfielder completed a highly satisfactory first term, taking the eye with his dynamic box-to-box presence while helping to secure the League and FA Cup double. In 1994/95 he seemed to plateau a little, overshadowed perhaps by fellow dreadnought Paul Ince, and it was 1995/96 before he was revealed in all his glory. Revelling in the extra responsibility entailed by the departure of the England star, he reached new heights of consistent excellence, a standard he has maintained, even embellished, in subsequent seasons. Blemishes? Apart from occasional temperamental lapse, there appear to be none.

Indeed, seven years into his United career, it could hardly be clearer why Fergie had pursued the former boxer, Gaelic

footballer, sprinter and marathon runner since he had first surfaced at Nottingham Forest. Yet back in '93, after clocking in at Old Trafford, the sought-after 21-year-old was confronted by a few early home truths.

They were imparted on that most revealing of arenas, the practice pitch, where his general sharpness and aspects of his technique were found wanting. To his credit, Roy worked prodigiously to improve and reacted to the challenge with disarming self-deprecation, declaring: 'I just run around a lot.' True, limitless stamina allied to pace and aggression is important to his input, but any objective observer would go on to speak of far, far more natural ability than he would mention himself.

A further, frequently underrated Keane attribute is versatility. He could hold down a central defensive role for many years hence, such is his aerial prowess, tackling expertise and soccer knowhow, but it would be a terrible waste.

Roy is in his element at the hub of midfield, sometimes building and sometimes destroying, but always controlling. What an unstoppable force he can look on those archetypal lung-bursting surges from deep, one stirring early example coming at Maine Road in November 1993, when he steamed into the area to slam home Denis Irwin's searching cross without breaking stride, thus claiming all three points from a derby that had seemed lost. A less flamboyant, but even more priceless example of his worth came against Liverpool at Wembley in 1996 when he neutralised the attacking flair of McManaman and company, ruthlessly and with crushing totality, to be hailed as man of the match.

When, as a teenager, he wrote to most top English clubs asking for a trial, he didn't bother with United because he didn't think he was good enough. As it turned out, the price of a stamp could have saved the Red Devils a fortune. Understandably, when club and player sat down to contract talks in the summer of 1999, he was much more sure of his worth. The ensuing saga dragged on until December, when the plc shattered its wage structure to retain its inspirational captain, leaving the fans – who pay his wages – to breathe a huge sigh of relief. On the field, though it seemed barely credible, Roy Keane scaled new peaks, scoring more goals than ever before, and being feted as Football of the Year by both writers and his fellow players. Had either award gone elsewhere, it would have been a sheer travesty.

1992/93–

247 **48**
GAMES GOALS

BORN ● Leytonstone, London, 2.5.75.
HONOURS ● European Cup 98/9. League Championship 95/6, 96/7, 98/9, 99/00. FA Cup 95/6, 98/9. 28 England caps.
OTHER CLUBS ● (96–). Preston North End on loan 94/5 (5, 2).

The power and dexterity with which he strikes a football sets him apart from his peers.

David Beckham is special. Not because of his untold wealth, or the extravagant trappings of his fame, or the widespread obsession with the trivia of a lifestyle divorced from everyday reality. He is special because he creates moments of wonder on a football field, flashes of beauty that remain vivid in the memory long after a match, or a season, is over. He is not the perfect player, yet there are occasions on which he can lift sporting endeavour to truly rarified heights. That cannot be said of many performers in the modern game and so, despite the oceans of tediously irrelevant media fluff which so often suffocate the original cause of his celebrity, Beckham the footballer deserves to be cherished.

David Beckham

There is strength of character to be admired, too. In a previous edition of this book, reference was made to David's need to curb his temperamental excesses, no matter how understandable they might be for a boy scrutinised so relentlessly by the public eye. That was written before his infamous indiscretion against Argentina during France '98, an incident which catapulted the slim Londoner and his family into a nightmare of moronic and astonishingly venomous vilification. He might have quailed and retreated, but he battled on, his form somewhat muted at first but improving dramatically thereafter, until he had earned the respect of all right-minded observers. Admittedly, the tetchy streak persists, but its effect has been minimal and practically irrelevant when compared to his ravishing overall contribution.

David's progress has been of the storybook variety since he left home, practically in West Ham's backyard, to join United as a skinny but delectably skilful 16-year-old in July 1991. Within ten months he had helped to win the FA Youth Cup, then made his senior debut in September 1992. There followed two years in the reserves, learning his trade while adding physical strength to his bountiful natural gifts, which he paraded impressively against Galatasaray in December 1994. That night his coolly taken goal and all-round expertise served notice of what might be expected of young David Beckham.

Duly in 1995/96 he began to deliver. Deployed on the right in the void created by the departure of Andrei Kanchelskis, he made an exhilarating contribution to United's second League and FA Cup double. But it was in 1996/97 that the words Beckham and star began to be used in meaningful conjunction. A scintillating Charity Shield show against Newcastle was followed by his celebrated long-distance miracle against Wimbledon. In the weeks thereafter, though United spluttered, the 21-year-old shone so brightly that he was picked for England.

What sets him apart from his peers? There is the power and dexterity with which he strikes a football, whether towards goal or a colleague, a golden knack that has seen him dubbed the world's finest crosser and premier free-kick specialist; then there is the panoramic vision of his passing, its astonishing accuracy over vast distances, and an invaluable facility for disguising the direction of delivery. Add to that an undimmed eagerness to learn, a phenomenal work rate and the combination of zest and initiative which characterises his entire game, and the picture of a head-turning entertainer takes on increasingly sharp focus. But even such a near-comprehensive catalogue of qualities does not tell the entire tale. There is one more characteristic, far from evident from his conversation, that rounds off the Beckham phenomenon. David is not an arrogant boy – far from it – but there is an arrogance in his play, a certain sureness which proclaims, even on a poor day, that here is a man who can change the course of events.

His best position? Some say only central midfield offers maximum scope to his immense gifts, though more now maintain that he is most effective wide on the right, where he has become the Reds' principal goal-maker, not matching Kanchelskis for speed but outstripping the Ukrainian for soccer intelligence. The challenge for David Beckham, as he approaches his prime, is to go on improving. Certainly he was doing so in 1999/2000, during which he was named as runner-up to Rivaldo in both World and European Footballer of the Year polls and voted Europe's most valuable player by the continent's top coaches.

Though a February spat with Sir Alex Ferguson provoked speculation about a move, soon club and player were declaring their undying love for each other, and any imminent fracture in a mutually gratifying relationship appeared unlikely. So let's ignore the hype and concentrate on the football. After all, the lad is rather good at it!

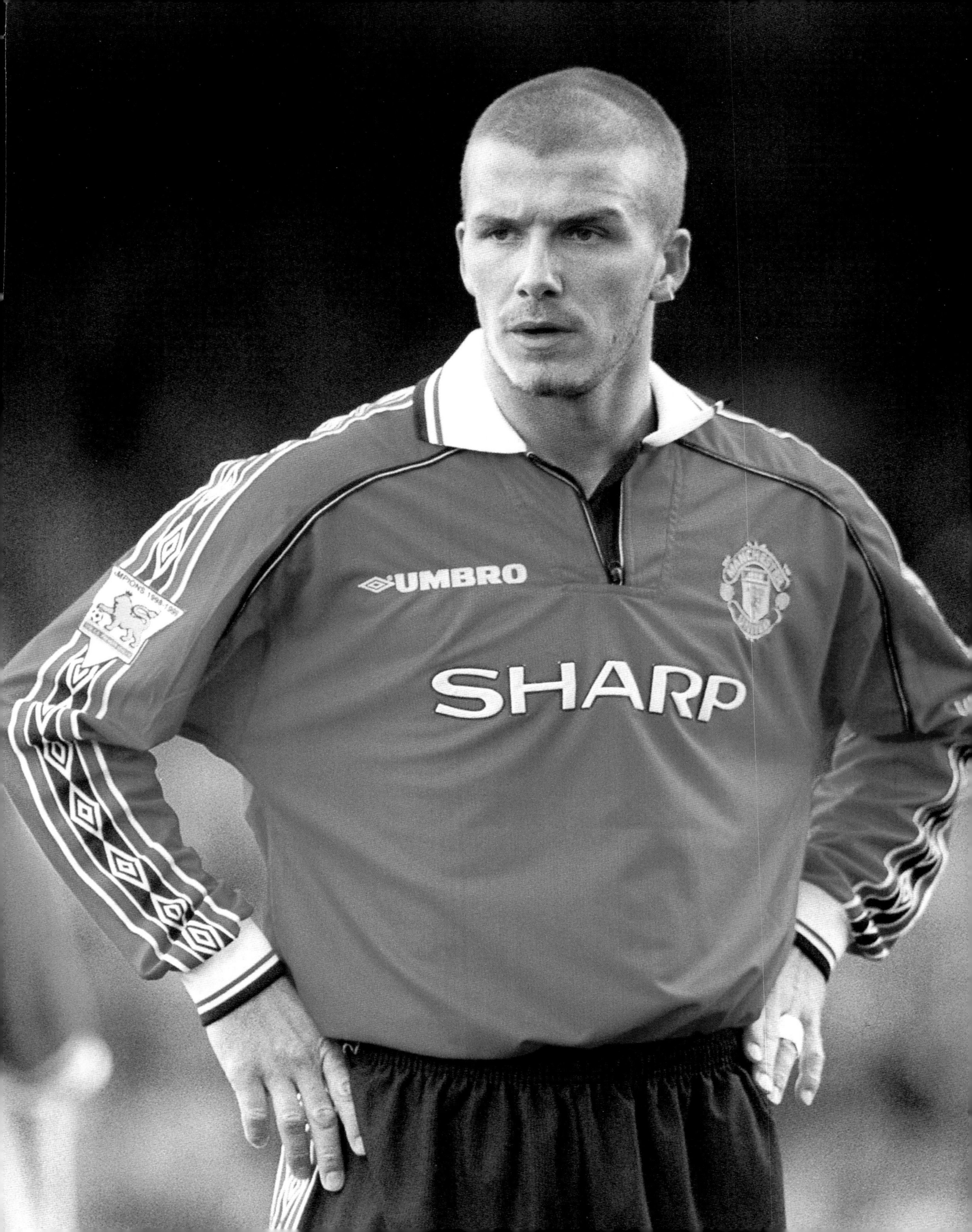
UMBRO
SHARP

Faced with adversity, he merely rolled his sleeves a little higher and concentrated all the harder.

1998/99–

99	1
GAMES	GOALS

BORN Kampen, Holland, 17.7.72.
HONOURS European Cup 98/9. League Championship 98/9,99/00. FA Cup 98/9. Holland caps.
OTHER CLUBS FC Zwolle, Cambuur Leeuwarden, Willem II, PSV Eindhoven, all Holland.

Some stoppers are endowed with Herculean physical strength and colossal presence, others take to the field armed with prodigious mental toughness, while yet more are blessed with speed, intelligence and an assured technique. However, those who would do battle with Jaap Stam – he of the Goliath-like frame topped with that sternly chiselled, imperious glare – face a rare and daunting combination of all those attributes. That is why, come the end of his second season as a Red Devil, it was hard to imagine a more complete defender anywhere in the world.

Jaap Stam

In the view of no less an authority than Johan Cruyff, his fellow Dutchman merited that accolade already when PSV Eindhoven asked Manchester United £15 million for their man-mountain in the spring of 1998. Eventually, thanks in part to the player's determination to join the club he had supported as a boy and his absence of greed during financial deliberations, a deal was struck for £10.75 million, still enough to make him the costliest defender on the planet.

Thereafter, having taken his place on that unenviable pedestal, Jaap became a natural target for media snipers who dwelt mercilessly on a handful of errors during Holland's progress to the World Cup semi-finals. Then followed further ill-judged ridicule as he strove to adjust to the hectic pace of the English game and headlines calling the United manager's judgement into doubt – 'Alex In Blunderland' was a typical example – became commonplace.

Naturally, there were teething troubles, particularly growing accustomed to the Reds' offside tactics while not operating in a settled central defensive partnership. However neither Stam, nor those who appreciated the massive extent of his ability, allowed their heads to drop; faced with adversity, he merely rolled his sleeves a little higher and concentrated all the harder. The situation echoed initial criticism of Gary Pallister and the cheap, vacuous 'donkey' treatment once meted out to Tony Adams and, sure enough, the Dutchman prevailed in sim-

ilar triumphant manner to the two Englishmen.

Before long he struck a vein of consistent form that had his erstwhile detractors queueing to lavish praise and he was even touted as a contender to become Footballer of the Year. It was easy to see why: Jaap's vast strength made it virtually impossible to muscle him out of any challenge, he was deceptively quick and nimble for such a big man and he was a decisive timer of tackles, usually attempting to place his body between opponent and ball and then turning away in possession, rather than committing himself by diving in rashly. He read the game with immense perception, he could control instantly a ball plummeting from the sky, and he could pass with calm accuracy. In addition, if he made a mistake he was not outwardly upset by it, just getting on with the job in hand with a minimum of fuss.

During the momentous spring of 1999, Stam exerted a towering influence as United achieved their treble, and he was never mightier than in the tumultuous semi-final clashes with Arsenal and Juventus, emerging as a quiet leader, a performer to be trusted implicitly. Duly he was voted the outstanding defender of that Champions League campaign and Premiership managers nominated him as the player they coveted above all others.

Though 1999/2000 brought occasional moments of vulnerability as he sought to build understandings with newcomers Mark Bosnich and Mickael Silvestre, Jaap remained the benchmark by which all other stoppers were judged, and his stature was emphasised by his appointment as deputy skipper to Roy Keane.

Stam was a late developer, not turning professional until he was 19 and once returning from an inconclusive trial with Sheffield Wednesday as a homesick teenager. Since then he has helped PSV lift the Dutch title, been voted Holland's player of the year in 1998 and then achieved his heart's desire by committing the prime years of his career to Old Trafford. Pallister was a difficult act to follow but, early in his English sojourn, Jaap Stam was hailed by Sir Bobby Charlton as one of the finest centre-halves in United's history, thus placing him alongside the likes of Chilton and Foulkes, Bruce and Pally himself. But if he maintains his initial rate of progress, soon the rough-hewn, undemonstrative son of a provincial carpenter may find himself in a category all of his own.

JESPER BLOMQVIST

1998/99–

38 GAMES **1** GOALS

BORN	Tavelsjo, Sweden, 5.2.74.
HONOURS	European Cup 98/9. League Championship 98/9. Sweden caps.
OTHER CLUBS	Tavelsjo IK, Sweden; UMEA, Sweden; IFK Gothenburg, Sweden, 92/3-96/7 (71, 18); AC Milan, Italy, 96/7 (20, 1); Parma, Italy, 97/8 (28, 1).

Alex Ferguson believed that lack of high-quality left-flank cover for Ryan Giggs cost the Red Devils dearly when the Welshman was injured in the spring of 1998 – and so, that summer, he bought Jesper Blomqvist.

When he paid Parma £4.4 million for the one-time whizz-kid of Swedish football, Alex was acquiring a player he had coveted for several years, perhaps since an uncomfortable evening in Gothenburg in November 1994, when Jesper had tortured the out-of-position David May and reduced United's Champions League dreams to tatters.

Now, after several failed attempts to sign him, the Old Trafford club were getting a more mature, experienced performer with four Swedish title medals to his credit, even if he had not made the impact expected of him in Italy.

Initially Jesper expressed reservations about the move, not wanting to languish in the shadow of a star, but reached agreement after hearing that the option of playing Ryan in the centre was under active consideration. As it turned out through a variety of circumstances, the newcomer received plenty of opportunities and there were instances when, if hardly a like-for-like replacement, he earned his corn as a credible alternative to Giggs.

After an understandably tentative start, Jesper grew in confidence and revealed flair and guile aplenty during the autumn, as well as a willingness to tackle back, albeit clumsily on occasion. At Southampton and in Brondby he demonstrated the capacity to beat defenders before dispatching delightfully perceptive passes, but it was in the return match with the Danes that he enjoyed his most outstanding moment, embarking on a run from his own half past three opponents before freeing David Beckham to set up a goal for Dwight Yorke.

However, it was not always thus. Sometimes he lacked penetration, proving indecisive when in menacing positions, notably at Middlesbrough in May 1999. His critics reckoned that he cut inside too much, yet without the goal sense to justify it. Still, none could question his effort and there was the mitigating factor of a niggling long-term foot problem which limited his effectiveness in the European Cup Final.

The best of Blomqvist, it was hoped, would be seen in 1999/2000, but a knee injury suffered in a late-summer Hong Kong friendly sidelined him for the whole campaign. Since then the arrival of Quinton Fortune has intensified the competition on United's left side, and Jesper faced a testing challenge as 2000/2001 got under way.

Unlike certain of his predecessors who were long on talent but short on nerve, Wes Brown is not afraid to play for Manchester United. Indeed, of the myriad attributes screaming for attention in the footballing make-up of the rookie defender, it is his utter imperturbability that is the most compelling.

No matter how colossal the occasion, how frenetic the hype or how daunting the challenge, he remains a monument to self-possession, a quality underscored emphatically by the composed manner in which he dealt with a serious injury in the summer of 1999.

That Brown sang-froid was vividly evident during one of the most assured senior debuts ever witnessed at Old Trafford. The tall, lithe 19-year-old was called on as a substitute for David May against Leeds in May 1998, and he shone against such strong and pacy operators as Jimmy Floyd Hasselbaink and Harry Kewell. In front of 55,000 fans and a massive TV audience he was ready to put his foot on the ball, pass it with distinction and even go past opponents with a sway of his hips and a burst of acceleration which belied his relaxed style.

Come 1998/99 and Wes was ready for a settled first-team run, thus leapfrogging the likes of Michael Clegg and John Curtis, and he impressed hugely with his combination of technique, judgement and athleticism, both at the back and marauding down the right flank. At times, he appeared a tad too casual for some observers, but that was an illusion caused by his easy, loose-limbed gait, and errors were few.

Generally Wes played at right-back but his natural position is in the centre of defence, and Alex Ferguson has predicted he will become an ideal long-term partner for Jaap Stam. However, the United boss was wary of overtaxing his prodigy in his first full season in the squad, preferring the experienced May when injuries caused a vacancy alongside the Dutchman as the Premiership scrap reached a crescendo.

Also, it should be noted that when Wes won his first England cap after only 12 League starts, a record, in all honesty he did not appear ready for the international stage.

Thus it was recognised that continued grooming was necessary, but that process was cruelly interrupted by knee damage sustained during preparation for 1999/2000. At first it was believed that an operation would not be necessary, but eventually he went under the surgeon's knife and missed the whole season.

Still, there is no doubt that, given successful rehabilitation, the rudiments of a truly exceptional performer remain in place. 'Golden Brown' chorus the supporters, and they are right.

WESLEY BROWN

1997/98–

23	0
GAMES	GOALS

BORN   Manchester, 16.3.79.
HONOURS   League Championship 98/9. 1 England cap (99–).

Dwight emerged as United's laughing cavalier, his infectious zest embellishing his bountiful ability.

1998/99–

96 **52**
GAMES GOALS

BORN Canaan, Tobago, 3.11.71.
HONOURS European Cup 98/9. League Championship 98/9,
99/00. FA Cup 98/9. Trinidad and Tobago caps.
OTHER CLUBS Aston Villa 89/90-98/9 (231, 75).

With the utmost respect to Dwight Yorke's admirable achievments during his nine years at Villa Park, it's fair to say that there was hardly communal rejoicing among Manchester United fans when Alex Ferguson paid a club record £12.6 million for the Tobagan striker in August 1999. The Reds had been linked with a succession of international stars – the likes of Gabriel Batistuta and Patrick Kluivert – and, in all honesty, Dwight's name would not have appeared on many laymen's lists of top transfer targets. Indeed, when the tiresomely protracted negotiations culminated in the Villa favourite becoming the sixth most expensive footballer in history, there was widespread condemnation of the deal. The sanity of the game in general, and the Red Devils' boss in particular, was called into question.

Dwight Yorke

Oh, we of little faith! During 1998/99 the fee looked less exorbitant with each of Yorke's 29 goals as the effervescent newcomer illuminated the United attack with a capacity for the unexpected which had been largely lacking since the departure of Eric Cantona. Dwight emerged as Old Trafford's laughing cavalier, his infectious zest embellishing his bountiful ability with a feelgood factor and an all-too-rare sense of enjoyment which was refreshingly welcome in the pressurised, stress-laden world that top-level football has become.

Throughout most of that epoch-making campaign, Yorke exuded impudence without arrogance. Clever, unorthodox and endlessly audacious, he augmented his lavish skills with industry, courage and resilience. Apart from his exceptional strike rate, he impressed as an all-rounder who could drop deep to telling effect, a legacy from a midfield stint during his Aston Villa days. With his subtle movement and assured control, he offered an ever-present passing option, while his potent partnership with Andy Cole has been rightly eulogised. Their high-speed choreography, their bewildering cocktail of dummies, step-overs and some of the slickest one-two passing combinations ever seen at Old Trafford, gave the attack a pulsating and

much-needed new dimension.

But while the chemistry between Dwight and Andy both on and off the pitch made them the manager's first-choice combination, the Tobagan demonstrated that he could thrive alongside Ole Gunnar Solskjaer and Teddy Sheringham as well, while link-ups with Ryan Giggs and Paul Scholes meant he had been half of no less than five frontline duos before the end of September.

Variety was a feature, too, of the Yorke goal catalogue. Fierce drives and adroit volleys were supplemented by subtle dinks and routine tap-ins while, though not outstandingly powerful in the air, he displayed a priceless knack of sneaking unnoticed between defenders. Some of Europe's most feted rearguards fell victim to this last-mentioned speciality, notably Inter Milan at Old Trafford (twice), Barcelona at the Nou Camp and Juventus in Turin.

But if one goal summed up the joyous appeal of Dwight Yorke it was the second of his brace against Chelsea at Stamford Bridge in the FA Cup quarter-final replay. After a typical piece of persistence by Cole, the ball ran loose some 25 yards out in the inside-right channel. There seemed little immediate danger to Ed De Goey's goal but Dwight delivered an instant chip with the outside of his right foot which sent the ball arcing unerringly over the stranded 'keeper to nestle in the far corner of the net. It was a moment of sheer incandescent brilliance, fit to grace any stage on any occasion, and it ended that game as a meaningful contest.

Perhaps inevitably after enjoying such a buoyant start to life as a Red Devil, Yorke suffered a late springtime hiccup to his form, when the goals ceased to flow and his touch seemed suddenly uncertain. Happily he was back on song for the climax of a tumultuous campaign in which he had exceeded virtually all expectations except, presumably, those of the man who mattered most. Yet again, the judgement of Alex Ferguson had been vindicated handsomely.

There followed, though, a further and more prolonged blip in 1999/2000. After starting with all his characteristic spontaneity and bounce, Dwight apparently succumbed to 'second season syndrome', a notional condition which has afflicted many footballers elevated suddenly to superstardom. For months he was a travesty of his former self, seemingly devoid of confidence, but he recovered ebulliently, becoming the first United man since Brian McClair in 1987/88 to net 20 League goals in a single term.

JONATHAN GREENING ▼

1998/99–

15	0
GAMES	GOALS

BORN ○ Scarborough, Yorkshire, 2.1.78.
OTHER CLUBS ○ York City 96/7–97/8 (25, 2).

At Bootham Crescent, Jonathan Greening was viewed as exceptional, a boy wonder; at Old Trafford, he is merely one of many starlets striving for a berth in the big time. However, the former Minsterman appears a possibility for long-tem graduation, despite a contract dispute which called his future into question.

Sir Alex Ferguson entertained lofty hopes for Jonathan, who arrived in Manchester in March 1998, York City banking a reported £350,000 with more to come depending on his progress. It was a significant investment for a teenager with only five League starts to his name.

Since then, despite being granted only a handful of senior outings and never quite seizing the day, the tall, willowy striker cum wide midfielder has done enough to suggest that the basics of a Premiership footballer are in place. Though there are rough edges to be honed – notably a tendency to dwell too long in possession – Jonathan is quick and long-striding, blessed with deft control and a bewildering body-swerve, and he carries a fierce shot. In addition, the England under-21 international is willing to graft, witness his chasing and dispossessing of David Ginola after Nicky Butt had been beaten at White Hart Lane in December 1998.

Happily, a rapprochement between club and player seemed imminent as this book went to print.

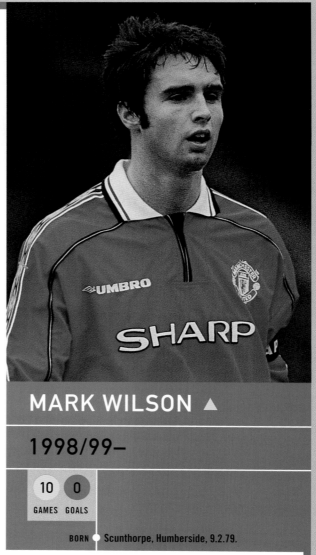

MARK WILSON ▲

1998/99–

10	0
GAMES	GOALS

BORN ○ Scunthorpe, Humberside, 9.2.79.

An eminent Old Trafford insider predicted at the outset of 1999/2000 that Mark Wilson would consolidate his place in the senior squad by season's end. It didn't happen, and the task facing the tall midfielder will not become any easier, but, at the time of writing, the door was not closed.

Mark is an assured, all-purpose performer whose game boasts a natural authority. Snappily combative in the tackle, he tracks back and tidies up efficiently, while being ever ready to embark on enterprising forward runs. A neat passer who is comfortable on the ball, he packs a powerful shot, too, as he demonstrated with a sizzling strike in the Eric Cantona testimonial match.

Alex Ferguson demonstrated his confidence in Mark by blooding him at senior level as a substitute away to Brondby in October 1998, the teenaged Humbersider responding with composed competence.

Thereafter he did well on the 1999 summer tour of Australia and the Far East, and earned a trip to Rio for the Club World Championship, but since then he has been unable to take the next step forward. However, talk of a move to Portsmouth in March 2000 came to nothing and Mark Wilson could continue to nurse dreams of an Old Trafford future.

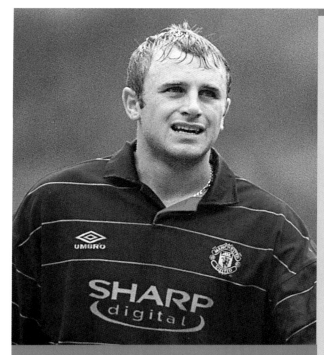

RONNIE WALLWORK ▲

1997/98–

9	0
GAMES	GOALS

BORN — Manchester 10.9.77.
OTHER CLUBS — Carlisle United on loan 97/8 (10, 1); Stockport County on loan 97/8 (7, 0); Royal Antwerp, Belgium, on loan 98/9.

'He will be a first-team player, no doubt. He is a great reader of the game, a fine passer and tough mentally.' For Ronnie Wallwork these were comforting words at nightmare's end, particularly as they came from Sir Alex Ferguson.

The bad dream in question was the young central defender's life ban imposed after an alleged attack on a Belgian referee towards the end of 1998/99, when he had been on loan with Royal Antwerp.

The draconian sentence was rescinded on appeal, but only after several months of torment and Ronnie's characteristic single-mindedness was illustrated graphically by his convincing performance as a midfield holding player when rising from the Anfield bench to replace Nicky Butt in September 1999 – just six days before the hearing that would determine his future.

Yet for all his power and competence that day, it is at the heart of the back four rather than just in front of it that the muscular Mancunian habitually thrives. Not the tallest but hugely determined, endlessly industrious and deceptively skilful, Ronnie was a boyhood United fan who has been at the club since he was ten. The likelihood is that he will remain part of the Old Trafford scenery for many seasons to come.

DANNY HIGGINBOTHAM ▼

1997/98–

7	0
GAMES	GOALS

BORN — Manchester 29.12.78.
OTHER CLUBS — Royal Antwerp, Belgium, 98/9.

The standing ovation accorded to Danny Higginbotham when a sharp attack of cramp removed him from the action shortly before the end of his home Premiership debut against Leicester City in November 1999 was tumultuous even by Old Trafford standards.

It was a fitting reward for a practically foot-perfect performance which underscored the huge potential of the tall, self-possessed left-back. Indeed, his composure was in evidence in the opening minute when his first touch produced a concerted handball appeal from the Foxes, but the referee waved play on and Danny remained utterly unfazed.

The young, left-sided Mancunian is firm, neat and sensible in his defensive duties, but it is his ability to control and then use the ball creatively – perhaps a legacy of his schoolboy days as a winger – which commands the eye.

During a lengthy loan spell with Royal Antwerp in 1998/99, Danny became something of a cult figure with local fans after contributing winning goals in consecutive matches. It was a shame that his Belgian sojourn was to end with a ban after he became involved, along with Ronnie Wallwork, in an alleged altercation with a referee, but with that controversy behind him the future looks bright for Danny Higginbotham.

RAIMOND VAN DER GOUW

1996/97–

42 GAMES **0** GOALS

BORN	Oldenzaal, Holland, 24.3.63.
HONOURS	League Championship 99/00.
OTHER CLUBS	Go Ahead Eagles 85/6-87/8; Vitesse Arnhem 88/9-95/6, both Holland.

During the first half of 1999/2000, with Manchester United striving to adjust to life without Peter Schemichel, the safest pair of hands at Old Trafford belonged to Raimond van der Gouw.

In contrast to Mark Bosnich and Massimo Taibi, both of whom proved fitfully errant, the tall, lithe Dutchman gave several short sequences of solid displays interspersed with a couple of stunning ones, notably in the landmark triumph at Highbury and the home win against Valencia.

Each time, though, Raimond would give way, thus occasioning considerable frustration to United fans intolerant of the newcomers' uncertainty and mightily impressed by the consistent, unflashy competence of the man who had spent three seasons as steady understudy to the giant Dane, no doubt learning plenty in the process.

Perhaps, had Van der Gouw not been closer to his fortieth birthday than his thirtieth, he might have prevailed. As it was, he stepped up again when Bosnich was omitted in March, performing splendidly against Liverpool at Old Trafford before dropping an uncharacteristic clanger in Bordeaux, then slipping quietly back to the bench.

When the Red Devils had sought a goalkeeping number-two in the summer of 1996, they were not looking for an ambitious young buck who would be straining to supplant Schmeichel as premier custodian. What they required was an experienced deputy whose reassuring presence would mean that any enforced absence by Peter need not be viewed as an unmitigated calamity. For such a purpose, Raimond proved ideal.

His first-team opportunities were limited throughout most of 1996/97, though he did enough on his rare outings to confirm his all-round competence and cool temperament. True, he could not equal the immense physical presence of Schmeichel but that was hardly surprising and, crucially, when he was really needed Raimond was not found wanting.

Stepping into the breach when Peter was unfit for the first leg of the European Cup semi-final confrontation with Borussia Dortmund, Van der Gouw excelled, making several fine saves before being beaten once, by a deflected shot. It was only his fourth senior outing for United but the 34-year-old had played 17 times in European competition for his previous club, Vitesse Arnhem, and it showed. A season later, in similar circumstances, he excelled again, making three blinding stops at home to Monaco in the quarter-final.

Apparently happy in the supporting role, which he has combined successfully with his work as a goalkeeping coach alongside Tony Coton, Raimond has proved to be an admirable acquisition. What a pity that he wasn't just a few years younger when Schmeichel left the club.

It would be wonderful to report that Mark Bosnich had slotted seamlessly into the Manchester United defence and that Peter Schmeichel had barely been missed. If only it were true.

Not that the massively self-assured Australian has been a flop, exactly, since arriving from Aston Villa to commence his second spell at Old Trafford in the summer of 1999. Indeed, it is fair to accentuate the positive regarding his rollercoaster progress as the near-omnipotent Dane's successor, because there has been plenty of it.

For example, no one could fairly deny that his exceptional display at the Bernabeu kept the Reds in contention in their European Cup quarter-final with Real Madrid, and United would not have lifted the Inter-Continental Cup in Tokyo but for his succession of fabulous saves which thwarted Palmeiras. Similarly, he performed superbly in the white heat of Elland Road, a major factor in a crucial victory.

Undoubtedly Mark is a magnificent shot-stopper, arguably the most acrobatic and sharp-witted in the English game. He is faultlessly courageous when diving at feet; he presents a formidable barrier in one-on-one situations, and he is endlessly determined.

However, there is a flip side. For all his confidence, Bosnich does not dominate his box. When crosses come in there is every chance of an ineffectual flap, such as the one which gifted a goal to Paul Ince at Middlesbrough in April, and colleagues appear uncertain of his intentions. Though there have been mitigating factors, such as the need to bed in the new central defensive partnership of Stam and Silvestre, it is unusual for table-toppers to concede more goals than the five teams below them. Yet that was the case in the spring of 2000, and a considerable portion of the responsibility must rest with the goalkeeper.

In addition, despite his protestations to the contrary, Mark's kicking was abysmal at times, his feeble dispatches frequently placing United under instant and unnecessary pressure. True, he was handicapped by an early-season hamstring injury, but even when he was fit his kicking was inconsistent, at best.

Mark, who served United briefly as a teenager during the Ron Atkinson era before work-permit problems forced him to move, returned on a free transfer under the Bosman ruling, but failed to impress in his early outings.

Then, amid widely voiced doubts about his attitude, came his injury, the signing of Massimo Taibi and a string of fine displays from the solid Raimond van der Gouw. Suddenly Mark appeared to be third in the pecking order, and his gutsy recovery from that unenviable position is to be applauded. But, surely, improvement is needed if the ebullient six-footer is to become a long-term fixture between the Red Devils' posts.

MARK BOSNICH

1989/90–1990/91 & 1999/2000–

 36 **0**

GAMES **GOALS**

BORN ◉ Sydney, Australia, 13.1.72.
HONOURS ◉ League Championship 99/00; Australia caps.
OTHER CLUBS ◉ Croatia Sydney, Australia; Aston Villa 91/2-98/9 (179, 0).

MICKAEL SILVESTRE

1999/2000–

37	0
GAMES	GOALS

BORN Chambray-Les-Tours, France, 9.8.77.
HONOURS League Championship 99/00.
OTHER CLUBS Rennes, France, 95/6-97/8; Internazionale of Milan 98/9.

Mickael Silvestre is not the finished article; far from it. But despite a tendency to cause palpitations among the Old Trafford faithful through his deceptively casual air when the ball is at his feet and an opponent is bearing down on him, the pacy, polished French defender has the makings of a Manchester United stalwart for years to come.

As a 21-year-old Mickael had impressed for Internazionale against the Reds in the Milan leg of the 1999 European Cup quarter-final, but he was unhappy with his deployment as a wing-back and soon Liverpool and United were locked in a battle for his signature.

At first, the French connection appeared to make Gerard Houllier favourite to prevail, but an assurance from Sir Alex Ferguson that Silvestre would be given opportunities in his favoured role as a centre-half paved the way for a £3.5 million move to Manchester.

Ironically, just days later, Mickael made his Premiership debut at Anfield as a left-back! Predictably enough, he was booed every time he touched the ball but he wasn't fazed in the slightest, taking the eye with his athleticism, authority and control during a thrilling 3-2 victory.

Clearly the new recruit was an immensely accomplished all-round footballer, as powerful in the air as he was composed on the deck, but soon that characteristic sang froid emerged as a potential problem. Several times he was caught in possession by nippy opponents – one instance cost United a home victory over Southampton, when he was robbed by Marian Pahars, who set up Matt Le Tissier's equaliser – and his concentration was called into question.

Thereafter he was granted his wish of moving to the heart of the rearguard alongside Jaap Stam, but while his passing, tackling and, above all, his speed earned plaudits, there were some disturbingly shaky moments. Occasionally these were the result of his heavy bias towards his left foot, which offered welcome balance to the defence but, once or twice, limited his options when under pressure.

In fairness to Mickael, who is a model professional and eager to learn, he needed time to adjust to the frenetic pace of the English game, and it didn't help that the Reds' goalkeeping situation was unsettled throughout the first half of the season.

In general, the positive outweighed the negative and there were some serenely majestic performances, notably against Leeds at Elland Road. At times he was omitted from the side, but always with the intention of a comeback, and as 1999/2000 approached its climax, the shaven-headed six-footer was making steady progress.

Still, despite his stated preference for a central berth, many shrewd observers reckon he is better deployed at left-back, and that may yet be where his future lies. Whatever, time is on his side, and the best of Mickael Silvestre is yet to come.

MASSIMO TAIBI ▲

1999/2000–

4	0
GAMES	GOALS

BORN Palermo, Italy, 18.2.70.
OTHER CLUBS Licata, AC Milan (twice), Como Calcio, Piacenza, Venezia, Reggina on loan, all Italy.

He was big, he was oozing with self-belief and if he made a mistake he tended to look elsewhere to place the blame. But that was not what the headline-writer had in mind when he penned 'United hail new Schmeichel' following Massimo Taibi's debut against Liverpool.

That morning at Anfield in August 1999, the 6ft 3in Italian – signed for £4.5 million from Venezia because Mark Bosnich was afflicted by injury and indifferent form – made a succession of brilliant saves and the visitors departed with three hard-won points. Apart from one horrible blunder, when he failed to catch a cross and allowed Sami Hyypia to head into an empty net, it had been a triumphant entry and instant stardom seemed to beckon.

In fact, misery was in store. After an uneventful encounter with Wimbledon, Massimo dropped a colossal clanger at home to Southampton, allowing a soft shot from Matt Le Tissier to squirm embarrassingly through his grasp. Still worse was to come at Stamford Bridge where he conceded five, starting with a carbon copy of his Merseyside bloomer, this time letting in Gus Poyet after only 28 seconds. It couldn't go on. Soon Taibi was dispatched to Reggina on loan for the rest of the season, explaining that he had been unused to the bombardment of crosses which is part of the English game and vowing that he would return to prove his critics wrong. Good luck Massimo, you'll need it.

QUINTON FORTUNE ▼

1999/2000–

12	4
GAMES	GOALS

BORN Cape Town, South Africa, 21.5.77.
HONOURS South Africa caps.
OTHER CLUBS Atletico Madrid, Spain.

Quinton Fortune faces a daunting challenge if he is to win long-term membership of Manchester United's starry squad, but there is something about the young South African which suggests he is made of the right stuff to win through.

The solidly built left-sided midfielder is blessed with pace and balance, an assured touch and a knack of finding the net, but beyond that there is an indefinable spark, a hunger to succeed which emanates, perhaps, from his origins in a poor township.

After being recruited for £2 million from Atletico Madrid in August 1999, Quinton suffered ankle problems which made it difficult to achieve an early impact. But, with Jesper Blomqvist sidelined by injury, the left-sided newcomer gradually emerged as a presentable deputy for Ryan Giggs.

He scored on his first Premiership start, at home to Bradford City on Boxing Day, then bolstered his confidence with two smart finishes against South Melbourne at the Maracana. Thereafter he made the most of occasional outings, earning lavish praise for his flighted crosses and the feisty attitude which permeated his game.

Versatile enough to slot in as a full-back or a striker at need, and highly influential in central midfield for his country, Quinton Fortune can reflect on a commendable first term as a Red Devil.

LUKE CHADWICK ▼

1999/2000–

1	0
GAMES	GOALS

BORN ● Cambridge, 18.11.80.
OTHER CLUBS ● Royal Antwerp, Belgium, on loan 99/00.

Luke Chadwick is a tall, dashing, right-sided attacker whose vast potential was once viewed with more pleasure at Highbury than at Old Trafford. However, having been affiliated to Arsenal at 14, he moved up to Manchester, where his talents have developed to gratifying effect.

Though he had still not progressed beyond the Red Devils' reserves, in August 1999 Luke earned England under-21 recognition, displaying considerable flair and scoring on his debut, a 5-0 triumph over Luxembourg.

Since then he has made his first-team entrance, albeit in difficult circumstances as part of a virtual second-string United line-up which was overwhelmed by full-strength Aston Villa in the League Cup in October.

Even more valuable, perhaps, has been Luke's experience on loan to Royal Antwerp, for whom he also netted on debut, then showed encouraging form as the club rode high at the summit of the Belgian Second Division.

Back at Old Trafford, he will face ferociously intense competition for a senior berth, but his bountiful natural ability gives Luke Chadwick a fighting chance of making the grade.

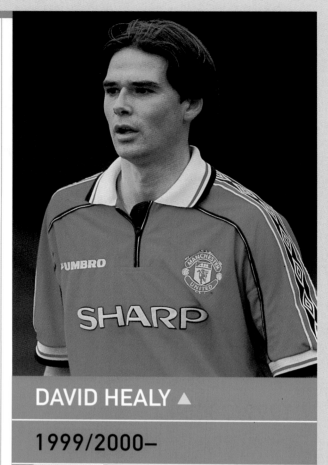

DAVID HEALY ▲

1999/2000–

1	0
GAMES	GOALS

BORN ● Downpatrick, Northern Ireland, 5.8.79.
HONOURS ● 3 Northern Ireland caps (2000-).
OTHER CLUBS ● Port Vale on loan 99/00 (16, 3).

Rookie marksman David Healy had enjoyed only one senior outing for Manchester United, and that as a substitute, when he made a startling impact on the full international stage.

Called up by former Red Devil Sammy McIlroy for his first game in charge of Northern Ireland in February 2000, David responded by scoring two goals and setting up the other in a 3-1 victory in Luxembourg.

Afterwards Sammy described his sparky young countryman as 'a bit special' but added sensibly: 'We're not going to put pressure on him by going overboard, but he's level-headed and I can't see him flinching at anything. I'm not going to say he's the answer to our prayers but it's a great start.'

Healy further emphasised his immense potential with another strike in his second international, against Malta, and by several goals during a springtime spell on loan with Port Vale which boosted the Potteries club's valiant but unavailing struggle to avoid relegation to the Second Division.

David is quick and skilful, and he has a priceless instinct for being in the right place at the right time. He should go far.

MICHAEL TWISS

1997/98–

MIDFIELDER

2 GAMES **0** GOALS

BORN:
Salford, Manchester,
26.12.77.

OTHER CLUBS:
Sheffield United on loan
98/9 (12, 1).

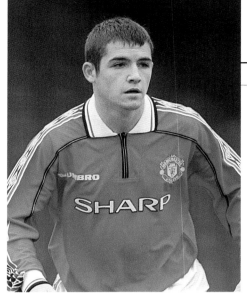

ALEX NOTMAN

1998/99–

FORWARD.

1 GAMES **0** GOALS

BORN:
Edinburgh, 10.12.79.

OTHER CLUBS:
Sheffield United on loan
99/00 (10, 3).

ERIK NEVLAND

1997/98– 1998/99

FORWARD

5 GAMES **1** GOALS

BORN:
Stavanger, Norway,
10.11.77.

OTHER CLUBS:
Viking Stavanger, Norway,
95/6–96/7; IFK Gothenburg,
Norway, 98/9 on loan; Viking
Stavanger 99/00–.

JOHN O'SHEA

1999/2000–

DEFENDER

1 GAMES **0** GOALS

BORN:
Waterford, Republic of
Ireland, 30.4.81.

OTHER CLUBS:
Bournemouth on loan 99/00
(10, 1).

RICHARD WELLENS

1999/2000

MIDFIELDER

1 GAMES **0** GOALS

BORN:
Manchester, 26.3.80.

OTHER CLUBS:
Blackpool 99/00– (8, 0).

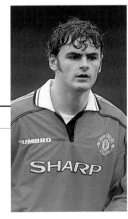

PAUL RACHUBKA

1999/2000–

GOALKEEPER

1 GAMES **0** GOALS

BORN:
San Luis Obispo, California, USA, 21.5.81.

NICK CULKIN

1999/2000–

GOALKEEPER

1 GAMES **0** GOALS

BORN:
York, 6.7.78.

OTHER CLUBS:
Hull City on loan 99/00 (4, 0).

JIMMY MURPHY

COACH: 1945–1955
ASSISTANT MANAGER: 1955–1971
ACTING MANAGER: February–August 1958

Some of the greatest players ever to come out of British football owed a huge debt to Jimmy Murphy. The forthright little Welshman joined Matt Busby at Old Trafford in 1945 with special responsibility for nurturing young talent, and started a production line which turned out the likes of Duncan Edwards, Bobby Charlton and George Best.

Working in harness with the loyal Bert Whalley, a former United player who was to die at Munich, Jimmy loomed large in the life of the club's juniors. He was sergeant major, father confessor and psychologist, driving when necessary, cajoling when it was called for, always passionate in his love for the game.

Perhaps Jimmy's most memorable achievement was in leading the Reds to Wembley in the aftermath of the Munich air crash while Matt Busby fought for his life. They lost to Bolton Wanderers but United's acting boss, who had been promoted from coach to assistant manager in 1955 and had a spell in charge of Wales, had truly performed a soccer miracle.

Like Matt, Jimmy turned down lucrative offers to take control of other clubs in this country and abroad. The tireless lieutenant preferred to stay at Old Trafford, marching shoulder to shoulder into history alongside the man who gave him a job after the war.

Jimmy Murphy was Matt's first signing for United – and unquestionably his most important. He remained a much-loved figure at the ground until shortly before his death, at the age of 81, in 1989.

WILF McGUINNESS

CHIEF COACH: April 1969–June 1970
MANAGER: June 1970–December 1970

When Wilf McGuinness was plucked from the relative obscurity of the Old Trafford coaching staff and entrusted with United's future, he was seen by many as the luckiest man in football. However, with the benefit of hindsight there is a strong case for believing that, far from fortunate, he was on a hiding to nothing.

Some of the team's best players were on the brink of decline and many of the youngsters were not good enough. A series of forays into the transfer market for quality replacements proved abortive. With such a catalogue of disadvantages, and with a legend to live up to, he needed to command the respect and support of his players from the outset. In failing to do so he lost his first and most vital battle.

Confrontations with senior first-teamers did nothing to build confidence and performances slumped. He chose the same match to drop both Denis Law and Bobby Charlton but results did not improve.

Finally Matt Busby, who had recommended Wilf for the job, resumed at the helm and the man who had been with United for 17 years as player and backroom boy left to coach in Greece.

Wilf need not be ashamed of his record: three semi-finals (two League Cup, one FA Cup) and two eighth places in the First Division would have been hailed as success by other employers. But not United, a club for whom – as he said on the day he was deposed – he would willingly bleed. Matt's desire for continuity, for a successor from within the United 'family', perhaps led him to make a rare error of judgement. Wilf McGuinness was simply the innocent victim.

FRANK O'FARRELL

MANAGER: June 1971–December 1972

He came a stranger and he left a stranger: that was Denis Law's succinct epitaph to the frustrating reign of Frank O'Farrell. Law was voicing a popular view that the immaculate Irishman, destined for the sack after 18 months, was too remote and used his office as a retreat.

Like Ron Atkinson later, Frank was not the board's first choice, but they were impressed by his steady climb up the managerial ladder, reaching Leicester via Weymouth and Torquay. Ironically in view of this proven stability, his United team was to catapult from one end of the First Division to the other within a year.

Many aspects of his tenure were difficult. He was unfortunate to be in control as George Best's discontent came to a head; he was attacked for shelling out £200,000 for Third Division striker Ted MacDougall (though he could point to the astute capture of Martin Buchan); and his relationship with the board sometimes appeared strained. The Best saga – would he leave or wouldn't he? – was like a running sore and must have been both distracting and debilitating.

Yet Frank could not have hoped for a better start. By Christmas in his first season United were five points clear of the pack and had entertained royally at times. But pundits predicted a fall and, sure enough, a woeful run of defeats deposited the team in mid-table.

The next campaign proved worse. Points were dropped, injuries piled up and gloom settled over Old Trafford. By December talk was turning to – say it softly – relegation. Frank was curtly dismissed and left claiming that he could have done the job given time. It was a sad exit.

TOMMY DOCHERTY

MANAGER: December 1972–July 1977

Three years of struggle and confusion had squeezed the magic out of Manchester United. Tommy Docherty put it back, though the transformation was not without trauma. Traditionalists were appalled when the volatile troubleshooter breezed in, determined to blow away the cobwebs together with many of the playing staff.

In his first few months he was like a man possessed. He averted relegation and lived up to a lurid reputation gained in charge of five clubs and his native Scotland. The air crackled with one-liners and players came and went with bewildering rapidity. But the next term brought catastrophe as a very poor United went down. The Doc expected the sack; instead he got a crate of champagne from the board. Clearly he enjoyed backing that his predecessors would have envied.

Critics predicted a lengthy stay in the lower flight but Tommy's team confounded them, leading the table for the whole campaign. And what a breath of fresh air the new United proved back in Division One. They played stirring, adventurous football and just missed the double. Next season came FA Cup triumph and more honours seemed certain. But news broke of the Doc's love for the club physio's wife, and he was sacked.

During his reign he had changed a demoralised outfit into a major force and moved the club's bank balance from red to black. But his was not a serene tenure. There were well-publicised rows with Law, Crerand, Buchan, Stepney, Macari and Morgan and he made powerful enemies. Many fans, though, agreed with Steve Coppell, who said of Tommy's exit: 'Managers are not made in heaven. In the end United were the losers.'

DAVE SEXTON

MANAGER: July 1977–April 1981

'I've got to be honest and say the image of Manchester United overawed me, but this job is the peak of ambition for any manager.' That remark by softly-spoken Dave Sexton shortly after taking control at Old Trafford perhaps furnishes a clue to subsequent events.

There is no denying that he is a top-class coach and an original thinker, a modest character of integrity and dedication. Ask anyone in football about Dave and they will talk with respect about a lovely man. As a manager he knew success with Chelsea and QPR; but was he the right personality for the huge stage of Old Trafford, constantly under the media microscope, continually pressured by the fervour of the fans?

His supporters can rightly claim that he took United higher in the League than anyone since Matt Busby (second place in 1979/80), that he nearly lifted the FA Cup in 1979 and that his team recorded seven straight wins prior to his sacking. They can point also to his strength of purpose shown, in differing circumstances, by his contentious sales of terrace favourites Gordon Hill and Andy Ritchie. Against all that can be ranged three mid-table finishes in four seasons, never mind the over-expensive purchase and questionable use of Garry Birtles.

A huge problem was surmounting the fans' affection for the Doc. With a team which played measured (some said dull) rather than flamboyant football, and a cool manner which also alienated many pressmen, he never stood a chance in that vital department. Dave Sexton attempted a quiet revolution at Old Trafford. He didn't realise he was tilting at an impossible windmill.

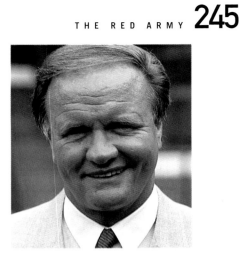

RON ATKINSON

MANAGER: July 1981–November 1986

For a few heady months Ron Atkinson looked more likely than any of his four ill-fated predecessors to do the job for which they had all been hired – to bring home that elusive League Championship. In the autumn of 1985 United made their best-ever start.

Ron's men won their first ten games and remained undefeated until November, playing a potent brand of exuberant, attacking football. Robson and company were irresistible; the title was there for the taking.

Then bleak reality took over, first in the form of a crushing injury list, then in the inevitable shape of Liverpool. This time, though, it really was hard to deny that, with just an even break in the matter of injuries, Ron might have pinned that pennant to the Reds' flagpole. Instead the general air of disillusionment hung over into the following season, the team slumped and Ron was gone.

He had arrived five and a half years earlier, apparently as fourth choice. An engaging extrovert who had achieved much with little at Cambridge and West Bromwich, Ron was seen by the board, perhaps, as an acceptable blend of Docherty's brash flair and Sexton's stability. His United were to play entertaining football with the hint of a swagger.

Ron never lacked courage and plunged into the transfer market to land some of the League's best players. In that he didn't win the title, it didn't pay off. But his side never finished out of the top four and there was the little matter of two FA Cups.

The Champagne Charlie image, beloved of the tabloids, was irrelevant; Ron knew his business right enough. He just failed to meet his ultimate challenge.

Early in the year 2000, Sir Alex Ferguson was voted the greatest football manager of all time, a verdict from which few neutral judges would demur. How could they? The sheer weight of his achievement is convincing enough. But what makes this driven man awesomely unique is the burning intensity of his desire for ever more success, the unshakeable belief that he will attain it no matter what the odds against him and, most telling of all, his priceless ability to inspire those same qualities in his players. Any hint of complacency is crushed; the self-satisfied are culled; the next game, the next challenge, are all that matters.

Alex Ferguson

MANAGER: November 1986–

As the man who ended 26 years of Championship failure by leading Manchester United to six titles in eight seasons – with three League and FA Cup doubles thrown in for good measure – and also captured the European Cup and a once-in-a-lifetime treble in unforgettable fashion, he has written his own ticket to Old Trafford immortality.

Sir Alex has built two United sides which have combined style with steel, glamour with character, and has reaped royal reward for his creations. Lifting 13 major honours in the space of 11 campaigns is a record not even his predecessor could match, and the Red Devils' modern master – his rage to succeed still burning fiercely at the age of 58 and with a contract in his pocket which takes him to 2002 – has much more to give.

In soccer terms, then, Ferguson has achieved true greatness, but there was a time when the man Bobby Charlton championed from the boardroom to take over from Ron Atkinson in November 1986 seemed in danger of leaving Old Trafford as a flop. The former toolmaking union official had arrived as the first United boss to have proved himself conclusively elsewhere, his Aberdeen side having loosened the grip of Celtic and Rangers on Scottish football. Ferguson's first job was to lift the Reds away from the foot of the table and this he accomplished, but many problems remained. United's reputation as a social club, rather than a football club, was not altogether without foundation and Alex tackled the situation head-on. In addition, he revamped the youth system and paid minute attention to every detail of club life. Fresh players arrived for 1987/88 and the new combination finished as League runners-up, but 1988/89 brought dour anti-climax. The side was hard-working, methodical, disciplined – and dull.

More expensive team surgery followed but by January 1990 United were struggling horribly and chants of 'Fergie Out' became commonplace. Though chairman Martin Edwards has denied it, the manager's job must have been under dire threat had there been an early exit from the FA Cup. But they won that trophy, then the European Cup Winners' Cup and, in 1991/92, the League Cup, though that was overshadowed by allowing a title that had seemed in their grasp to slip away to Elland Road. Alex was criticised for being too tense, and for communicating pressure to his players, and many believed that recovery from such a setback would prove beyond him.

However, season 1992/93 was to bring the perfect riposte in the shape of the League Championship. Adopting an approach that, outwardly at least, was more relaxed, he finally secured the prize for which United had pined so painfully. In retrospect, the turning point was the unplanned acquisition of Eric Cantona, whom he signed after a chance inquiry made when the Leeds chairman telephoned on other business. But the way the Scot capitalised on that good fortune, realising that the brilliant French maverick must be the hub of his team, was inspired.

Come 1993/94 and his classy machine was purring along more smoothly, more joyously than ever and by late autumn there was talk of an unprecedented domestic treble. Then came trouble. Prickly reactions to public criticism, which rained on his head as sendings-off and bookings threatened to scupper the entire campaign, mushroomed into full-scale paranoia. Results declined alarmingly, the League Cup Final was lost and Blackburn reduced a 16-point chasm to goal difference. But, happily, Alex regained his poise and United their equilibrium to lift the League and FA Cup double.

Inevitably perhaps, 1994/95 was anti-climactic, though only just. The title was conceded by one point and the FA Cup Final by a single goal, though the main event of the season was the debilitating Cantona affair. The way Fergie handled the storm which broke after the Frenchman attacked a 'fan' at Selhurst Park, and his subtle coaxing of Eric to remain in the Old Trafford fold, was management at its best. After that trauma, the outcry surrounding the sales of Hughes, Ince and Kanchelskis in the summer of 1995 would have brought lesser men to their knees. Typically cussedly, but a good deal more imperturbably than in the past, Alex dug in to attain arguably his most remarkable triumph. He replaced the departing stars with boys from his youth team and, after being advised by TV pundit Alan Hansen that 'you win nothing with kids', his new team completed the club's second League and FA Cup double.

Season 1996/97 brought another tilt at his European Cup windmill and a fourth Championship in five seasons, then came a rare trophyless term. And so to 1998/99, which began with the much-criticised Manchester United plc coughing up some £28 million to reinforce the squad and ended in the soccer equivalent of the Promised Land. Despite the distraction of the abortive BSkyB takeover bid and the loss of right-hand man Brian Kidd, Alex rotated his massive squad brilliantly, harnessing extravagant flair to unquenchable spirit and compiling a prodigious 33-match unbeaten run that secured the title, the FA Cup and, at long last, the European Cup.

After annihilating his rivals to claim another Premiership crown in 1999/2000, this fearsome, honest, wholly remarkable man, whose public persona can shift from charming warmth to stubbornness and raw aggression and whose psychological mind games can reduce rivals to apoplexy, is scheduled to carry on the struggle for another two years. Whatever the future holds – and there have been reports of a strained relationship with his chairman – Sir Alex Ferguson has earned for himself the lasting devotion of all who, like him, love Manchester United. He deserves nothing less. As for the inevitable prospect of replacing him in the not-too-distant future, it doesn't bear contemplation.

PLAYERS' STATISTICS

Player	Season	LEAGUE			FA CUP			LEAGUE CUP			EUROPE			CWC			TOTAL		
		Ap	Sb	Gl	Ap	Sb	Gl	Ap	Sb	Gl	Ap	Sb	Gl	Ap	Sb	Gl	Ap	Sb	Gl
Albiston A	74-87	364	(15)	6	36	(0)	0	38	(2)	1	26	(1)	0	0	(0)	0	464	(18)	7
Appleton M	1996	0	(0)	0	0	(0)	0	1	(1)	0	0	(0)	0	0	(0)	0	1	(1)	0
Anderson T	72-73	13	(6)	2	0	(0)	0	0	(0)	0	0	(0)	0	0	(0)	0	13	(6)	2
Anderson V	87-90	50	(4)	2	7	(0)	1	6	(1)	1	1	(0)	0	0	(0)	0	64	(5)	4
Anderson W	63-66	7	(2)	0	2	(0)	0	0	(0)	0	1	(0)	0	0	(0)	0	10	(2)	0
Aston J	64-71	139	(16)	25	5	(2)	1	12	(3)	0	8	(0)	1	0	(0)	0	164	(21)	27
Bailey G	78-86	294	(0)	0	31	(0)	0	28	(0)	0	20	(0)	0	0	(0)	0	373	(0)	0
Baldwin T	1974	2	(0)	0	0	(0)	0	0	(0)	0	0	(0)	0	0	(0)	0	2	(0)	0
Barnes P	85-86	19	(1)	2	0	(0)	0	5	(0)	2	0	(0)	0	0	(0)	0	24	(1)	4
Beardsley P	1982	0	(0)	0	0	(0)	0	1	(0)	0	0	(0)	0	0	(0)	0	1	(0)	0
Beardsmore R	88-91	30	(26)	4	4	(4)	0	3	(1)	0	2	(3)	0	0	(0)	0	39	(34)	4
Beckham D	92-	158	(17)	36	16	(2)	5	5	(2)	0	45	(0)	7	1	(1)	0	225	(22)	48
Bent G	54-56	12	(0)	0	0	(0)	0	0	(0)	0	0	(0)	0	0	(0)	0	12	(0)	0
Berg H	97-	49	(16)	2	7	(0)	0	3	(0)	0	19	(4)	1	1	(0)	0	79	(20)	3
Berry J	51-57	247	(0)	37	15	(0)	4	0	(0)	0	11	(0)	3	0	(0)	0	273	(0)	44
Best G	63-73	361	(0)	137	46	(0)	21	25	(0)	9	34	(0)	11	0	(0)	0	466	(0)	178
Bielby P	1973	2	(2)	0	0	(0)	0	0	(0)	0	0	(0)	0	0	(0)	0	2	(2)	0
Birtles G	80-81	57	(1)	11	4	(0)	1	2	(0)	0	0	(0)	0	0	(0)	0	63	(1)	12
Blackmore C	83-92	150	(36)	19	15	(6)	1	23	(2)	3	11	(0)	2	0	(0)	0	199	(44)	25
Blanchflower J	51-57	105	(0)	26	6	(0)	1	0	(0)	0	5	(0)	0	0	(0)	0	116	(0)	27
Blomqvist J	98-	20	(5)	1	3	(2)	0	0	(1)	0	6	(1)	0	0	(0)	0	29	9	1
Bosnich M	89-90 & 99-	26	(0)	0	0	(0)	0	1	(0)	0	7	(0)	0	2	(0)	0	36	(0)	0
Bradley W	58-61	63	(0)	20	3	(0)	1	0	(0)	0	0	(0)	0	0	(0)	0	66	(0)	21
Bratt H	1960	0	(0)	0	0	(0)	0	1	(0)	0	0	(0)	0	0	(0)	0	1	(0)	0
Brazil A	84-85	18	(13)	8	0	(1)	0	4	(3)	3	2	(0)	1	0	(0)	0	24	(17)	12
Brazil D	88-89	0	(2)	0	0	(0)	0	0	(0)	0	0	(0)	0	0	(0)	0	0	(2)	0
Brennan S	57-69	291	(1)	3	36	(0)	3	4	(0)	0	24	(0)	0	0	(0)	0	355	(1)	6
Briggs R	60-61	9	(0)	0	2	(0)	0	0	(0)	0	0	(0)	0	0	(0)	0	11	(0)	0
Brown W	97-	12	(4)	0	2	(0)	0	0	(1)	0	3	(1)	0	0	(0)	0	17	(6)	0
Bruce S	87-95	309	(0)	36	41	(0)	3	32	(2)	6	25	(1)	6	0	(0)	0	407	(3)	51
Buchan G	1973	0	(3)	0	0	(0)	0	0	(1)	0	0	(0)	0	0	(0)	0	0	(4)	0
Buchan M	71-82	376	(0)	4	39	(0)	0	30	(0)	0	10	(0)	0	0	(0)	0	455	(0)	4
Burns F	67-71	111	(10)	6	11	(1)	0	10	(1)	1	10	(1)	0	0	(0)	0	142	(13)	7
Butt N	92-	140	(37)	16	16	(2)	1	5	(0)	0	30	(8)	0	2	(0)	1	193	(47)	18
Byrne R	51-57	245	(0)	17	18	(0)	2	0	(0)	0	14	(0)	0	0	(0)	0	277	(0)	19
Cantona E	92-96	142	(1)	64	17	(0)	10	6	(0)	1	16	(0)	5	0	(0)	0	181	(1)	80
Cantwell N	60-66	123	(0)	6	14	(0)	2	0	(0)	0	7	(0)	0	0	(0)	0	144	(0)	8
Carolan J	58-60	66	(0)	0	4	(0)	0	1	(0)	0	0	(0)	0	0	(0)	0	71	(0)	0
Casper C	94-96	0	(2)	0	1	(0)	0	3	(0)	0	0	(1)	0	0	(0)	0	4	(3)	0
Chadwick L	99-	0	(0)	0	0	(0)	0	1	(0)	0	0	(0)	0	0	(0)	0	1	(0)	0
Charlton R	56-72	604	(2)	199	79	(0)	19	24	(0)	7	45	(0)	22	0	(0)	0	752	(2)	247
Chisnall P	61-63	35	(0)	8	8	(0)	1	0	(0)	0	4	(0)	1	0	(0)	0	47	(0)	10
Clark J	1976	0	(1)	0	0	(0)	0	0	(0)	0	0	(0)	0	0	(0)	0	0	(1)	0
Clayton G	1956	2	(0)	0	0	(0)	0	0	(0)	0	0	(0)	0	0	(0)	0	2	(0)	0

PLAYERS' STATISTICS

Player	Season	LEAGUE			FA CUP			LEAGUE CUP			EUROPE			CWC			TOTAL		
		Ap	Sb	Gl	Ap	Sb	Gl	Ap	Sb	Gl	Ap	Sb	Gl	Ap	Sb	Gl	Ap	Sb	Gl
Clegg M	96-	4	(5)	0	3	(0)	0	5	(0)	0	1	(2)	0	0	(0)	0	13	(7)	0
Cole A	94-	139	(26)	80	18	(2)	9	2	(0)	0	32	(4)	14	2	(0)	0	193	32	103
Colman E	55-57	85	(0)	1	9	(0)	0	0	(0)	0	13	(0)	1	0	(0)	0	107	(0)	2
Connaughton J	1971	3	(0)	0	0	(0)	0	0	(0)	0	0	(0)	0	0	(0)	0	3	(0)	0
Connell T	1978	2	(0)	0	0	(0)	0	0	(0)	0	0	(0)	0	0	(0)	0	2	(0)	0
Connelly J	64-66	79	(1)	22	13	(0)	2	1	(0)	0	19	(0)	11	0	(0)	0	112	(1)	35
Cooke T	95-96	1	(3)	0	0	(0)	0	1	(2)	1	0	(1)	0	0	(0)	0	2	6	1
Cope R	56-60	93	(0)	2	10	(0)	0	1	(0)	0	2	(0)	0	0	(0)	0	106	(0)	2
Coppell S	74-82	320	(2)	54	36	(0)	4	25	(0)	9	11	(1)	3	0	(0)	0	395	(3)	70
Coyne P	1975	1	(1)	1	0	(0)	0	0	(0)	0	0	(0)	0	0	(0)	0	1	(1)	1
Crerand P	62-70	304	(0)	10	43	(0)	4	4	(0)	0	41	(0)	1	0	(0)	0	392	(0)	15
Crompton J	45-55	191	(0)	0	20	(0)	0	0	(0)	0	0	(0)	0	0	(0)	0	211	(0)	0
Crooks G	1983	6	(1)	2	0	(0)	0	0	(0)	0	0	(0)	0	0	(0)	0	6	(1)	2
Crowther S	57-58	13	(0)	0	5	(0)	0	0	(0)	0	2	(0)	0	0	(0)	0	20	(0)	0
Cruyff J	96-99	15	(18)	8	0	(1)	0	5	(0)	0	4	(7)	0	1	(1)	0	25	(27)	8
Culkin N	99-	0	(1)	0	0	(0)	0	0	(0)	0	0	(0)	0	0	(0)	0	0	(1)	0
Cunningham L	1982	3	(2)	1	0	(0)	0	0	(0)	0	0	(0)	0	0	(0)	0	3	(2)	1
Curtis J	97-	4	(9)	0	0	(0)	0	5	(0)	0	0	(0)	0	0	(0)	0	0	(9)	0
Daly G	73-76	107	(4)	23	9	(1)	5	17	(0)	4	4	(0)	0	0	(0)	0	137	(5)	32
Davenport P	85-88	73	(19)	22	2	(2)	0	8	(2)	4	0	(0)	0	0	(0)	0	83	(23)	26
Davies A	81-83	6	(1)	0	2	(0)	0	0	(0)	0	0	(1)	1	0	(0)	0	8	(2)	1
Davies R	1974	0	(8)	0	0	(2)	0	0	(0)	0	0	(0)	0	0	(0)	0	0	(10)	0
Davies S	94-96	4	(7)	0	0	(0)	0	3	(2)	0	3	(1)	1	0	(0)	0	10	(10)	1
Davies W	1972	15	(1)	4	1	(0)	0	0	(0)	0	0	(0)	0	0	(0)	0	16	(1)	4
Dawson A	56-61	80	(0)	45	10	(0)	8	3	(3)	1	0	(0)	0	0	(0)	0	93	(0)	54
Dempsey M	83-85	1	(0)	0	0	(0)	0	0	(0)	0	0	(1)	0	0	(0)	0	1	(1)	0
Doherty J	52-57	25	(0)	7	1	(0)	0	0	(0)	0	0	(0)	0	0	(0)	0	26	(0)	7
Donaghy M	88-91	76	(13)	0	10	(0)	0	9	(5)	0	2	(3)	0	0	(0)	0	97	(21)	0
Donald I	1972	4	(0)	0	0	(0)	0	2	(0)	0	0	(0)	0	0	(0)	0	6	(0)	0
Dublin D	92-93	4	(8)	2	1	(1)	0	1	(1)	1	0	(1)	0	0	(0)	0	6	(11)	3
Dunne A	60-72	414	(0)	2	54	(1)	0	21	(0)	0	40	(0)	0	0	(0)	0	529	(1)	2
Dunne P	64-65	45	(0)	0	7	(0)	0	1	(0)	0	13	(0)	0	0	(0)	0	66	(0)	0
Duxbury M	80-89	274	(25)	6	20	(5)	1	32	(2)	0	17	(1)	0	0	(0)	0	343	(33)	7
Edwards D	52-57	151	(0)	20	12	(0)	1	0	0	0	12	(0)	0	0	(0)	0	175	(2)	21
Edwards P	69-72	52	(2)	0	10	(0)	0	4	(0)	1	0	(0)	0	0	(0)	0	66	(2)	1
Ferguson D	90-93	20	(7)	0	0	(0)	0	2	(1)	0	0	(0)	0	0	(0)	0	22	(8)	0
Fitzpatrick J	64-72	111	(6)	8	11	(0)	1	12	(0)	1	7	(0)	0	0	(0)	0	141	(6)	10
Fletcher P	72-73	2	(5)	0	0	(0)	0	0	(0)	0	0	(0)	0	0	(0)	0	2	(5)	0
Foggon A	1976	0	(3)	0	0	(0)	0	0	(0)	0	0	(0)	0	0	(0)	0	0	(3)	0
Forsyth A	72-77	99	(2)	4	10	(0)	1	7	(0)	0	0	(1)	0	0	(0)	0	116	(3)	5
Fortune Q	99-	4	(2)	2	0	(0)	0	0	(0)	0	1	(3)	0	1	(1)	2	6	(6)	4
Foulkes W	52-69	563	(3)	7	61	(0)	0	3	(0)	2	52	(0)	2	0	(0)	0	679	(3)	9
Garton W	84-88	39	(2)	0	3	(0)	0	5	(1)	0	0	(1)	0	0	(0)	0	47	(4)	0
Gaskell, D	57-66	96	(0)	0	16	(0)	0	1	(0)	0	5	(0)	0	0	(0)	0	118	(0)	0

PLAYERS' STATISTICS

Player	Season	LEAGUE			FA CUP			LEAGUE CUP			EUROPE			CWC			TOTAL		
		Ap	Sb	Gl	Ap	Sb	Gl	Ap	Sb	Gl	Ap	Sb	Gl	Ap	Sb	Gl	Ap	Sb	Gl
Gibson C	85-89	74	(5)	9	8	(1)	0	7	(0)	0	0	(0)	0	0	(0)	0	89	(6)	9
Gibson T	85-86	14	(9)	1	1	(1)	0	0	(2)	0	0	(0)	0	0	(0)	0	15	(12)	1
Gidman J	81-85	94	(1)	4	9	(0)	0	5	(0)	0	7	(2)	0	0	(0)	0	115	(3)	4
Giggs R	90-	267	(23)	59	34	(3)	7	17	(4)	6	43	(1)	11	2	(0)	0	363	(31)	83
Giles J	59-62	99	(0)	10	13	(0)	2	2	(0)	1	0	(0)	0	0	(0)	0	114	(0)	13
Gill A	86-88	5	(5)	1	2	(2)	1	0	(0)	0	0	(0)	0	0	(0)	0	7	(7)	2
Gillespie K	92-94	3	(6)	1	1	(1)	1	3	(0)	0	0	(0)	0	0	(0)	0	7	(7)	2
Givens D	1969	4	(4)	1	0	(0)	0	1	(0)	0	0	(0)	0	0	(0)	0	5	(4)	1
Goodwin F	54-59	95	(0)	7	8	(0)	1	0	(0)	0	3	(0)	0	0	(0)	0	106	(0)	8
Gowling A	67-71	64	(7)	18	6	(2)	2	7	(1)	1	0	(0)	0	0	(0)	0	77	(10)	21
Graham A	83-84	33	(4)	5	1	(0)	0	6	(0)	1	6	(1)	1	0	(0)	0	46	(5)	7
Graham D	87-88	1	(0)	0	0	(1)	1	0	(1)	0	0	(0)	0	0	(0)	0	1	(2)	1
Graham G	72-74	41	(2)	2	2	(0)	0	1	(0)	0	0	(0)	0	0	(0)	0	44	(2)	2
Greaves I	54-59	67	(0)	0	6	(0)	0	0	(0)	0	2	(0)	0	0	(0)	0	75	(0)	0
Greenhoff B	73-78	218	(3)	13	24	(0)	2	19	(0)	2	6	(0)	0	0	(0)	0	267	(3)	17
Greenhoff J	76-80	94	(3)	26	18	(1)	9	4	(0)	1	2	(0)	0	0	(0)	0	118	(4)	36
Greening J	98-	1	(6)	0	0	(1)	0	4	(0)	0	1	(1)	0	1	(0)	0	7	(8)	0
Gregg H	57-66	210	(0)	0	24	(0)	0	2	(0)	0	11	(0)	0	0	(0)	0	247	(0)	0
Griffiths C	1973	7	(0)	0	0	(0)	0	0	(0)	0	0	(0)	0	0	(0)	0	7	(0)	0
Grimes A	77-82	62	(28)	10	5	(0)	1	6	(0)	0	4	(2)	0	0	(0)	0	77	(30)	11
Grimshaw A	1975	0	(1)	0	0	(0)	0	0	(1)	0	0	(0)	0	0	(0)	0	0	(2)	0
Harrop R	57-58	10	(0)	0	1	(0)	0	0	(0)	0	0	(0)	0	0	(0)	0	11	(0)	0
Hawksworth A	1957	1	(0)	0	0	(0)	0	0	(0)	0	0	(0)	0	0	(0)	0	1	(0)	0
Haydock F	60-62	6	(0)	0	0	(0)	0	0	(0)	0	0	(0)	0	0	(0)	0	6	(0)	0
Healy D	99-	0	(0)	0	0	(0)	0	0	(1)	0	0	(0)	0	0	(0)	0	0	(1)	0
Herd D	61-67	201	(1)	114	35	(0)	15	1	(0)	1	25	(0)	14	0	(0)	0	262	(1)	144
Heron T	57-60	3	(0)	0	0	(0)	0	0	(0)	0	0	(0)	0	0	(0)	0	3	(0)	0
Higginbotham D	97-	2	(2)	0	0	(0)	0	1	(0)	0	0	(1)	0	1	(0)	0	4	(3)	0
Higgins M	1985	6	(0)	0	2	(0)	0	0	(0)	0	0	(0)	0	0	(0)	0	8	(0)	0
Hill G	75-77	100	(1)	39	17	(0)	6	7	(0)	4	8	(0)	2	0	(0)	0	132	(1)	51
Hogg G	83-87	82	(1)	1	8	(0)	0	7	(1)	0	10	(0)	0	0	(0)	0	107	(2)	1
Holton J	72-74	63	(0)	5	2	(0)	0	4	(0)	0	0	(0)	0	0	(0)	0	69	(0)	5
Houston S	73-79	204	(1)	13	22	(0)	1	16	(0)	2	6	(1)	0	0	(0)	0	248	(2)	16
Hughes M	83-85 & 88-94	336	(9)	120	45	(1)	17	37	(1)	16	30	(3)	9	0	(0)	0	448	(14)	162
Hunter R	1958	1	(0)	0	0	(0)	0	0	(0)	0	0	(0)	0	0	(0)	0	1	(0)	0
Ince P	89-94	203	(3)	25	26	(1)	1	23	(1)	2	20	(0)	0	0	(0)	0	272	(5)	28
Irwin D	90-	326	(9)	22	41	(1)	7	28	(3)	0	58	(0)	2	2	(0)	0	455	(13)	31
Jackson T	75-76	18	(1)	0	0	(0)	0	4	(0)	0	0	(0)	0	0	(0)	0	22	(1)	0
James S	68-74	129	(0)	4	12	(0)	0	17	(1)	0	2	(0)	0	0	(0)	0	160	(1)	4
Johnsen R	96-	65	(13)	5	8	(2)	1	2	(0)	0	20	(2)	0	0	(0)	0	95	(17)	6
Jones M	50-57	103	(0)	1	7	(0)	0	0	(0)	0	10	(0)	0	0	(0)	0	120	(0)	1
Jones P	1957	1	(0)	0	0	(0)	0	0	(0)	0	0	(0)	0	0	(0)	0	1	(0)	0
Jordan J	77-80	109	(0)	37	11	(1)	2	4	(0)	2	1	(0)	0	0	(0)	0	125	(1)	41
Jovanovic N	79-80	20	(1)	4	1	(0)	0	2	(0)	0	2	(0)	0	0	(0)	0	25	(1)	4

PLAYERS' STATISTICS

Player	Season	LEAGUE Ap	Sb	Gl	FA CUP Ap	Sb	Gl	LEAGUE CUP Ap	Sb	Gl	EUROPE Ap	Sb	Gl	CWC Ap	Sb	Gl	TOTAL Ap	Sb	Gl
Kanchelskis A	90-94	96	(27)	28	11	(1)	4	15	(1)	3	7	(0)	1	0	(0)	0	129	(29)	36
Keane R	93-	177	(8)	24	29	(1)	1	9	(2)	0	40	(0)	12	2	(0)	0	257	(11)	37
Kelly J	1975	0	(1)	0	0	(0)	0	0	(0)	0	0	(0)	0	0	(0)	0	0	(1)	0
Kidd B	67-73	195	(8)	52	24	(1)	8	20	(0)	7	16	(0)	3	0	(0)	0	255	(9)	70
Kinsey A	1964	0	(0)	0	1	(0)	1	0	(0)	0	0	(0)	0	0	(0)	0	1	(0)	1
Kopel F	67-68	8	(2)	0	1	(0)	0	0	(0)	0	1	(0)	0	0	(0)	0	10	(2)	0
Law D	62-72	305	(4)	171	44	(2)	34	11	(0)	3	33	(0)	28	0	(0)	0	393	(6)	236
Lawton N	59-62	36	(0)	6	7	(0)	0	1	(0)	0	0	(0)	0	0	(0)	0	44	(0)	6
Leighton J	89-90	73	(0)	0	14	(0)	0	7	(0)	0	0	(0)	0	0	(0)	0	94	(0)	0
Lewis E	52-55	20	(0)	9	4	(0)	2	0	(0)	0	0	(0)	0	0	(0)	0	24	(0)	11
Macari L	72-83	311	(18)	78	31	(3)	8	22	(5)	10	9	(1)	1	0	(0)	0	373	(27)	97
McCalliog J	73-74	31	(0)	7	1	(0)	0	5	(1)	0	0	(0)	0	0	(0)	0	37	(1)	7
McClair B	87-97	296	(59)	88	39	(6)	4	44	(1)	19	17	(6)	5	0	(0)	0	396	(72)	126
McCreery D	74-78	48	(38)	7	1	(6)	0	4	(4)	1	4	(3)	0	0	(0)	0	57	(51)	8
MacDougall E	1972	18	(0)	5	0	(0)	0	0	(0)	0	0	(0)	0	0	(0)	0	18	(0)	5
McGarvey S	80-82	13	(12)	3	0	(0)	0	0	(0)	0	0	(0)	0	0	(0)	0	13	(12)	3
McGibbon P	1995	0	(0)	0	0	(0)	0	1	(0)	0	0	(0)	0	0	(0)	0	1	(0)	0
McGrath C	76-80	12	(16)	1	0	(0)	0	0	(2)	0	3	(1)	0	0	(0)	0	15	(19)	1
McGrath P	82-88	159	(4)	12	15	(3)	2	13	(0)	2	4	(0)	0	0	(0)	0	191	(7)	16
McGuinness W	55-59	81	(0)	2	2	(0)	0	0	(0)	0	2	(0)	0	0	(0)	0	85	(0)	2
McIlroy S	71-81	320	(22)	57	35	(3)	6	25	(3)	6	10	(0)	2	0	(0)	0	390	(28)	71
McKee C	1993	1	(0)	0	0	(0)	0	0	(0)	0	0	(0)	0	0	(0)	0	1	(0)	0
McMillan S	61-62	15	(0)	6	0	(0)	0	0	(0)	0	0	(0)	0	0	(0)	0	15	(0)	6
McQueen G	77-84	184	(0)	20	21	(0)	2	16	(0)	4	7	(0)	0	0	(0)	0	228	(0)	26
Maiorana G	88-89	2	(5)	0	0	(0)	0	0	(1)	0	0	(0)	0	0	(0)	0	2	(6)	0
Martin L	87-93	56	(17)	1	13	(1)	1	8	(2)	0	6	(6)	0	0	(0)	0	83	(25)	2
Martin M	72-74	33	(7)	2	2	(0)	0	1	(0)	0	0	(0)	0	0	(0)	0	36	(7)	2
May D	94-	65	(15)	6	6	(0)	0	7	(0)	1	12	(1)	1	0	(0)	0	90	(16)	8
Milne R	88-89	19	(4)	3	7	(0)	0	0	(0)	0	0	(0)	0	0	(0)	0	26	(4)	3
Moir I	60-64	45	(0)	5	0	(0)	0	0	(0)	0	0	(0)	0	0	(0)	0	45	(0)	5
Moore G	1963	18	(0)	4	1	(0)	1	0	(0)	0	0	(0)	0	0	(0)	0	19	(0)	5
Moore I	71-73	39	(0)	11	0	(0)	0	4	(0)	1	0	(0)	0	0	(0)	0	43	(0)	12
Moran K	78-87	228	(3)	21	17	(0)	1	24	(1)	2	13	(1)	0	0	(0)	0	282	(5)	24
Morgan W	68-74	236	(2)	25	27	(0)	4	24	(1)	3	4	(0)	1	0	(0)	0	291	(3)	33
Morgans K	57-60	17	(0)	0	2	(0)	0	0	(0)	0	4	(0)	0	0	(0)	0	23	(0)	0
Moses R	81-87	143	(7)	7	11	(0)	1	22	(2)	4	12	(1)	0	0	(0)	0	188	(10)	12
Muhren A	82-84	65	(5)	13	8	(0)	1	11	(0)	1	8	(0)	3	0	(0)	0	92	(5)	18
Mulryne P	97-98	1	(0)	0	0	(0)	0	3	(0)	0	0	(0)	0	0	(0)	0	4	(0)	0
Neville G	92-	167	(4)	2	21	(2)	0	4	(1)	0	41	(3)	0	2	(0)	0	235	(10)	2
Neville P	94-	105	(26)	1	14	(4)	0	5	(1)	0	18	(9)	1	2	(1)	0	144	(41)	2
Nevland E	97-98	0	(1)	0	2	(0)	0	0	(2)	1	0	(0)	0	0	(0)	0	2	(3)	1
Nicholl J	74-81	188	(9)	3	22	(4)	1	14	(0)	1	10	(0)	1	0	(0)	0	234	(13)	6
Nicholson J	60-62	58	(0)	5	7	(0)	1	3	(0)	0	0	(0)	0	0	(0)	0	68	(0)	6
Noble R	65-66	31	(0)	0	2	(0)	0	0	(0)	0	0	(0)	0	0	(0)	0	33	(0)	0

PLAYERS' STATISTICS

Player	Season	LEAGUE			FA CUP			LEAGUE CUP			EUROPE			CWC			TOTAL		
		Ap	Sb	Gl	Ap	Sb	Gl	Ap	Sb	Gl	Ap	Sb	Gl	Ap	Sb	Gl	Ap	Sb	Gl
Notman A	98-	0	(0)	0	0	(0)	0	0	(1)	0	0	(0)	0	0	(1)	0	0	(1)	0
O'Brien L	86-88	16	(15)	2	0	(2)	0	1	(2)	0	0	(0)	0	0	(0)	0	17	(19)	2
O'Kane J	94-96	1	(1)	0	1	(0)	0	2	(1)	0	1	(0)	0	0	(0)	0	5	(2)	0
O'Neil T	70-72	54	(0)	0	7	(0)	0	7	(0)	0	0	(0)	0	0	(0)	0	68	(0)	0
O'Shea J	99-	0	(0)	0	0	(0)	0	1	(0)	0	0	(0)	0	0	(0)	0	1	(0)	0
Olsen J	84-88	119	(20)	21	13	(3)	2	10	(3)	1	6	(1)	0	0	(0)	0	148	(27)	24
Pallister G	89-97	314	(3)	12	38	(0)	2	36	(9)	0	39	(1)	1	0	(0)	0	427	(4)	15
Parker P	91-95	100	(5)	1	14	(1)	1	15	(0)	0	7	(3)	0	0	(0)	0	136	(9)	2
Paterson S	76-79	3	(3)	0	0	(0)	0	2	(0)	0	0	(2)	0	0	(0)	0	5	(5)	0
Pears S	1984	4	(0)	0	1	(0)	0	0	(0)	0	0	(0)	0	0	(0)	0	5	(0)	0
Pearson M	57-62	68	(0)	12	7	(0)	1	3	(0)	1	2	(0)	0	0	(0)	0	80	(0)	14
Pearson S	74-78	138	(1)	55	22	(0)	5	12	(0)	5	6	(0)	1	0	(0)	0	178	(1)	66
Pegg D	52-57	127	(0)	24	9	(0)	0	0	(0)	0	12	(0)	4	0	(0)	0	148	(0)	28
Phelan M	89-93	88	(14)	2	10	(0)	1	14	(2)	0	14	(3)	0	0	(0)	0	126	(19)	3
Pilkington K	94-97	4	(2)	0	1	(0)	0	1	(0)	0	0	(0)	0	0	(0)	0	6	(2)	0
Pinner M	1960	4	(0)	0	0	(0)	0	0	(0)	0	0	(0)	0	0	(0)	0	4	(0)	0
Poborsky K	96-97	18	(14)	5	2	(0)	0	3	(0)	1	5	(5)	0	0	(0)	0	28	(19)	6
Prunier W	1995	2	(0)	0	0	(0)	0	0	(0)	0	0	(0)	0	0	(0)	0	2	(0)	0
Quixall A	58-63	165	(0)	50	14	(0)	4	1	(0)	2	3	(0)	0	0	(0)	0	183	(0)	56
Rachubka P	99-	0	(0)	0	0	(0)	0	0	(0)	0	0	(0)	0	0	(1)	0	0	(1)	0
Rimmer J	67-72	34	(0)	0	3	(0)	0	6	(0)	0	2	(1)	0	0	(0)	0	45	(1)	0
Ritchie A	77-80	26	(7)	13	3	(1)	0	3	(2)	0	0	(0)	0	0	(0)	0	32	(10)	13
Robins M	88-91	19	(29)	11	4	(4)	3	0	(7)	2	4	(2)	1	0	(0)	0	27	(42)	17
Robson B	81-93	326	(20)	74	33	(2)	10	50	(1)	5	26	(1)	8	0	(0)	0	435	(24)	97
Roche P	74-81	46	(0)	0	4	(0)	0	3	(0)	0	0	(0)	0	0	(0)	0	53	(0)	0
Rogers M	1977	1	(0)	0	0	(0)	0	0	(0)	0	0	(0)	0	0	(0)	0	1	(0)	0
Ryan J	65-69	21	(3)	4	1	(0)	0	0	(0)	0	2	(0)	0	0	(0)	0	24	(3)	4
Sadler D	63-73	266	(6)	22	22	(1)	1	22	(0)	1	16	(0)	3	0	(0)	0	326	(7)	27
Sartori C	68-71	26	(13)	4	9	(0)	1	3	(2)	0	2	(0)	1	0	(0)	0	40	(15)	6
Scanlon A	54-60	115	(0)	34	6	(0)	1	3	(0)	0	3	(0)	0	0	(0)	0	127	(0)	35
Schmeichel P	91-98	292	(0)	0	41	(0)	0	17	(0)	0	42	(0)	1	0	(0)	0	392	(0)	1
Scholes P	94-	117	(43)	42	8	(7)	4	6	(2)	5	28	(10)	10	0	(0)	0	159	(62)	61
Scott J	52-56	3	(0)	0	0	(0)	0	0	(0)	0	0	(0)	0	0	(0)	0	3	(0)	0
Sealey L	89-90&93	33	(0)	0	4	(1)	0	9	(0)	0	8	(0)	0	0	(0)	0	54	(1)	0
Setters M	59-64	159	(0)	12	25	(0)	1	2	(0)	0	7	(0)	1	0	(0)	0	193	(0)	14
Sharpe L	88-95	160	(33)	21	22	(7)	3	15	(8)	9	15	(2)	3	0	(0)	0	212	(50)	36
Sheringham E	97-	50	(25)	16	3	(4)	4	1	(0)	1	12	(8)	4	0	(2)	0	66	(39)	25
Sidebottom A	72-74	16	(0)	0	2	(0)	0	2	(0)	0	0	(0)	0	0	(0)	0	20	(0)	0
Silvestre M	99-	30	(1)	0	0	(0)	0	0	(0)	0	2	(2)	0	2	(2)	0	34	(3)	0
Sivebaek J	85-86	29	(2)	1	2	(0)	0	1	(0)	0	0	(0)	0	0	(0)	0	32	(2)	1
Sloan T	78-80	4	(7)	0	0	(0)	0	0	(1)	0	0	(0)	0	0	(0)	0	4	(8)	0
Solskjaer O	96-	64	(38)	47	5	(8)	3	4	(0)	3	16	(17)	7	2	(1)	0	91	(64)	60
Stam J	98-	63	(0)	1	6	(1)	0	0	(0)	0	26	(0)	0	2	(0)	0	97	(1)	1
Stapleton F	81-86	204	(19)	60	21	(0)	7	26	(1)	6	14	(1)	5	0	(0)	0	265	(21)	78

PLAYERS' STATISTICS

Player	Season	LEAGUE			FA CUP			LEAGUE CUP			EUROPE			CWC			TOTAL		
		Ap	Sb	Gl	Ap	Sb	Gl	Ap	Sb	Gl	Ap	Sb	Gl	Ap	Sb	Gl	Ap	Sb	Gl
Stepney A	66-77	433	(0)	2	44	(0)	0	35	(0)	0	23	(0)	0	0	(0)	0	535	(0)	2
Stiles N	60-70	311	(0)	17	38	(0)	0	7	(0)	0	36	(0)	2	0	(0)	0	392	(0)	19
Strachan G	84-88	155	(5)	33	22	(0)	2	12	(1)	1	6	(0)	2	0	(0)	0	195	(6)	38
Taibi M	99-	4	(0)	0	0	(0)	0	0	(0)	0	0	(0)	0	0	(0)	0	4	(0)	0
Taylor E	57-58	22	(0)	2	6	(0)	1	0	(0)	0	2	(0)	1	0	(0)	0	30	(0)	4
Taylor T	52-57	166	(0)	112	9	(0)	5	0	(0)	0	14	(0)	11	0	(0)	0	189	(0)	128
Thomas M	78-80	90	(0)	11	13	(0)	2	5	(0)	2	2	(0)	0	0	(0)	0	110	(0)	15
Thornley B	93-97	1	(8)	0	2	(0)	0	3	(0)	0	0	(0)	0	0	(0)	0	6	(8)	0
Tomlinson G	94-	0	(0)	0	0	(0)	0	0	(2)	0	0	(0)	0	0	(0)	0	0	(2)	0
Tranter W	1963	1	(0)	0	0	(0)	0	0	(0)	0	0	(0)	0	0	(0)	0	1	(0)	0
Turner C	85-87	64	(0)	0	8	(0)	0	7	(0)	0	0	(0)	0	0	(0)	0	79	(0)	0
Twiss M	97-	0	(0)	0	0	(1)	0	1	(0)	0	0	(0)	0	0	(0)	0	1	(1)	0
Ure I	69-70	47	(0)	1	8	(0)	0	10	(0)	0	0	(0)	0	0	(0)	0	65	(0)	1
Van Der Gouw R	96-	21	(5)	0	0	(0)	0	6	(0)	0	9	(0)	0	1	(0)	0	37	(5)	0
Viollet D	52-61	259	(0)	159	18	(0)	5	2	(0)	1	12	(0)	13	0	(0)	0	291	(0)	178
Waldron C	1976	3	(0)	0	0	(0)	0	1	(0)	0	0	(0)	0	0	(0)	0	4	(0)	0
Walker D	1962	1	(0)	0	0	(0)	0	0	(0)	0	0	(0)	0	0	(0)	0	1	(0)	0
Wallace D	89-92	36	(11)	6	7	(2)	2	4	(3)	3	5	(2)	0	0	(0)	0	52	(18)	11
Wallwork R	97-	0	(6)	0	0	(0)	0	1	(1)	0	0	(0)	0	1	(0)	0	2	(7)	0
Walsh G	86-94	49	(1)	0	0	(0)	0	7	(0)	0	6	(0)	0	0	(0)	0	62	(1)	0
Watson W	70-72	11	(0)	0	0	(0)	0	3	(0)	0	0	(0)	0	0	(0)	0	14	(0)	0
Wealands J	82-83	7	(0)	0	0	(0)	0	1	(0)	0	0	(0)	0	0	(0)	0	8	(0)	0
Webb N	89-92	70	(5)	8	9	(0)	1	14	(0)	1	11	(0)	1	0	(0)	0	104	(5)	11
Webster C	53-58	65	(0)	26	9	(0)	4	0	(0)	0	5	(0)	1	0	(0)	0	79	(0)	31
Wellens R	1999	0	(0)	0	0	(0)	0	0	(1)	0	0	(0)	0	0	(0)	0	0	(1)	0
Whelan A	1980	0	(1)	0	0	(0)	0	0	(0)	0	0	(0)	0	0	(0)	0	0	(1)	0
Whelan L	54-57	79	(0)	43	6	(0)	4	0	(0)	0	11	(0)	5	0	(0)	0	96	(0)	52
Whitefoot J	49-55	93	(0)	0	2	(0)	0	0	(0)	0	0	(0)	0	0	(0)	0	95	(0)	0
Whitehurst W	1955	1	(0)	0	0	(0)	0	0	(0)	0	0	(0)	0	0	(0)	0	1	(0)	0
Whiteside N	81-88	193	(13)	47	24	(0)	10	26	(3)	9	11	(2)	1	0	(0)	0	254	(18)	67
Whitworth N	1990	1	(0)	0	0	(0)	0	0	(0)	0	0	(0)	0	0	(0)	0	1	(0)	0
Wilkins R	79-83	158	(2)	7	10	(0)	1	14	(1)	1	8	(0)	1	0	(0)	0	190	(3)	10
Wilkinson I	1991	0	(0)	0	0	(0)	0	1	(0)	0	0	(0)	0	0	(0)	0	1	(0)	0
Wilson D	1988	0	(4)	0	0	(2)	0	0	(0)	0	0	(0)	0	0	(0)	0	0	(6)	0
Wilson M	98	1	(2)	0	0	(0)	0	2	(0)	0	2	(2)	0	1	(0)	0	6	(4)	0
Wood N	85-86	2	(1)	0	0	(0)	0	0	(1)	0	0	(0)	0	0	(0)	0	2	(2)	0
Wood R	49-58	178	(0)	0	15	(0)	0	0	(0)	0	12	(0)	0	0	(0)	0	205	(0)	0
Wratten P	1990	0	(2)	0	0	(0)	0	0	(0)	0	0	(0)	0	0	(0)	0	0	(2)	0
Yorke D	98-	61	(3)	68	5	(3)	3	0	(0)	0	20	(21)	10	2	(0)	1	88	(8)	52
Young A	70-75	69	(14)	1	5	(0)	0	5	(4)	0	0	(0)	0	0	(0)	0	79	(18)	1

CWC = Club World Championship

Dates shown indicate the first year of each season. Thus 70-77 means 1970/71 to 1977/78. A single entry indicates one season only, eg 1964 refers to 1964/65.

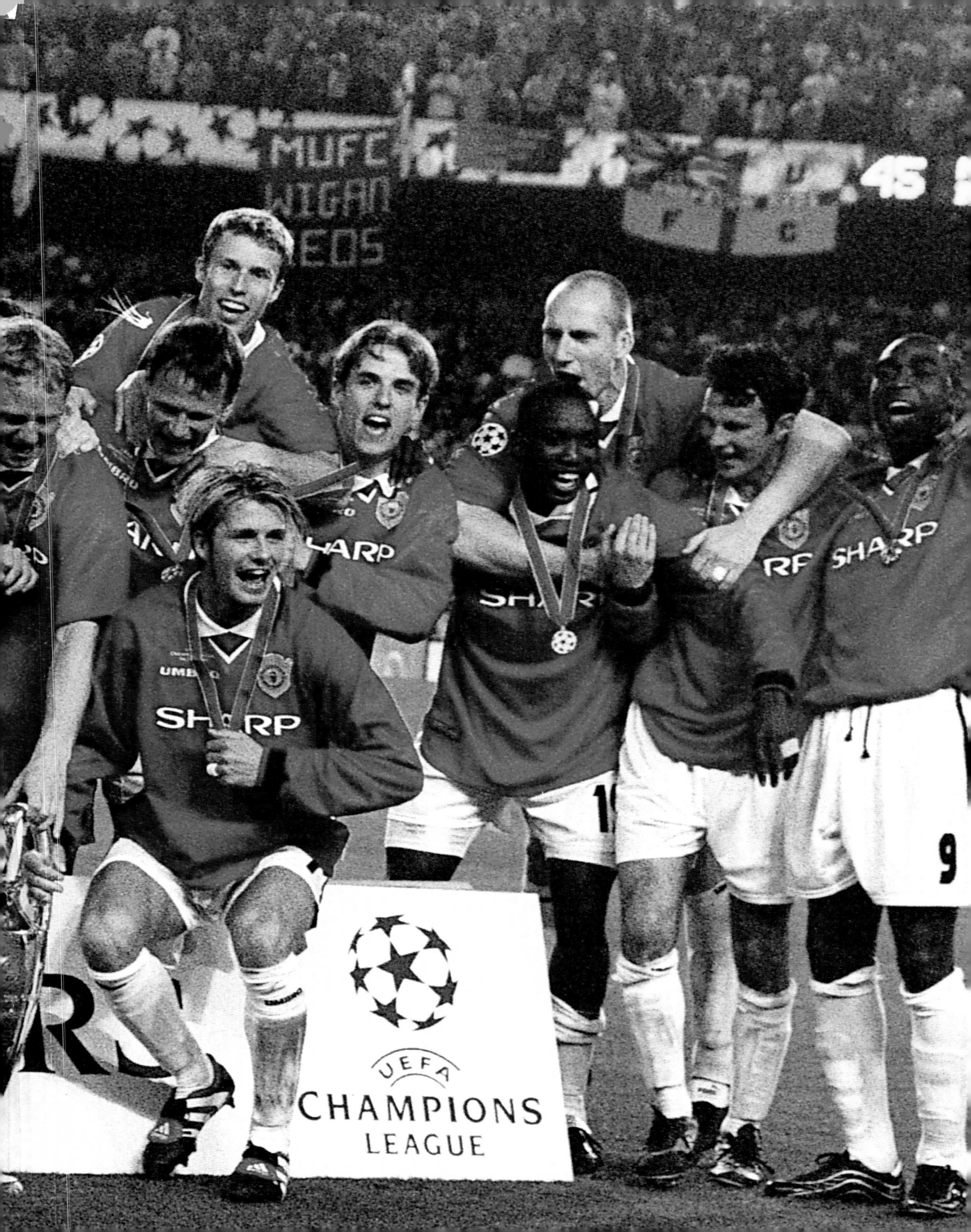
MUFC
WIGAN
UEFA
CHAMPIONS
LEAGUE
SHARP
UMBRO

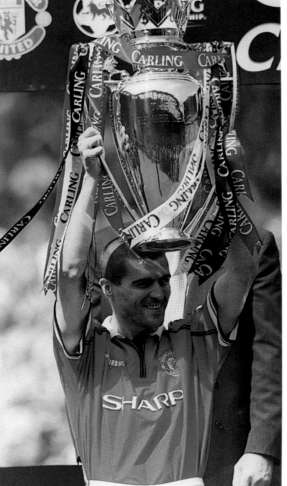

Manchester United made history in the spring of 1999 by achieving the unprecedented treble of League Championship, FA Cup and European Cup.

Left: Skipper Roy Keane hoists the 1999/2000 Premiership Trophy.

Above: Wembley scorers Sheringham and Scholes celebrate after victory over Newcastle in the 1999 FA Cup.

Previous page: Communal rejoicing after the stunning events in Barcelona had turned dreams into reality.